AF881208

About IFPRI

The International Food Policy Research Institute (IFPRI), established in 1975, provides research-based policy solutions to sustainably reduce poverty and end hunger and malnutrition. The Institute conducts research, communicates results, optimizes partnerships, and builds capacity to ensure sustainable food production, promote healthy food systems, improve markets and trade, transform agriculture, build resilience, and strengthen institutions and governance. Gender is considered in all of the Institute's work. IFPRI collaborates with partners around the world, including development implementers, public institutions, the private sector, and farmers' organizations.

About IFPRI's Peer Review Process

IFPRI books are policy-relevant publications based on original and innovative research conducted at IFPRI. All manuscripts submitted for publication as IFPRI books undergo an extensive review procedure that is managed by IFPRI's Publications Review Committee (PRC). Upon submission to the PRC, the manuscript is reviewed by a PRC member. Once the manuscript is considered ready for external review, the PRC submits it to at least two external reviewers who are chosen for their familiarity with the subject matter and the country setting. Upon receipt of these blind external peer reviews, the PRC provides the author with an editorial decision and, when necessary, instructions for revision based on the external reviews. The PRC reassesses the revised manuscript and makes a recommendation regarding publication to the director general of IFPRI. With the director general's approval, the manuscript enters the editorial and production phase to become an IFPRI book.

Nutrition and Economic Development

Exploring Egypt's Exceptionalism and the Role of Food Subsidies

Olivier Ecker, Perrihan Al-Riffai, Clemens Breisinger,
and Rawia El-Batrawy

Copyright © 2016 International Food Policy Research Institute. All rights reserved.
Contact ifpri-copyright@cgiar.org for permission to reproduce.

Any opinions stated herein are those of the author(s) and are not necessarily representative of or endorsed by the International Food Policy Research Institute.

The boundaries and names shown and the designations used in the map or elsewhere in this publication do not imply official endorsement or acceptance by the International Food Policy Research Institute (IFPRI).

International Food Policy Research Institute
2033 K Street, NW
Washington, DC 20006-1002, USA
Telephone: 202-862-5600

Library of Congress
Cataloging in Publication Program
101 Independence Avenue, S.E.
Washington, DC 20540-4283

DOI: 10.2499/9780896292383

Library of Congress Cataloging-in-Publication Data

Names: Ecker, Olivier, author. | Al-Riffai, Perrihan, author. | Breisinger, Clemens, author. | El-Batrawy, Rawia, author.
Title: Nutrition and economic development : exploring Egypt's exceptionalism and the role of food subsidies / by Olivier Ecker, Perrihan Al-Riffai, Clemens Breisinger, and Rawia El-Batrawy.
Description: Washington, DC : International Food Policy Research Institute, [2016] | Includes bibliographical references and index.
Identifiers: LCCN 2016044755 (print) | LCCN 2016046490 (ebook) | ISBN 9780896292383 (pbk. : alk. paper) | ISBN 9780896292437 (e-book)
Subjects: LCSH: Food industry and trade—Subsidies—Egypt. | Nutrition policy—Egypt. | Egypt—Economic policy.
Classification: LCC HD9017.E32 E25 2016 (print) | LCC HD9017.E32 (ebook) | DDC 338.1/962—dc23
LC record available at https://lccn.loc.gov/2016044755

Cover Design: James Sample, IFPRI
Project Manager: John Whitehead, IFPRI
Book Layout: BookMatters

Executive Summary

Egypt faces two major nutritional challenges of public health concern with critical implications for development and economic prosperity. These are the double burden of malnutrition and the growth-nutrition disconnect. This study documents and explores the two nutritional challenges and highlights the importance of addressing them urgently and decisively.

According to 2011 estimates, 31 percent of Egyptian children ages 6–59 months are stunted—a prevalence rate that is usually seen only in developing countries with much lower national income levels than Egypt's. Egypt also ranks among the countries with the highest rates of female overweight and obesity in the world, with 73 percent of all (nonpregnant) women 20 years of age and older being overweight and 34 percent being obese. The prevalence of overweight among children (29 percent) is almost as high as the prevalence of child stunting. The double burden of malnutrition—that is, the coexistence of under- and overnutrition—occurs not only at the national level but also at the family level and even the individual level: 22 percent of the children who are stunted have a mother who is overweight, and 14 percent of children suffer from both stunting and overweight at the same time. Surprisingly, chronic child undernutrition, child and maternal overnutrition, and the double burden of malnutrition are prevalent at similar rates among the poorest and the richest income quintiles of the population as well as in urban and rural areas. Despite high economic growth, the prevalence rate of child stunting increased significantly and steadily throughout the 2000s—an atypical trend for a country outside wartime.

This study identifies four potential key drivers of Egypt's two—probably interlinked—nutritional challenges, which, in combination, may have led to the country's exceptionalism. These are the nutrition transition, economic crises and rising poverty, the food subsidy system, and insufficient nutrition-sensitive investment. Although the high rates of female overnutrition may be partly attributable to the nutrition transition, and part of the increase in child stunting may be due to the succession of recent economic crises, these factors are insufficient to explain Egypt's exceptionalism and observed patterns of malnutrition among the Egyptian population. The main hypothesis of this study is that Egypt's large food subsidy system has been ineffective in reducing undernutrition; in fact, it may have contributed to sustaining and even aggravating both nutrition challenges. At least until the reform in 2014–2015, both the Baladi bread and flour program and the ration-card program incentivized the consumption of calorie-overladen and unbalanced diets as a result of providing calorie-rich foods at very low and constant prices and with quotas much above dietary recommendations. In addition to these hypothesized direct nutritional effects, the food subsidy system may have another adverse, indirect effect on nutrition: the public budget allocated to food subsidies is unavailable for possibly more nutrition-beneficial spending, such as for child and maternal nutrition-specific interventions.

To provide supportive evidence for the main hypothesis, the econometric analysis uses propensity score matching approaches for binary and continuous treatment variables and data from the 2010–2011 Egypt Household Income, Expenditure, and Consumption Survey (HIECS) to investigate the direct effects of food subsidies on child and maternal nutrition, the double burden of malnutrition at the individual and the family level, and household diet quality. The estimation results suggest that that the ration-card program (in place until May 2014) considerably affects under- and overnutrition mainly in urban areas. The Baladi bread and flour program has notable effects on overnutrition in both urban and rural areas. The nutritional effect of the ration-card program is generally larger than that of the Baladi bread and flour program. Consistent with the main hypothesis, there is no statistically significant indication that higher food subsidies lead to improved nutritional outcomes. On the contrary, higher food subsidies increase the risk of malnutrition among both children and their mothers, particularly related to overnutrition. In urban areas, the probability of child overweight and the probability of maternal overweight increase with the subsidy levels that the families acquire from the ration-card program. And maternal overnutrition is more common among beneficiary families of the ration-card program than among nonbeneficiary families. Urban mothers' risk of overweight also tends to increase with increasing Baladi bread and flour subsidies. Moreover, the estimated dose-response functions show a tendency toward increasing probabilities of child stunting and the double burden of child malnutrition with increasing ration-card-program subsidy levels in urban areas. The (binary) propensity score matching (PSM) estimations indicate that, on average, the risk of child stunting is still lower among urban beneficiary households of the ration-card program than among urban nonbeneficiary households. Thus, the ration-card program has no uniformly negative effect on child nutrition; it is rather the received subsidy level that matters for child malnutrition. However, regarding maternal overnutrition, the program has only adverse effects. The estimation results for household diet quality indicators confirm that the ration-card program seems to indeed adversely affect nutrition in urban areas through incentivizing diets that are unbalanced, especially regarding the frequency of consuming micronutrient-rich foods.

In conclusion, the findings of this book consistently suggest that—in addition to the well-known economic rationale for reforming the Egyptian food subsidy system—there are strong reasons to reform food subsidies due to nutrition and public health concerns. From a nutritional perspective, primarily the ration-card program that was in place until May 2014 incentivized overconsumption of calorie-rich and unbalanced diets, especially among urban beneficiaries. In June 2014, Egypt's new government began to fundamentally reform the food subsidy system with the aims of alleviating its considerable and rapidly growing fiscal burden on the country's budget and of increasing its effectiveness as a social protection instrument. The recent changes mark important steps toward a voucher-based system and provide the basis for implementing a more targeted approach. Although nutrition concerns may have played no (decisive) role in the reform debate, the already implemented modifications, and especially the changes to the ration-card program, can be expected to have positive dietary effects. They tend to reduce—but not fully remove—the incentives for overconsuming calorie-rich and micronutrient-poor diets.

Given Egypt's persistent and exceptional nutritional challenges, future food subsidy reform steps should consider nutritional implications from the onset. In fact, there may be scope to transform the current subsidy system into a key policy instrument in the fight against malnutrition. Follow-up impact evaluation studies can provide important evidence on income, dietary, and nutritional implications of different reform alternatives and thereby help to create a more nutrition-sensitive social safety net in Egypt.

Keywords: propensity score, dose-response model, double burden of malnutrition, growth-nutrition disconnect, child stunting, overweight, food subsidy, food assistance, Baladi bread, ration card, Egypt

Contents

Figures, Tables, and Boxes

Figures

Tables

Boxes

Foreword

Our knowledge about the importance of good nutrition for economic development has been growing rapidly in recent years. Research has shown that malnutrition during the early years of life leads to lower educational achievements and lower incomes later in life, with negative implications for societies as a whole. While progress has been made in reducing undernutrition in several countries, overweight, obesity, and related noncommunicable diseases have become growing concerns.

Egypt is one of the countries that is grappling with both under- and overnutrition at the same time. In *Nutrition and Economic Development: Exploring Egypt's Exceptionalism and the Role of Food Subsidies*, the authors argue that the recent aggravation of the double burden of malnutrition in Egypt can be explained by a combination of several driving factors: economic growth has been largely disconnected from nutrition improvements; poverty has risen as a result of a succession of recent crises; nutrition-sensitive public investments (such as in basic healthcare and safe drinking water and sanitation) and nutritional awareness and education programs have been insufficient; and the population has faced a rapid nutrition transition due to changing diets and lifestyle.

Further, as one of this book's main contributions to the discussion on nutrition and social protection in developing countries, the authors show that the Egyptian food subsidy system, as it was in place until May 2014, helped to aggravate the double burden of malnutrition. Higher food subsidies increase the risk of malnutrition among both children and their mothers, particularly related to overnutrition. Thus—in addition to the conventional arguments for food subsidy reforms related to their high fiscal costs and often untargeted nature—the authors provide an additional argument for subsidy reform.

Since the preliminary results of this book were first presented in Cairo in early 2013, the Egyptian government has started to fundamentally reform the food subsidy system, in line with several of this book's recommendations. In the long run, an important question for policy makers will be whether to follow the path of countries such as Algeria, Jordan, and Mexico, by replacing food subsidies with (conditional) income transfers, or to maintain (targeted) food subsidies as the United States and India, for example, have done. For the short run, the authors make concrete suggestions as to how to make the current system more nutrition-sensitive, including smarter subsidy targeting, need-based selection of subsidized products, food fortification, and nutritional education. Follow-up analyses to monitor the economic and nutritional benefits and costs of the reforming system and the willingness of policy makers to learn and adjust will be important for success.

Shenggen Fan
Director General, IFPRI

Acknowledgments

This study benefited from the comments and suggestions of many people. We are particularly thankful to Dina Magdy Armanious, Heba El-Laithy, and Sherine Al-Shawarby from Cairo University; Abraham Abatneh, Riham Abuismail, Gian-Pietro Bordignon, Nora Soliman, and Jane Waite from the World Food Programme (WFP); Nadim Khouri (formerly United Nations Economic and Social Commission for Western Asia); Jean-François Maystadt from the University of Lancaster; Michela Bia from the Luxembourg Institute of Socio-Economic Research; and Harold Alderman, Daniel Gilligan, Katrina Kosec, and Jef Leroy from the International Food Policy Research Institute (IFPRI). We highly appreciate the provision of poverty and inequality estimates by Heba El-Laithy and the support of Khaled Maher from the Egypt Central Agency for Public Mobilization and Statistics (CAPMAS) in providing the applied datasets of the 2010–2011 Egypt Household Income, Expenditure, and Consumption Survey. We thank Marc Nene from Tufts University for his research assistance. We are also very thankful to IFPRI's Publications Review Committee, its Chair Gershon Feder, and two anonymous reviewers for their critical and valuable comments and suggestions. We gratefully acknowledge the editing and design of this book by IFPRI's visual design and production team, particularly Jamed Falik, James Sample, and John Whitehead, and the great support of IFPRI's communications team, led by Katrin Park. We thank BookMatters for their work in producing the book.

Preliminary results of our study were presented at the Hidden Hunger Congress in Stuttgart (Germany) in March 2013; in seminars in Cairo at CAPMAS in September 2014, the Faculty of Economics and Political Science of Cairo University in May 2013, and the United States Agency for International Development in May 2013 and January 2015; in seminars at IFPRI in Washington, DC, in August 2013 and at the Georg-August University of Goettingen (Germany) in February 2015; and in a joint WFP-CAPMAS-IFPRI workshop in Cairo in January 2013. We thank all participants in these events for their comments.

We gratefully acknowledge financial support from the International Fund for Agricultural Development and the CGIAR Research Program on Policies, Institutions, and Markets.

Chapter 1

INTRODUCTION

Good nutrition is widely regarded as one of the key factors for advancing human well-being and economic prosperity.[1] Recent research clearly shows that malnutrition—and especially undernutrition—is not only a consequence of poverty, food insecurity, and disease but also one of the reasons for the lack of progress in economic development throughout the developing world (IFPRI 2014).[2] Undernutrition slows economic growth and deepens poverty through productivity losses from poor physical performance and cognitive capacity (World Bank 2006). Productivity losses to individuals are estimated at more than 10 percent of lifetime earnings, and productivity losses to the gross domestic product (GDP) in developing countries are at least 2–3 percent annually (Horton 1999; World Bank 2006). These economic costs vary considerably by country and may exceed 10 percent of GDP in countries with high prevalence rates of undernutrition and relatively high per capita workforce productivity (Horton and Ross 2003; IFPRI 2014).

Losses in household income potential and GDP are due to impaired cognitive abilities, which are especially relevant in more advanced economies

1 Malnutrition is a chronic condition caused by under- or overconsumption of any or several essential macro- or micronutrients or by adverse health conditions affecting nutrient absorption or storage in the human body. According to Mayer (1976), four forms of malnutrition can be differentiated: (1) protein-energy undernutrition (caused by dietary deficiencies in carbohydrates and/or proteins and frequently referred to as "hunger"), (2) micronutrient undernutrition (caused by dietary mineral and vitamin deficiencies, frequently referred to as "hidden hunger"), (3) overnutrition (mostly resulting from overconsumption of carbohydrates), and (4) secondary malnutrition (that is, under- or overnutrition primarily caused by illness or disease). This book looks at both ends of the malnutrition spectrum and therefore differentiates terminologically between under- and overnutrition.

2 "Poverty is pronounced deprivation in well-being. . . . It includes low incomes and the inability to acquire the basic goods and services necessary for survival with dignity" (World Bank 2012, adapted from Haughton and Khandker 2009).

"Food security exists when all people, at all times, have physical, social and economic access to sufficient, safe and nutritious food to meet their dietary needs and food preferences for an active and healthy life" (FAO 1996, par. 1). The "four pillars of food security are availability, access, utilization, and stability" and "the nutritional dimension is integral to the concept" (FAO 2009, fn. 1).

(Hoddinott et al. 2008; Selowsky and Taylor 1973). Chronically undernourished children tend to have lower intelligence quotient (IQ) scores, by 5 to 11 points, and worse school performance compared to their well-nourished peers (Caulfield et al. 2006; World Bank 2006). Undernutrition among young children and women of reproductive age is of particular concern from a societal perspective, because prevalence rates among them are highest; their nutritional status is most crucial for the prosperity of the next generation; and nutritional interventions are most effective during the window of opportunity in the life cycle, comprising the time of pregnancy and the first two years of life (Bryce et al. 2008; Engle et al. 2007; Victora et al. 2008). In addition to losses in GDP, both under- and overnutrition also increase healthcare costs (World Bank 2006), thus contributing an additional burden to often strained budgets and potentially drawing resources away from other urgently needed social or developmental expenditures.

While undernutrition is still the main nutritional problem in the developing world, overnutrition is rapidly on the rise in many countries. The global prevalence of obesity nearly doubled between 1980 and 2008, reaching 14 percent among women and 10 percent among men (Finucane et al. 2011; Stevens et al. 2012). Along with North America, two developing regions—the Middle East and North Africa (MENA) and Latin America and the Caribbean (LAC)—exhibit the highest prevalence of obesity, with rates among women of more than 30 percent (Finucane et al. 2011; Stevens et al. 2012).

Rising rates of overnutrition often go along with a growing prevalence of noncommunicable diseases (NCDs), which entails substantially increasing healthcare costs and productivity losses to the individual and the society (Finkelstein, Fiebelkorn, and Wang 2003; Finkelstein, Ruhm, and Kosa 2005; Popkin et al. 2006; Trogdon et al. 2008). For example, the costs attributable to overweight and obesity in China are expected to rise from about US$50 billion in 2000 (or 4 percent of gross national product [GNP]) to about US$112 billion in 2025 (or 9 percent of GNP) (Popkin et al. 2006). Deaths related to NCDs are projected to increase by 15 percent worldwide between 2010 and 2020, with the greatest increases expected to exceed 20 percent in MENA, Africa south of the Sahara, and Southeast Asia (WHO 2011).

The rapid rise of overnutrition, combined with the relatively slow decline of undernutrition, has led in recent years to a new nutritional challenge of growing public health concern in several developing countries. The coexistence of over- and undernutrition—often referred to as "the double burden of malnutrition"—has been particularly prevalent in middle-income countries and especially those in the MENA and LAC regions.

A possible explanation for the rise of the double burden of malnutrition is a rapid "nutrition transition." This phenomenon describes the shift in dietary patterns and physical activity levels that emerges from economic growth and transformation in combination with technological advances (especially in communications and transportation) (Popkin 1993, 1994). Rapid shifts in dietary patterns and eating habits such as toward more processed foods and eating outside the home, in combination with a reduced physical workload from increasingly sedentary economic activities and a lack of physical exercise have increased overweight and obesity at a faster rate than undernutrition has been reduced (Prentice 2006; Schmidhuber and Shetty 2005; Shrimpton and Rokx 2012). In fact, several MENA countries, including Egypt—the most populous country in the region—have been going through a substantial nutrition transition since the mid-1970s, associated with rapid economic development (Galal 2002).

There is growing evidence that in addition to the nutrition transition, economic and social policies and programs may contribute to the rapid rise of overnutrition and the double burden of malnutrition in developing countries. For example, Asfaw (2006, 2007a, 2007b) finds that women's body mass indexes (BMIs) and the probability of female overweight and obesity in Egypt increase as prices of the foods that are subsidized under the national food subsidy system fall. And Leroy et al. (2013) show that cash and in-kind transfers lead to excess weight gain in a population of women in rural Mexico with a high prevalence of overweight. These case study findings are supported by evidence from studies in high-income countries, and particularly studies on the effects of the United States' Food Stamp Program on overweight and obesity (e.g., Chen, Yen, and Eastwood 2005; Meyerhoefer and Pylypchuk 2008; Ver Ploeg et al. 2007; Zagorsky and Smith 2009).

This book contributes to the literature on the effects of social policies and public programs on contemporary nutritional problems, using Egypt as a case study country. Specifically, our study serves two objectives: First, it provides a comprehensive overview of Egypt's two major nutritional challenges—which are exceptionally pronounced in Egypt compared to other developing countries—and their potential key drivers. These two nutritional challenges are (1) the double burden of malnutrition and (2) the phenomenon of high, decades-long economic growth that, contrary to expectations, was not accompanied by declining prevalence rates of chronic (child) undernutrition—a challenge referred to as the "growth-nutrition disconnect." Second, our study econometrically investigates causal relationships between one of the potential key drivers—consumer food subsidies—and nutritional outcomes. We hypothesize that Egypt's large and long-standing food subsidy system has contributed to sustaining and even aggravating both nutritional challenges.

To serve the first objective, we document that the double burden of malnutrition and the growth-nutrition disconnect are indeed exceptionally pronounced in Egypt compared to other developing countries, describe the respective patterns of malnutrition among the Egyptian population, and elaborate on four—possibly interlinked—factors that often have been hypothesized to cause or to contribute to the high prevalence of malnutrition in Egypt. In addition to the global phenomenon of the nutrition transition, they include rising poverty resulting from a succession of economic crises, the food subsidy system, and insufficient nutrition-sensitive investments.

The analysis in the first part of the book draws on a combination of literature reviews and descriptive statistics that we derived from various cross-country databases, official data sources, and cross-sectional household surveys, including several rounds of the Demographics and Health Survey (DHS) (MOH, El-Zanaty and Associates, and Macro International 2008; MOHP, NPC, and ORC Macro 2000; MOHP et al. 2003; MOHP et al. 2005). In the second part, we turn to the second objective by focusing on the causal effects of the Egyptian food subsidies on nutrition and the double burden of malnutrition in particular. For the main empirical analysis, we use both a quasi-experimental design and unique cross-sectional household survey datasets—compiled from the 2010–2011 Egypt Household Income, Expenditure, and Consumption Survey (HIECS) (CAPMAS and WFP 2011)—to estimate the hypothesized direct effects of the food subsidy system on child under- and overnutrition, maternal overnutrition, the coexistence of under- and overnutrition in the same children and the same child-mother pairs, and household diet quality. Providing statistical evidence for the existence of the causal relationships between received food subsidies and nutritional outcomes is fundamental for the hypothesized role of the food subsidy system as a driver of the double burden of malnutrition. In addition, a potential adverse effect of food subsidies on chronic child undernutrition is likely to contribute to the observed growth-nutrition disconnect.

We chose Egypt as a case study because the two nutritional challenges of the double burden of malnutrition and the growth-nutrition disconnect are much more pronounced in Egypt than in other developing countries and because addressing them through the reform of existing policies and programs can be expected to make a critical contribution to accelerating the country's economic and social development. Probably the most important ongoing social policy reform in Egypt is a substantial revision of the food subsidy system. We hope that the findings from our study will be useful for informing the ongoing food subsidy reform process and policies related to the country's social safety net in general. Because implications of food subsidies for nutrition and public health seem to have been hardly considered in past reforms, our study may offer a new perspective and an additional rationale for further changes and fundamental modifications.

From a public health perspective, the double burden of malnutrition is of particular concern. Almost every third Egyptian child under five years of age is chronically undernourished (according to 2011 estimates)—a prevalence rate that is more characteristic of developing countries with much lower national income levels than Egypt's. Egypt has also one of the highest female overweight rates in the world, affecting 78 percent of all (nonpregnant) ever-married women 15–49 years of age, while almost 40 percent are obese (El-Zanaty and Way 2009).[3] In addition, contrary to the global trend of decreasing undernutrition accompanying economic growth, chronic child undernutrition significantly increased over at least the first decade of the 2000s, despite high economic growth. A decade-average GDP growth of 4.8 percent was associated with an increase in the prevalence rate of child stunting, from 24.6 percent in 2000 to 31.2 percent in 2011. Although a few other developing countries have experienced increasing chronic child undernutrition in the face of economic growth in the 2000s, the magnitude of this growth-nutrition disconnect in Egypt is exceptional relative to other countries in the MENA region and other developing countries worldwide (as we will show in this book).

We argue that although the nutrition transition is an underlying development that has facilitated Egypt's contemporary nutritional challenges, it falls short of explaining Egypt's exceptionalism in the double burden of malnutrition. A common presumed explanation for the increase in the prevalence of child stunting is the cumulative impact of a succession of recent economic crises. These crises include the devaluation of the Egyptian pound (EGP) in 2003; the avian influenza epidemic in 2006; the global food, fuel, and financial crises of 2007–2009; and the macroeconomic instability caused by the revolution in the spring of 2011. Although these shocks have contributed to the continuous increase in (monetary) poverty, they fail to convincingly explain why child stunting increased most among the richest wealth/income

3 Adults are classified as overweight if their body mass indexes (BMIs) are 25 or larger, and as obese, if their BMIs are 30 or larger.

quintile of the Egyptian population and remained (nearly) stable among the poorest quintile (as we will show in this book).

We further argue that Egypt's large food subsidy system has been ineffective in reducing child and maternal undernutrition, and hypothesize that it has contributed to sustaining and even aggravating both nutritional challenges. The existence and the design of the food subsidy system may hence provide an explanation for the country's exceptionalism in the global comparison. The rationale for this hypothesis is twofold.

First, the food subsidy system may discourage good nutrition and possibly contribute directly to malnutrition—and to the double burden of malnutrition in particular—through incentivizing overconsumption of cheap, calorie-rich foods and unbalanced diets. Ample availability of cheap calories through subsidization creates an incentive for their consumption in excess, causing overweight and obesity. Calorie consumption above physiological requirement levels does not improve children's physical growth, while retardation in child growth in Egypt has been caused by insufficient micronutrient intakes from inadequate diets (possibly in addition to poor health conditions). Rapid increases of overweight and obesity and slow reduction, stagnation, or even increase of child stunting over past decades led to the double burden of malnutrition. In addition, inadequate reduction of—or even an increase in—child stunting despite high economic growth formed part of the growth-nutrition disconnect. The coverage and benefits of the Egyptian food subsidy system have been large and were even expanded in the 2000s—partly in response to the recent economic crises.

Second, the food subsidy system constitutes a heavy burden on the public budget (in addition to the even more sizeable fuel subsidies), so funds are unavailable for possibly more nutrition-beneficial investments. In this way, the subsidy system may maintain and aggravate malnutrition indirectly. This potential indirect effect of the food subsidies is omitted from our main empirical analysis because of a lack of the data required to conduct such an investigation.

Following this line of argumentation, the book is structured as follows. The second chapter analyzes the double burden of malnutrition and the growth-nutrition disconnect by comparing Egypt's situation with that of other developing countries and by exploring within-country differences between regions and population groups and over time. The third chapter investigates the potential key socioeconomic drivers of Egypt's exceptionalism. These potential drivers include the nutrition transition, the succession of recent economic crises, the food subsidy system, and the lack of nutrition-sensitive investment. The fourth chapter presents the main empirical analysis of the hypothesized nutritional effects of the Egyptian food subsidy system. It explains the applied methodology, describes the data from the 2010–2011 HIECS that were used, and presents the estimation results. The fifth chapter concludes the book by summarizing the main findings and discussing implications for policy and research.

Chapter 2

NUTRITIONAL CHALLENGES FOR ECONOMIC DEVELOPMENT

From an economic development perspective, malnutrition among women of reproductive age and among young children is of particular concern. This is because prevalence rates tend to be highest among these groups, their nutritional well-being is most crucial for future generations' prosperity, and targeted interventions have been found to be most cost-effective during the period from pregnancy to when a child is 24 months of age (Bryce et al. 2008; Engle et al. 2007; Horton et al. 2010).

Malnutrition among pregnant women can have serious long-term effects because of the biological intergenerational transmission of malnutrition in utero (see below). And malnourished mothers tend to be less able to provide sufficient and nutritious breast milk and adequate care to their children, which, in turn, increases the children's risk of being malnourished. Malnutrition during early childhood reduces cognitive and physical capacity and productivity in children's later life, so children born from malnourished mothers tend to be economically disadvantaged from the beginning compared to their well-nourished peers.

Due to the importance of maternal and child nutrition for economic and social development, our analysis focuses mainly on the nutritional status of preschool children and of women of reproductive age—especially the children's mothers. Nutritional status is determined by anthropometric measures. Anthropometric measurements, particularly for children under five years of age, have been shown to be reliable nutrition indicators and, more broadly, critical development indicators for several reasons.

First, focusing on young children, who are typically the weakest household members, captures aspects of intrahousehold distribution of resources (including food and care time) that are ignored when using household-level indicators such as poverty (as measured by household income) or food and nutrient consumption derived from standard household consumption surveys. Second, anthropometrics are measurements of the human body and hence indicators of nutritional (and health) outcomes (unlike food and nutrient consumption/intake). Third, they aggregately capture adequacy of food intake in terms of macro- and micronutrients, health status, and the interaction of nutrient absorption and diseases in the human body. Fourth, young children's nutritional status tends to be more responsive to changing living conditions and shocks than that of adults due to children's high physiological nutrient requirements for growth, special dietary needs, and high vulnerability to diseases common in underdeveloped settings. Fifth, high prevalence rates of malnourished children are often associated with poor delivery of basic public services (especially in the health sector), poor quality of drinking water and sanitation infrastructure, low educational levels, gender inequality, and high population growth rates.

Using selected anthropometric indicators, the following two sections examine the double burden of malnutrition and the growth-nutrition disconnect—Egypt's two main nutritional challenges—in detail.

The Double Burden of Malnutrition

Under- and overnutrition can coexist at the population, the family, and even the individual levels. Common forms of the double burden of malnutrition at the population level are high prevalence rates of stunting among children and overweight among adults; at the family level, stunted children with overweight mothers; and at the individual level, stunted but overweight children. Other common forms of the double burden of malnutrition include the coexistence of micronutrient deficiencies and overweight. Because this study is concerned with chronic malnutrition and the link to (future) economic development, it focuses on the coexistence of stunting among children under five years of age and overweight among them and among their mothers.

From a development policy analysis point of view, a situation where the double burden of malnutrition is prevalent at the population level but under- and overnutrition do not coexist in the same family or the same individual among a considerable share of the population may be of less concern compared to a situation where the double burden of malnutrition is also prevalent at the family and the individual levels. The former situation does not constitute a novel problem and may rather be an outcome of other, well-studied development challenges such as large inequalities in the distribution of wealth and access to public services. For example, one may imagine a situation in a country where undernutrition affects almost exclusively the poor and overnutrition almost exclusively the rich (Corsi, Kyu, and Subramanian 2011; Subramanian, Perkins, and Khan 2009). Because the problems of undernutrition and overnutrition are separate here, some policy implications from analyses looking at under- and overnutrition independently of each other should be transferable to this situation (given comparable settings).

However, such transferability of findings is inappropriate and can even lead to counterproductive policy recommendations where the double burden of malnutrition is also prevalent at the family and the individual levels, as in the case of Egypt (as we will show below). In such cases, households may face circumstances that can simultaneously contribute to both under- and overnutrition, and policies that influence these circumstances require careful consideration of their potential effects on both under- and overnutrition. Moreover, these circumstances must occur at large in order to result in prevalence rates of under- and overnutrition coexisting in families and individuals that are sufficiently high to be a public health concern.

Physiological Pathways to the Double Burden of Malnutrition

In the search for factors that cause and contribute to the double burden of malnutrition, it is important to note that there are genetic conditions that favor its manifestation and severity. Due to lack of suitable cohort data, we cannot estimate nutritional effects because of genetic factors and assess their importance relative to those of socioeconomic factors captured in our analyses (presented later in this book). Genetic conditions' contribution to the prevalence of malnutrition among the current generation, however, is likely to be of minor relevance for our study, which focuses on factors that can be influenced by policy changes in the present. Yet factors that cause and contribute to malnutrition in the current generation also increase the risk of malnutrition among future generations. The following literature review therefore describes such physiological pathways and draws particular attention to those that facilitate the phenomena of overweight mothers having stunted children and of stunted children being overweight at the same time.

The health literature provides robust evidence that under- and overnutrition is partly predetermined in utero. It also provides comprehensive evidence for several interlinked pathways by which fetal nutrition affects patterns of physical growth and body composition and increases the risk of nutrition-related noncommunicable diseases (NCDs) in the individuals' later lives. Most of these pathways build on or are consistent with Barker's well-known "mismatch hypothesis" (Barker 1988)—also known as "thrifty phenotype hypothesis" (Hales and Barker 1992, 2001). The hypothesis offers an explanation for the intergenerational transmission of malnutrition in terms of both over- and undernutrition and related NCDs. According to the hypothesis, poor nutrition during fetal life causes irreversible metabolic changes that are possibly designed to ensure survival in similar conditions as those faced in utero but increase the risk of nutritional diseases during adulthood when facing different conditions (Barker 1988).

To be specific, undernutrition during pregnancy in terms of macro- and micronutrient deficiencies is associated with higher risks of fetal growth retardation, premature birth, and low birth weight (Han et al. 2011; Haider and Bhutta 2012; Scholl and Hediger 1994; Yi, Han, and Ohrr 2013). Consistent with Barker's hypothesis, growth retardation can be seen as a mechanism to compensate for insufficient nutrient supply without compromising the development of vital organs. Low birth weight increases the risk of cardiovascular diseases, hypertension, and type 2 diabetes in adulthood—NCDs that are typically associated with overweight and obesity (Barker 2004).

Although overweight and obese women are less likely to give birth to low-weight babies (1,500–2,499 grams) than normal-weight women, they are more likely to give birth prematurely and to bear very low birth weight babies (< 1,500 grams), aggravating the risk of stillbirth (McDonald 2010). In addition, women with excess weight gain and associated symptoms of cardiovascular diseases during pregnancy are at an elevated risk of having children with these birth abnormalities (Eriksson et al. 1999; Gluckman and Hanson 2008). Being overweight during pregnancy can affect placental growth, leading to impaired nutrient supply to the fetus and thus fetal growth retardation as well (Wu et al. 2004).

It is worth noting here that low birth weight is an evident indicator of suboptimal intrauterine growth, but its absence does not necessarily imply optimal development for the fetus. Fetal undernutrition can affect cognitive development by causing structural damage to the brain and by impairing infant motor development and exploratory behavior (Victora et al. 2008). A cohort study from the United States suggests that differences in mean IQs are directly associated with birth weight, while each 0.5 IQ-point difference in male siblings at seven years of age corresponds to a 100-gram difference in birth weight, even within the normal birth weight range (Matte et al. 2001). Moreover, a systematic review study indicates that maternal obesity adversely affects breastfeeding success (Turcksin et al. 2014): compared with their normal-weight counterparts, obese women are less likely to intend to breastfeed. Maternal obesity is also associated with a delayed onset of milk secretion, a less adequate milk supply, and a decreased initiation and shortened duration of breastfeeding.

Undernutrition in utero and during infancy may also lead to permanent metabolic changes that increase the risk of overweight and obesity and related NCDs in adulthood (Barker 2004; Uauy et al. 2008). Children born from undernourished mothers may have developed a survival mechanism that allows them to better draw dietary energy from food and to more readily store it in their body as fat. However, when these individuals face a nutritional environment in childhood or adulthood that encourages obesity, they tend to gain weight faster than their healthy peers because of the prenatal metabolic programming (Hales and Barker 2001). In addition, people who were small at birth are more susceptible to hypertension and type 2 diabetes than people who were big. The development patterns of the two disorders are identical and coincide with that of coronary heart disease (Barker 2004). The risk of NCDs declines with increasing birth weight and rises with rapid weight gain in early childhood (Barker 2004; Koletzko et al. 2012).

Overnutrition during pregnancy may also cause permanent metabolic changes in the unborn that increase the risk of overweight and related NCDs later in life (Dabelea 2007; Dabelea et al. 2000; Freinkel 1980). The "fuel-mediated teratogenesis hypothesis" (Freinkel 1980) proposes that excess glucose supply in utero can give rise to irreversible dysfunctions of the body's control systems, including glucose intolerance, hunger regulation, and fat accumulation (Plagemann 2008). While maternal glucose is freely transferred to the fetus, maternal insulin does not cross the placenta, causing the fetus's pancreas to absorb high glucose levels by producing high volumes of insulin (Freinkel 1980). Although evidence from human studies is still limited, existing data point to a higher risk of diabetes in persons exposed to diabetes in utero, independent of adiposity and genetic predisposition of diabetes (Dabelea and Crume 2011). Yet the mechanism through which diabetes exposure in utero affects cardiovascular diseases is still not fully understood. Impaired insulin secretion has been proposed as a possible mechanism, considering that studies in newborns of diabetic mothers have revealed an enhanced insulin secretion in response to a glycemic stimulus. It is still unclear, however, if this is a transitory phenomenon or a symptom of impaired glucose tolerance later in life, when insulin resistance becomes important (Dabelea and Crume 2011). Nonetheless, there is compelling evidence that children from overweight women or women with excessive weight gain during pregnancy are at an increased risk of overweight and related NCDs, independent of genetic characteristics.

Finally, in utero growth retardation and low birth weight are associated with higher risks of postnatal child stunting and retarded head circumference growth, while children with reduced head circumference are more likely to be delayed in psychomotor development (Bove et al. 2012). Although stunting mainly manifests itself postnatally and usually peaks around 24 months (Victora et al. 2010), children born prematurely or small for gestational age are more likely to remain physically retarded in their growth compared to children born with normal stature and weight (Hediger et al. 1999; Karlberg and Albertsson-Wikland 1995; Leger et al. 1997; Strauss and Dietz 1998). Under suboptimal nutritional and health conditions, growth faltering cannot be caught up easily and may even accumulate over time, given the rapid development that children undergo, particularly during their first two years of life. Stunted children are more likely to become overweight in their later lives (Bove et al. 2012; El Taguri et al. 2009; Popkin et al. 1996; Schroeder, Martorell, and Flores 1999). Early evidence on the potential physiological mechanism involved in this process suggests that stunted children have a lower fat oxidation than their well-nourished peers and are therefore at higher risks of adiposity (Sawaya and Roberts 2003; Hoffman et al. 2000a, 2000b).

In conclusion, "chronic diseases are not the inevitable lot of humankind; they are the result of the changing pattern of human development," as Barker (2012; p. 185) puts it. Many children are malnourished and have an increased risk of NCDs in their later lives because their mothers were malnourished during pregnancy and lactation. In addition to the genetic loading, children with malnourished mothers have an increased risk of malnutrition because they tend to share the same or a similarly inadequate diet. Household diets are determined by household incomes, food prices, education, and many other factors—some of which can be influenced by economic and social policies.

Egypt's Double Burden of Malnutrition in the Global Comparison

The double burden of malnutrition is most pronounced in two developing regions, namely the MENA and LAC regions (Garrett and Ruel 2005). While undernutrition is still common in both regions, overnutrition has been rising rapidly in the wake of high economic growth and structural transformation in recent decades. In fact, along with North America, the MENA and LAC regions exhibit the highest prevalence of overweight and obesity, with rates among women (20 years of age and older) of more than 60 percent for overweight and 30 percent for obesity (Finucane et al. 2011; Stevens et al. 2012).

The prevalence of female overweight and obesity and the prevalence of child stunting are inversely correlated across countries. Considering that the countries are at different stages of economic development, the inverse relationship may also mark the typical course of decreasing child stunting and increasing female overweight and obesity that an average country follows throughout its development process. Our estimated functions suggest that the relationship has a flattened S-shaped curve (Figure 2.1 and Figure 2.2).

Yet several countries deviate from the general relationship. For example, relative to the prevalence of child stunting, the prevalence of female overweight and obesity is extremely high in Egypt, Guatemala, Iraq, Lesotho, Mexico, Panama, South Africa, and Saudi Arabia. Among these countries, the prevalence of child stunting exceeds 30 percent in Egypt, Guatemala, Lesotho, and South Africa. The gap between the actual prevalence rate of female overweight and obesity and the expected one given the actual child stunting rate is widest in Egypt, particularly for female obesity—the more severe form of overnutrition. Hence, according to this measure, the double burden of malnutrition (at the population level) in Egypt is most pronounced in the global comparison.

Egypt's prevalence of female overweight and obesity alone is among the highest in the world. Egypt ranks among the top 10 countries with the highest rate of obese women, ahead of the United States, Mexico, and Iraq and behind only Kuwait, Libya, Qatar, and some small Caribbean island states (Ng et al. 2014). Data from the Egypt DHSs in 2000, 2003, 2005, and 2008 suggest that a stable proportion of around 80 percent of all (nonpregnant) women 20–49 years of age were overweight between 2000 and 2008 (MOH, El-Zanaty and Associates, and Macro International 2008; MOHP, NPC, and ORC Macro 2000; MOHP et al. 2003; MOHP et al. 2005). The prevalence rate of female obesity in 2008 was about 40 percent, roughly the same as in 2000.[1] Considering a longer study period of 33 years, Ng et al. (2014) find the largest average increase in the female obesity rate to be in Egypt, followed by Saudi Arabia, Oman, Honduras, and Bahrain. Hence, the public health problem of chronic overnutrition and related NCDs in Egypt has increased considerably in severity in recent decades (Herman et al. 1995). In fact, Egypt has one of the highest death rates from cardiovascular diseases and diabetes in the developing world (Alwan et al. 2010). Abegunde et al. (2007) estimate that Egypt lost a cumulative US$1.26 billion to chronic diseases between 2005 and 2015; most of the loss is due to cardiovascular diseases and diabetes.

1 See Tables A.1 and A.2 in the Appendix.

FIGURE 2.1 Relationship between the prevalence of female overweight and child stunting

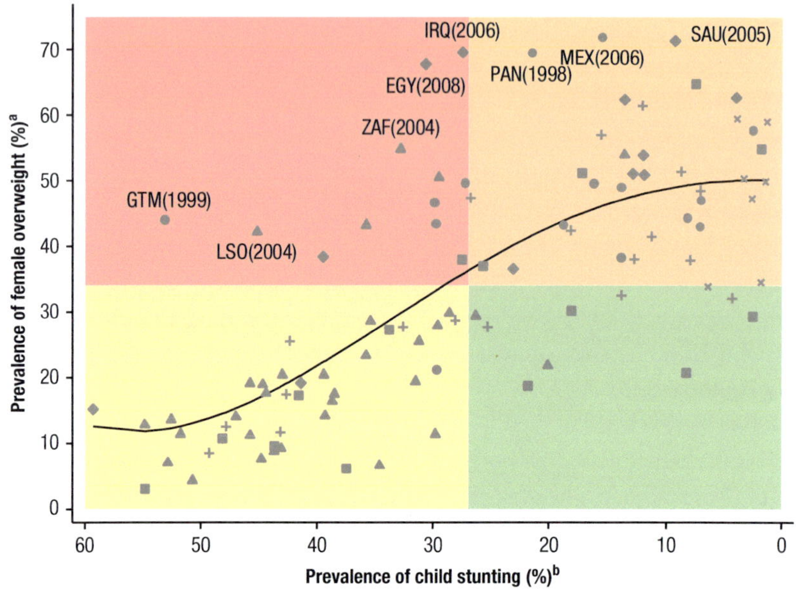

Source: Authors' estimation based on data from World Bank (2014).

Note: The sample includes the latest observations of the prevalence of female overweight and child stunting (measured within a period of less than five years) for 101 countries.

The regions are North America and Western Europe high-income countries (+); Arab world (♦); Africa south of the Sahara (▲); Latin America and Caribbean (•); East Asia and Pacific (▪); and West, Central, and South Asia and Eastern Europe (×).

Countries with a high prevalence of female overweight relative to their prevalence of child stunting include Egypt (EGY), Guatemala (GTM), Iraq (IRQ), Lesotho (LSO), Mexico (MEX), Panama (PAN), Saudi Arabia (SAU), and South Africa (ZAF).

The estimated relationship between the prevalence of female overweight and the prevalence of child stunting is obtained in two steps. In the first step, a nonparametric regression is applied to the data, and the estimated function is graphed to gain evidence on the form of a parametric function that yields the best data fit. A locally weighted regression is run, using Stata's "lowess" (locally weighted scatter plot smoothing) command. (The chosen bandwidth of the lowess curve is 0.8, which is Stata's standard bandwidth. The results of the nonparametric regression are not reported.) Based on the found shape of the curve, a fractional polynomial regression of degree 2 and a robust estimator of variance are applied to the data in the second step to determine the specific functional form and plot the predicted line of the relationship.

The estimated function is: $y = -1.370 * (((x/10)^3) - 19.556) + 0.668 * (((x/10)^3) * \ln(x/10) - 19.381) + 36.360$, where y is a country's female overweight rate, and x is its child stunting rate. Statistical significance and explanatory power of the model are high (F = 56.65, R-sq. = 0.536).

The sample means divide the sample into four quadrants, which group the countries according to the severity of the double burden of malnutrition. The color of the quadrant indicates the severity of the double burden of malnutrition, with green indicating low severity and red indicating high severity.

[a] The prevalence of female overweight is defined as the proportion of women 15 years of age and older with a body mass index (BMI) of 25 or higher.

[b] The prevalence rate of child stunting is defined as the proportion of children under five years of age with height-for-age z-scores (HAZs) below −2.

FIGURE 2.2 **Relationship between the prevalence of female obesity and child stunting**

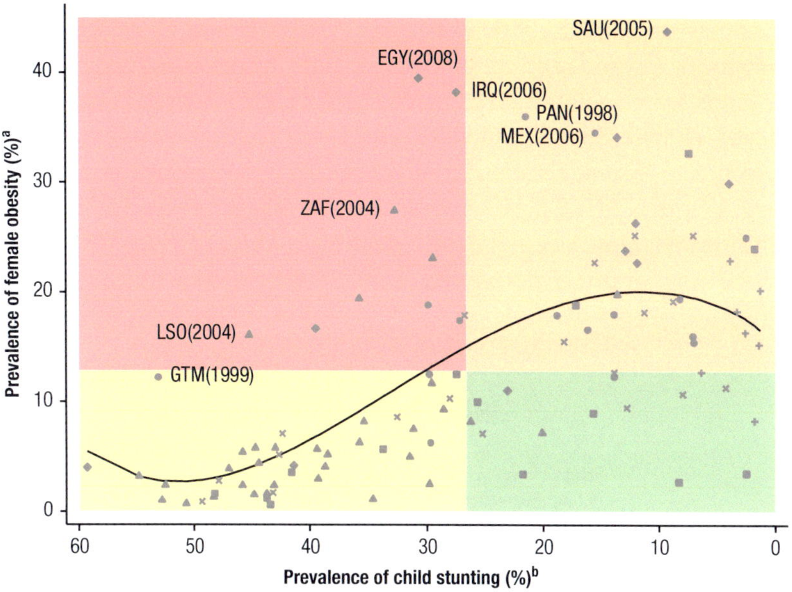

Source: Authors' estimation based on data from World Bank (2014).

Note: The sample includes the latest observations of the prevalence of female obesity and child stunting (measured within a period of less than five years) for 100 countries.

The regions are North America and Western Europe high-income countries (+); Arab world (♦); Africa south of the Sahara (▲); Latin America and Caribbean (•); East Asia and Pacific (▪); and West, Central, and South Asia and Eastern Europe (×).

Countries with a high prevalence of female obesity relative to their prevalence of child stunting include Egypt (EGY), Guatemala (GTM), Iraq (IRQ), Lesotho (LSO), Mexico (MEX), Panama (PAN), Saudi Arabia (SAU), and South Africa (ZAF).

The estimated relationship between the prevalence of female overweight and the prevalence of child stunting is obtained in two steps. In the first step, a nonparametric regression is applied to the data, and the estimated function is graphed to gain evidence on the form of a parametric function that yields the best data fit. A locally weighted regression is run, using Stata's "lowess" (locally weighted scatter plot smoothing) command. (The chosen bandwidth of the lowess curve is 0.8, which is Stata's standard bandwidth. The results of the nonparametric regression are not reported.) Based on the found shape of the curve, a fractional polynomial regression of degree 3 and a robust estimator of variance are applied to the data in the second step to determine the specific functional form and plot the predicted line of the relationship.

The estimated function is: $y = 7.119 * (((x/10)^{\wedge}0.5) - 1.633) - 1.095 * (((x/10)^{\wedge}3) - 18.957) + 0.546 * (((x/10)^{\wedge}3) * \ln(x/10) - 18.582) + 14.999$, where y is a country's prevalence rate of female obesity (in percent) and x is its prevalence rate of child stunting (in percent). Statistical significance and explanatory power of the model are moderately high ($F = 20.80$, R-sq. = 0.375).

The sample means divide the sample into four quadrants, which group the countries according to the severity of the double burden of malnutrition. The color of the quadrant indicates the severity of the double burden of malnutrition, with green indicating low severity and red indicating high severity.

[a] The prevalence of female obesity is defined as the proportion of women 15 years of age and older with a body mass index (BMI) of 30 or higher.

[b] The prevalence rate of child stunting is defined as the proportion of children under five years of age with height-for-age z-scores (HAZs) below –2.

Patterns of the Double Burden of Malnutrition within Egypt

Data from the HIECS in 2011 (CAPMAS and WFP 2011) suggest that almost every third young child in Egypt is stunted. Hence, their physical development is retarded as a result of inadequate nutrition and poor health conditions, which will remain a life-long health impairment in most cases—with all its implications for individual well-being and economic development. In addition to chronic child undernutrition, child overnutrition is widespread. The 2011 HIECS data suggest that overweight among children ages 6–59 months is almost as prevalent as stunting in this age group, while a large proportion suffer from stunting and overweight at the same time (Table 2.1).

TABLE 2.1 Prevalence patterns of the double burden of malnutrition in Egypt

	DBM at population level				DBM at family level	DBM at individual level
	Child stunting	Child overweight	Female overweight	Female obesity	Stunted child with overweight mother	Stunting and overweight in children
Total (%)	**31.2**	**29.2**	**72.6**	**33.9**	**22.3**	**14.0**
By region and residential area[a] (%)						
Metropolitan	30.8	29.5	74.0	33.9	26.9	15.6
Lower Egypt	27.1	30.7	78.3	40.9	20.6	12.7
Urban	24.7	27.1	78.5	39.7	20.4	11.9
Rural	27.8	31.7	78.2	41.4	20.7	12.9
Upper Egypt	34.7	27.0	65.6	25.8	21.5	14.3
Urban	39.2	28.1	71.5	29.4	25.6	16.2
Rural	33.4	26.7	62.8	24.1	20.2	13.7
By income quintile and residential area (%)						
Quintile 1 (poorest)	34.0	27.9	66.2	27.6	20.0	14.6
Quintile 2	32.3	28.9	71.2	32.4	22.2	15.0
Quintile 3	29.2	28.7	75.1	36.6	22.8	11.9
Quintile 4	27.2	26.6	75.3	37.5	20.3	12.5
Quintile 5 (richest)	33.1	33.7	75.0	35.5	26.1	15.9
Urban	31.9	28.8	74.3	34.2	25.3	15.1
Quintile 1 (poorest)	33.0	26.4	72.6	31.4	21.8	13.2
Quintile 2	32.3	29.9	77.0	36.7	25.5	16.6
Quintile 3	31.9	27.4	74.2	35.8	26.4	16.3
Quintile 4	33.0	30.4	76.1	36.2	29.9	14.1
Quintile 5 (richest)	29.4	30.1	71.6	30.7	22.9	15.4

	DBM at population level				DBM at family level	DBM at individual level
	Child stunting	Child overweight	Female overweight	Female obesity	Stunted child with overweight mother	Stunting and overweight in children
Rural	30.8	29.3	71.3	33.8	20.6	13.4
Quintile 1 (poorest)	32.3	27.1	62.3	25.5	17.6	13.9
Quintile 2	33.8	28.2	69.6	31.0	22.4	14.5
Quintile 3	30.7	31.6	71.0	33.4	22.4	12.1
Quintile 4	26.8	25.9	74.9	37.3	18.8	11.7
Quintile 5 (richest)	30.3	34.0	78.8	41.8	21.9	14.7

Source: Authors' calculation based on data from CAPMAS and WFP (2011).

Note: DBM = double burden of malnutrition.

The child stunting sample includes children ages 6–59 months with biologically plausible height-for-age z-scores (HAZs) (−6 ≤ HAZ ≤ 6) and has 3,852 observations. The child overweight sample includes children ages 6–59 months with biologically plausible body-mass-index-for-age z-scores (BMIZs) (−5 ≤ BMIZ ≤ 5) and has 3,631 observations. The female overweight/obesity sample includes nonpregnant women 20–49 years of age with biologically plausible body mass indexes (BMIs) (5.2 ≤ BMI ≤ 52.1) and has 9,778 observations. All others are subsamples of these samples with observations in both original samples. The child stunting and maternal overweight sample has 3,661 observations, and the child stunting and overweight sample has 3,577 observations.

The prevalence rate of child stunting is defined as the proportion of children with HAZs below −2, and the prevalence of child overweight is defined as the proportion of children with BMIZs of 2 or above. The prevalence of female overweight is defined as the proportion of women with BMIs of 25 or above, and the prevalence of female obesity is defined as the proportion of women with BMIs of 30 or above.

The household disaggregation by wealth/income quintile in the Demographic and Health Surveys samples (MOH, El-Zanaty and Associates, and Macro International 2008; Egypt, MOHP, NPC, and ORC Macro 2000; MOHP et al. 2003; MOHP et al. 2005) is based on the distribution of asset wealth (measured by a composite index), and the household disaggregation in the Household Income, Expenditure, and Consumption Survey sample (CAPMAS and WFP 2011) is based on the distribution of household income per capita.

[a] Prevalence rates for Frontier Governorates are not reported because of insufficient observations.

While 31.2 percent of the children are stunted, 29.2 percent are overweight.[2] Of those children who are stunted, about 45 percent are overweight. In total, 14.0 percent of all children ages 6–59 months are stunted and overweight. Children's height-for-age z-scores (HAZs; indicating stunting) are distinctly negatively and linearly correlated with their body-mass-index-for-age z-scores (BMIZs; indicating overweight and obesity) (Figure 2.3); the correlation coefficient is −0.431. Hence, in Egypt shorter children tend to be fatter than their taller peers. Note that child wasting (indicating acute child undernutrition)

2 Children are classified as stunted if their height-for-age z-scores (HAZs) are below −2 and as overweight if their body-mass-index-for-age z-scores (BMIZs) are 2 or above.

FIGURE 2.3 Relationship between children's BMIZs and HAZs in Egypt

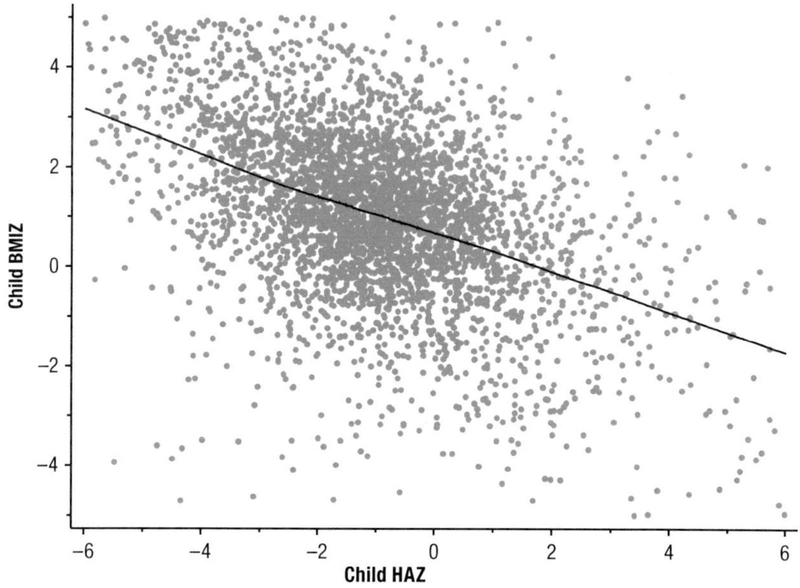

Source: Authors' estimation based on data from CAPMAS and WFP (2011).

Note: The sample includes children ages 6–59 months with biologically plausible body-mass-index-for-age z-scores (BMIZs) ($-5 \leq$ BMIZ ≤ 5) and height-for-age z-scores (HAZs) ($-6 \leq$ HAZ ≤ 6) and has 3,577 observations.

The relationship between children's BMIZs and HAZs is estimated nonparametrically, using a locally weighted regression estimation inbuilt in Stata. The chosen bandwidth is 0.8, which is Stata's default bandwidth of the "lowess" (locally weighted scatter plot smoothing) command.

and child underweight (indicating overall child undernutrition) have been low in Egypt, with national prevalence rates of below 8 percent since 2000.[3]

Moreover, the 2011 HIECS data (CAPMAS and WFP 2011) suggest that about 71 percent of all stunted Egyptian children have an overweight mother.[4] Out of all Egyptian child-mother pairs, 22.3 percent are child-mother pairs with a stunted child and an overweight mother (Table 2.1). According to the HIECS data, 72.6 percent of (nonpregnant) Egyptian women 20–49 years

3 Children are classified as wasted if their weight-for-height z-score (WHZ) is below −2 and as underweight if their weight-for-age z-score (WAZ) is below −2. For disaggregated prevalence rates of child nutrition indicators, see Tables A.3–A.6 in the Appendix.

4 The HIECS (CAPMAS and WFP 2011) does not explicitly indicate the child's mother. However, we are able to identify the likely mother—or female caretaker—using information from the household member characteristics module. See Box 4.2 in the subsection "Survey Data and Estimation Variables" below. In the following, we omit "caretaker" for ease of readability.

FIGURE 2.4 Relationship between women's BMIs and body heights in Egypt

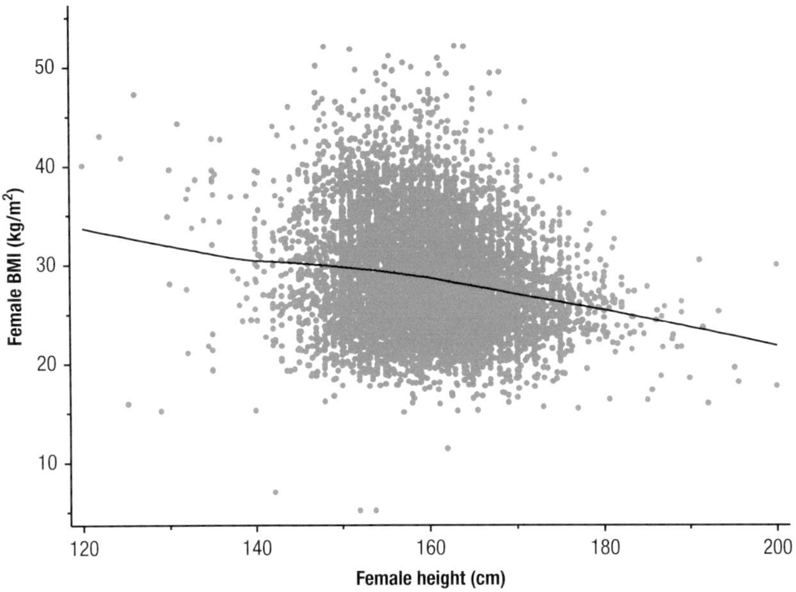

Source: Authors' estimation based on data from CAPMAS and WFP (2011).

Note: cm = centimeters; kg/m^2 = kilograms per square meter.

The sample includes nonpregnant women 20–49 years of age with biologically plausible body mass indexes (BMIs) ($5.2 \leq$ BMI ≤ 52.1) and has 9,778 observations.

The relationship between women's BMIs and heights is estimated nonparametrically using a locally weighted regression estimation inbuilt in Stata. The chosen bandwidth is 0.8, which is Stata's default bandwidth of the "lowess" (locally weighted scatter plot smoothing) command.

of age are overweight, and 33.9 percent are obese.[5] For these women, we also find a linear, negative relationship between their BMIs and absolute body heights (Figure 2.4), although the correlation, with a coefficient of −0.193, is less strong than that for children. Hence, shorter Egyptian women tend to be fatter than their taller peers. Note that stunting in women—which manifests itself mainly during early childhood—is not very prevalent in Egypt today. The 2011 HIECS data suggest that only 1.6 percent of all (nonpregnant) women 20–49 years of age are shorter than 145 centimeters (cm). And female underweight is almost nonexistent in Egypt. According to the HIECS

5 The 2011 HIECS data (CAPMAS and WFP 2011) indicate somewhat lower prevalence of female overweight and obesity than the 2008 DHS data (MOP, El-Zanaty and Associates, and Macro International 2008; MOHP, NPC, and ORC Macro 2000; MOHP et al. 2003; MOHP et al. 2005) did. These differences may partly be due to different survey years and sample populations.

data, 0.8 percent of all (nonpregnant) women 20–49 years of age are underweight.[6] DHS data from the survey rounds in 2000, 2003, 2005, and 2008 indicate that underweight affected less than 1 percent of all (nonpregnant) women throughout the 2000s (MOH, El-Zanaty and Associates, and Macro International 2008; MOHP, NPC, and ORC Macro 2000; MOHP et al. 2003; MOHP et al. 2005).

These first results have several important implications: The double burden of malnutrition in Egypt is not only highly prevalent at the population level but also at the family and the individual levels. The findings that under- and overnutrition exist in child-mother pairs and in the same children at considerable prevalence rates, and that individual body height and weight are negatively correlated among young children and women of reproductive age, suggest that lack of sufficient staple foods can be ruled out as a cause of widespread undernutrition. In other words, chronic hunger should not be an issue of public concern. This notion is also supported by low prevalence rates of wasting and underweight among children and of underweight among women.

Instead, these correlations point to a nutritional situation where calorie-rich foods are readily and cheaply available, which encourages overconsumption of these foods; where a large share of the population cannot afford or does not prefer a diversified diet dense in micronutrient-rich foods (such as meat, fish, dairy products, pulses, vegetables, and fruits); and where individual health conditions compromise optimal nutritional outcomes. The results also imply that the same circumstances in households' environments, the same behavior of their members, and the same individual characteristics may indeed contribute to both under- and overnutrition at the same time.

Furthermore, the HIECS data (CAPMAS and WFP 2011) show no distinct patterns in the prevalence of undernutrition, overnutrition, and the double burden of malnutrition between urban and rural areas and between regions (Table 2.1). This might be surprising given that there are clear economic development gaps between urban and rural areas, the Metropolitan areas and the rest of Egypt, and Lower and Upper Egypt. The regional patterns of some forms of malnutrition appear to even be inconsistent with those of economic development. For example, child stunting is somewhat more prevalent in the Metropolitan areas than in urban Lower Egypt—although less prevalent than in urban Upper Egypt. In Upper Egypt, the prevalence of child stunting is higher in urban areas than in rural areas. Female overweight and obesity are more prevalent in both urban and rural areas of Lower Egypt

6 Adults are classified as underweight if their BMIs are below 18.5.

than in the Metropolitan areas, whereas they are least prevalent in Upper Egypt. The double burden of malnutrition at the family and the individual levels is most prevalent in the Metropolitan areas and urban Upper Egypt.[7] The absence of distinct spatial prevalence patterns of under- and overnutrition and unexpectedly high prevalence rates in some parts of Egypt may be explained by the coverage of the food subsidy system, the local health environment, and differential impacts of the crises in the 2000s (Kavle et al. 2015a) to some extent.

Breaking down the malnutrition prevalence rates by income quintiles reveals no clear income-dependent patterns for any considered form of malnutrition—with the exception of female overnutrition in rural areas (Table 2.1).[8] Thus, unlike most other developing countries, Egypt shows no typical tendency of high rates of undernutrition among poor rural households and of high rates of overnutrition among rich urban households. In contrast, undernutrition and overnutrition are highly prevalent among both the poor and the rich at relatively similar rates. These results—obtained from the 2011 HIECS data (CAPMAS and WFP 2011)—are largely consistent with the patterns found in the DHSs conducted in the 2000s (MOH, El-Zanaty and Associates, and Macro International 2008; MOHP, NPC, and ORC Macro 2000; MOHP et al. 2003; MOHP et al. 2005).[9] In addition, the HIECS data also do not reveal, either in rural or in urban areas, obvious income-dependent patterns of the double burden of malnutrition at the family and the individual levels. Overall, these findings provide some initial evidence that household income (and monetary poverty) alone is unlikely to be the main driver of malnutrition in Egypt.

The next section explores how the prevalence of chronic child undernutrition—one component of the double burden of malnutrition—changed over time in Egypt relative to national economic growth and compared to other developing countries, as well as between different regions in Egypt and among different income/wealth groups of the Egyptian population.

---

7 See Tables A.7 and A.8 in the Appendix.

8 This also holds true when using household expenditure instead of household income for defining quintiles. In this study we use reported household incomes from the income section of the HIECS (CAPMAS and WFP 2011) because household expenditures are influenced by the amount of subsidies the households receive. We checked the robustness of all results using household expenditures instead of household incomes and did not find significant deviations. Note that the coefficient of the correlation of household income and expenditures is 0.906 across the entire sample (and 0.909 for urban households and 0.844 for rural households).

9 See Tables A.1–A.8 of the Appendix.

The Growth-Nutrition Disconnect

Economic growth leads to reduced undernutrition—at least in the long term—through two main routes. First, economic growth increases household incomes. Higher incomes allow households to purchase more and more nutritious food and to spend more on health, education, and housing that may result in improved nutrition indicators. Hence, the degree to which growth translates into reduced prevalence rates of undernutrition mainly depends on the proportion of the undernourished population that experiences income increases and the rates at which that population's income grows—in other words, it depends on the inclusiveness of economic growth.

Second, economic growth tends to increase the public budget through higher tax revenues, state-owned enterprises, and other revenue sources. These additional revenues provide fiscal space for income redistribution policies (affecting individual nutrition through the first route), investments in nutrition-sensitive infrastructure and public services (such as water and sanitation and basic healthcare), and health and nutrition-specific interventions (such as micronutrient supplementation and fortification and nutrition information and education programs). In addition, policies often play a critical role in influencing consumers' choices: they can either create an environment that encourages people to use increasing income for improving nutrition or that discourages them from nutrition-beneficial spending. An example of a policy that can incentivize unhealthy diets is food subsidies—as hypothesized in this book.

Thus, national policy can influence the degree to which economic growth translates into reduced prevalence rates of undernutrition through the amount of additional public budget generated from economic growth, the allocation and efficiency of the additional resources, the quality (and effectiveness) of the public services provided, and the design of policies enabling or interfering with nutritional improvement (Bryce et al 2008; Gillespie et al. 2013; Haddad et al. 2003; Smith and Haddad 2002).

Egypt's Chronic Child Undernutrition and Economic Growth in a Global Comparison

Relative to the national income level, chronic child undernutrition has been considerably more prevalent in Egypt than in most other developing countries—with the exception of a period in the late 1990s and early 2000s when it reached average prevalence rates (Figure 2.5). On a global level, countries' child stunting rate has declined, at decreasing margins, with increasing GDP

FIGURE 2.5 Relationship between the prevalence of chronic child undernutrition and national income

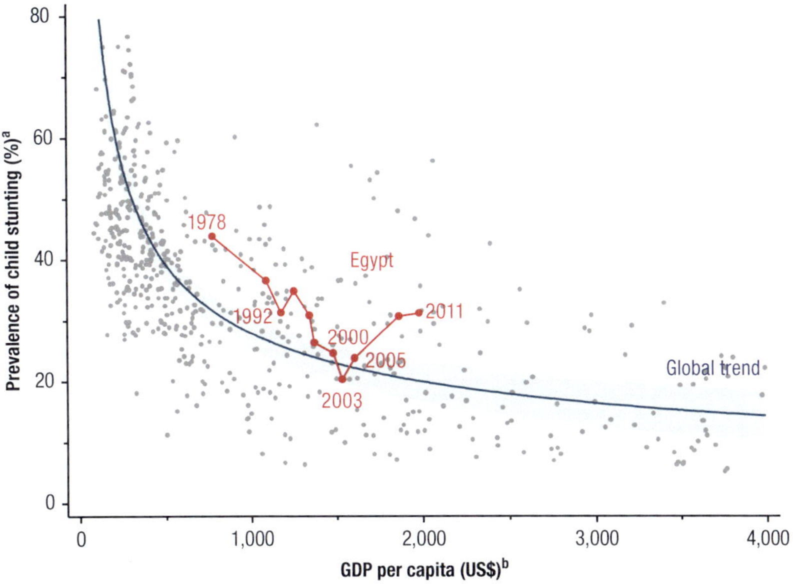

Source: Authors' estimation based on data from World Bank (2014), complemented with data from other sources. Child stunting rates for Egypt in 2011 are derived from CAPMAS and WFP (2011) data. Missing year observations of gross domestic product (GDP) per capita levels are replaced by computed GDP per capita levels, using GDP growth rates derived from IMF (2014) and UNSTAT (2014) and population data from UN-DESA (2014).

Note: The sample includes child stunting and GDP data for 141 countries with child stunting rates of 5 percent and above. The sample has a total of 628 observations, spanning the period from 1966 to 2012. The figure presents an excerpt, including countries with GDP per capita below US$4,000 (composing 89 percent of all observations).

The estimation of the "global trend" graph is bivariate and cross-country (based on the full sample) and includes two steps. In the first step, a nonparametric regression is applied, and the results are plotted to gain evidence on the general functional form of the relationship between the prevalence of child stunting and GDP per capita levels. A locally weighted regression is run, using Stata's "lowess" (locally weighted scatter plot smoothing) command. (The chosen bandwidth of the lowess curve is 0.8, which is Stata's standard bandwidth. The results of the nonparametric regression are not reported.) Given the shape of the curve, a fractional polynomial regression of degree 1 and a robust estimator of variance are applied to the data in the second step to determine the specific functional form and plot the predicted line of the relationship. The regression is weighted by population size.

The estimated function is: $y = 8.604 * (((x/10{,}000)\text{^}(-0.5)) - 2.385) + 21.220$, where y is a country's prevalence rate of child stunting (percentage) and x is its GDP per capita level in the same year. Statistical significance and explanatory power of the model are high (F = 124.7, R-sq. = 0.625). We tested alternative specifications of the functional form that had GDP per capita levels lagged by one to five years but found no clear evidence for general time lags. The shaded area around the global trend line marks the 95 percent confidence interval.

[a] The prevalence rate of child stunting is defined as the proportion of children under five years of age with height-for-age z-scores (HAZs) below −2.

[b] GDP per capita is measured at constant 2000 prices.

TABLE 2.2 Country comparison of child stunting reduction and economic growth

Country	Around 2010			Around 2000			Annual average change in the prevalence of child stunting (percentage points)	Annual average GDP per capita growth (%)	Arc child stunting-growth elasticity[c]
	Prevalence of child stunting (%)[a]	GDP per capita (US$)[b]	Year	Prevalence of child stunting (%)[a]	GDP per capita (US$)[b]	Year			
Egypt	**31.2**	**1,977**	**2011**	**24.6**	**1,476**	**2000**	**0.6**	**2.7**	**0.22**
Countries with similar stunting rates[d]									
Angola	29.2	563	2007	61.7	272	1996	–3.0	6.8	–0.43
Cameroon	32.6	666	2011	36.7	570	1998	–0.3	1.2	–0.26
Haiti	29.7	385	2006	28.3	424	2000	0.2	–1.6	–0.15
Honduras	29.9	1,354	2006	34.5	1,150	2001	–0.9	3.3	–0.28
Togo	29.8	266	2010	29.8	283	1998	0.0	–0.5	0.00
Zimbabwe	32.3	323	2010	33.7	556	1999	–0.1	–4.8	0.03
Countries with similar GDP per capita levels[e]									
Algeria	15.9	2,115	2005	23.6	1,794	2000	–1.5	3.3	–0.46
Azerbaijan	26.8	1,574	2006	24.1	655	2000	0.5	15.7	0.03
China	9.4	2,426	2010	17.8	949	2000	–0.8	9.8	–0.09
Guatemala	48.0	1,856	2009	50.0	1,717	2000	–0.2	0.9	–0.26
Morocco	14.9	1,941	2011	29.0	1,215	1997	–1.0	3.4	–0.30
Syria	27.5	1,509	2009	24.3	1,209	2000	0.4	2.5	0.14
Other Arab countries[f]									
Iraq	27.5	710	2006	28.3	1,063	2000	–0.1	–6.5	0.02
Jordan	8.3	2,577	2009	12.0	1,871	2002	–0.5	4.7	–0.11
Oman	9.8	11,192	2009	12.9	8,343	1999	–0.3	3.0	–0.10

Somalia	42.1	288	2006	29.2	277	2000	2.2	0.6	3.48
Sudan	38.3	582	2006	47.6	445	2000	–1.6	4.6	–0.34
Tunisia	9.0	2,776	2006	16.8	2,245	2000	–1.3	3.6	–0.36
West Bank and Gaza	11.8	984	2007	16.1	979	2002	–0.9	0.1	–7.54
Yemen	59.6	574	2006	59.3	508	1997	0.0	1.4	0.02
Other large developing countries[g]									
Bangladesh	41.4	588	2011	50.8	364	2000	–0.9	4.5	–0.19
Brazil	7.1	4,298	2007	13.5	3,628	1996	–0.6	1.6	–0.37
Ethiopia	44.2	230	2011	57.4	124	2000	–1.2	5.8	–0.21
India	47.9	622	2006	51.0	441	1999	–0.4	5.0	–0.09
Indonesia	39.2	1,145	2010	42.4	773	2000	–0.3	4.0	–0.08
Nigeria	36.0	566	2011	39.7	361	1999	–0.3	3.8	–0.08
Pakistan	43.0	672	2011	41.5	511	2001	0.2	2.8	0.05
Philippines	33.6	1,413	2011	38.3	1,017	1998	–0.4	2.6	–0.14
Vietnam	23.3	723	2010	43.4	402	2000	–2.0	6.1	–0.33

Source: Authors' calculation based on data from World Bank (2014), complemented with data from other sources. Child stunting rates for Egypt in 2011 are derived from CAPMAS and WFP (2011) data; child stunting rates for Yemen in 2006 are derived from CSO (2006) data. Missing year observations of gross domestic product (GDP) per capita levels are replaced by computed GDP per capita levels, using GDP growth rates derived from IMF (2014) and UNSTAT (2014) and population data from UN-DESA (2014).

Note: The sample includes countries with populations above 5 million people, a child health survey in the period 2005–2013, a child health survey in the period 1996–2004, a difference of at least five years between the two surveys, and GDP data reported for the years of the child health surveys.

[a] The prevalence rate of child stunting is defined as the proportion of children under five years of age with height-for-age z-scores (HAZs) below –2; [b] GDP per capita is measured in US dollars at constant 2000 prices; [c] Arc elasticities are presented in gray if countries experienced negative GDP per capita growth.

The sample includes 91 countries. The countries were selected according to the following criteria: [d] Countries with child stunting rates in the range of 2 percentage points around Egypt's rate; [e] Countries with GDP per capita levels in the range of US$500 around Egypt's GDP; [f] Arab countries that do not fall into the first two categories, where Arab countries include all 21 Arab League member states and Syria (which was suspended from the League in 2011); [g] Countries with populations over 80 million people that do not fall into the first two categories (Egypt's population in 2011 was 82.5 million).

per capita levels. Egypt followed this global trend throughout the 1980s and 1990s and even experienced over-proportionate reduction rates in the second half of the 1990s. However, Egypt's progress reversed in the early 2000s, and the prevalence of child stunting steadily increased throughout the 2000s. In fact, despite high economic growth in the 1990s and 2000s, child stunting in Egypt in 2011 (31.2 percent) was as prevalent as it was in 1992 (31.3 percent).[10]

Between 1992 and 2000, the prevalence of child stunting in Egypt declined by an average annual rate of 0.83 percentage points, so each 1 percent GDP per capita growth was associated with an average annual decrease in the child stunting rate of 0.29 percentage points. Globally, each 1 percent GDP per capita growth was associated with an average annual decrease in the child stunting rate of only 0.12 percentage points (at a GDP per capita level equivalent to Egypt's average GDP per capita during this period). However, between 2000 and 2011, the prevalence of child stunting in Egypt increased by an average annual rate of 0.60 percentage points, and each 1 percent GDP per capita growth in Egypt was associated with an average annual increase of 0.22 percentage points in the prevalence of child stunting (Table 2.2). In contrast, the global trend suggests an average annual decrease of 0.10 percentage points (at a GDP level equivalent to Egypt's period-average GDP per capita).

International comparisons confirm that Egypt's nutrition-growth disconnect is particularly pronounced (Table 2.2). Countries with prevalence rates of child stunting similar to Egypt's have considerably lower GDP per capita levels. Conversely, countries with similar GDP per capita levels have substantially lower prevalence rates of child stunting, with the exception of Guatemala—another country facing a pronounced double burden of malnutrition (Figure 2.1 and Figure 2.2). Further, only a few other countries experienced increasing chronic child undernutrition in the face of economic growth in the 2000s (Table 2.2). Most of these countries were affected by civil war or were in a postconflict transition period during the observation period—unlike Egypt. They include countries like Armenia, Azerbaijan, Macedonia, Pakistan, Sierra Leone, Somalia, Timor-Leste, and Yemen.

Patterns of Chronic Child Undernutrition within Egypt

In the 2000s, Egypt's prevalence rate of child stunting rose faster in urban areas than in rural areas (Figure 2.6a). Child stunting in 2011 was even slightly more prevalent in urban areas, whereas in most other developing

---

10 Egypt's decade-average GDP per capita growth rate was 2.3 percent in the 1990s and 3.0 percent in the 2000s.

FIGURE 2.6 Prevalence of child stunting in Egypt, by different subnational disaggregations, 2000–2011

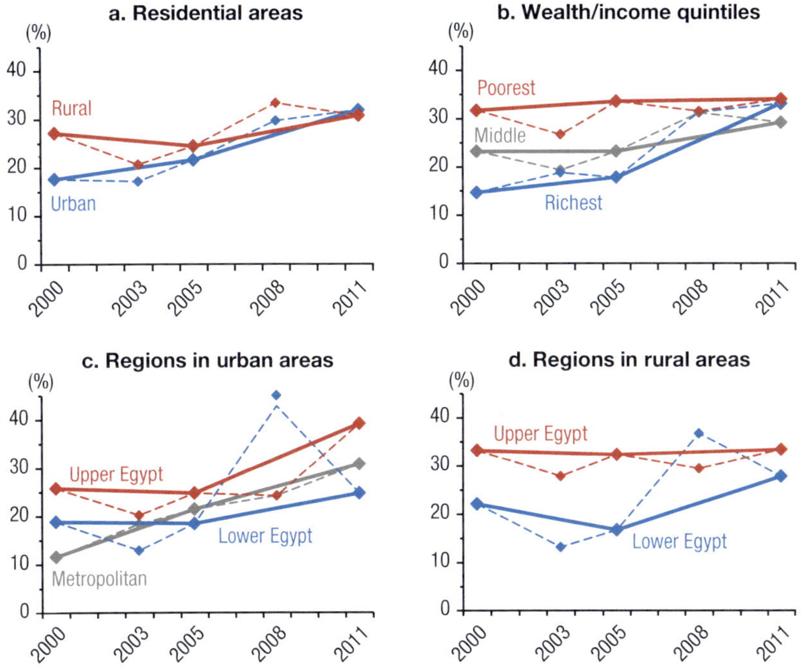

Source: Authors' estimation based on Demographic and Health Surveys (DHS) data (MOH, El-Zanaty and Associates, and Macro International 2008; MOHP, NPC, and ORC Macro 2000; MOHP et al. 2003; MOHP et al. 2005) and data from CAPMAS and WFP (2011).

Note: The samples include children ages 6–59 months with biologically plausible height-for-age z-scores (HAZs) (–6 ≤ HAZ ≤ 6). The prevalence rate of child stunting is defined as the proportion of children with HAZs below –2. The samples exclude the Frontier Governorate region because of insufficient observations.

The DHSs from 2000, 2005, and 2008 (MOH, El-Zanaty and Associates, and Macro International 2008; MOHP, NPC, and ORC Macro 2000; MOHP et al. 2003; MOHP et al. 2005) are standard DHSs; the respective samples contain 7,737, 10,352, and 8,196 observations. The 2003 DHS is an interim DHS, which oversampled Menia Governorate (in Upper Egypt) and the slum areas of Greater Cairo (in the Metropolitan area). The 2003 DHS sample contains 5,200 observations. The 2011 Household Income, Expenditure, and Consumption Survey (HIECS) sample (CAPMAS and WFP [2011]) contains 3,815 observations. The 2008 DHS data yield implausible subnational prevalence rates.

The solid lines connect "trusted" prevalence rates, derived from standard DHS and HIECS data. The dashed lines connect prevalence rates derived from all DHS and HIECS data.

countries, it has been considerably more prevalent in rural areas (Fotso 2007; Smith, Ruel, and Ndiaye 2005). Egypt's rural-urban gap closed over the past decade because children's nutrition deteriorated faster in urban areas than in rural areas and not because progress in reducing chronic child undernutrition in rural areas caught up with the advances made in urban areas. Rural-urban migration and rapid population growth in urban slums with a poor health environment may explain increasing child stunting in urban areas only to some extent. Compared to 2000, the increase in the prevalence rate of child stunting in 2011 was highest in the Metropolitan areas, where the slums are located (Figure 2.6c). However, child stunting also became considerably more prevalent in urban areas outside the big cities, and particularly in Upper Egypt. The rapid increase in urban Upper Egypt contributes to a widening north-south gap in child nutrition for urban areas.

The situation is quite different for rural areas. Throughout the 2000s, the prevalence rate of child stunting was fairly stable in rural Upper Egypt, at around 33 percent. It rapidly increased in rural Lower Egypt, at least between 2005 and 2011 (Figure 2.6d). Unlike for urban areas, this development has led to a narrowing of the north-south gap in child nutrition for rural areas. The 2011 child stunting rate in Upper Egypt is actually considerably lower in rural areas than in urban areas, which is the reverse of the situation in 2000 and the situation in Lower Egypt (Table 2.1 and Figure 2.6c and Figure 2.6d).

The difference in the prevalence rate of child stunting between the rich and the poor also narrowed throughout the 2000s, so the prevalence rate among the richest and poorest wealth/income quintiles was quite close in 2011 (Figure 2.6b). This narrowing is due to a rapidly increasing prevalence among the rich rather than a decreasing prevalence among the poor. In fact, the prevalence rate among the poorest wealth/income quintile increased only marginally. These results preliminarily suggest that child stunting is poorly correlated with household wealth/income across space and time.

The next chapter identifies four potential drivers that may explain part of these exceptional patterns.

Chapter 3

DRIVERS OF EGYPT'S EXCEPTIONALISM IN NUTRITION

This study argues that Egypt's exceptionalism in both the double burden of malnutrition and the growth-nutrition disconnect has been driven by four main, interacting developments: (1) the rapid nutrition transition—particularly the adoption of calorie-rich, unbalanced diets in combination with an increasingly sedentary lifestyle; (2) the succession of economic crises and increase in poverty over the past decade; (3) the expansion of the national food subsidy system; and (4) the underinvestment in nutrition-sensitive infrastructure and public services and nutrition-specific interventions. The following four sections explore these four potential drivers in detail.

Nutrition Transition and Implications for Malnutrition

A part of the two nutritional challenges that Egypt is facing may be attributable to the nutrition transition, which is present throughout most of the developing world; but it may not explain why they are extremely pronounced in Egypt. The nutrition transition refers to the shift in dietary patterns and physical activity levels that coincides with growing household income and other changes in economy, technology, demography, and epidemiology, and leads to changes in nutritional status and related diseases patterns (Popkin 1993, 1998, 2001). Hence, the nutrition transition describes a natural process in human history that is mainly driven by economic growth and transformation. The pace of the nutrition transition that developing countries go through today is much faster than what currently developed countries faced decades ago, mainly due to more rapid progress in technological advances and urbanization (Popkin 2002a, 2002b).

Five phases with distinct dietary and physical activity patterns have been differentiated, with each phase usually stretching over several generations

(Popkin 1993, 1994).[1] Today, most developing countries (and, still, several developed countries) are in the fourth phase, characterized by increasing degenerative diseases. Some of their governments—including the Egyptian government—struggle to set incentives that enable their people to overcome this phase and enter into the fifth phase, characterized by rising behavioral change in diet and lifestyle. Globally, developing countries are likely to bear the major burden of the nutrition transition in the coming decades (Schmidhuber and Shetty 2005).

Nutrition Transition in Developing Countries

In the course of economic development, undernutrition decreases with growing income at declining marginal rates (Figure 2.5; Smith and Haddad 2002; Haddad et al. 2003). At the same time, overnutrition increases with growing income in developing countries (and still in some developed countries). The relationship between overnutrition and income follows a bell-shaped curve over the entire process of the nutrition transition, with overnutrition being most prevalent during the fourth phase (Mendez, Monteiro, and Popkin 2005; Garrett and Ruel 2005; Ezzati et al. 2005). Ezzati et al. (2005) show that the mean BMI of a country's population increases rapidly until its GDP per capita reaches about I$ (international dollars) 5,000, then flattens and

---

1 Popkin (1994) identifies the following five phases of the nutrition transition:
1. Collection of food: The diet is typical for hunter-gatherer populations. It is high in carbohydrates and fiber and low in fat, especially saturated fat. The proportion of polyunsaturated fat in meat from wild animals is significantly higher than in meat from modern domesticated animals. Activity patterns are very high, and little obesity is found among hunter-gatherer societies.
2. Famine: The diet is much less varied—compared to that in the first phase—and is subject to larger variations and periods of acute food scarcity. These dietary changes likely lead to nutritional stress and a reduction in stature (the reduction is estimated to be about 4 inches). At later stages of this phase, social stratification intensifies, and dietary variation increases according to gender and social status. The types of physical activity change, but there is little change in activity levels during this period.
3. Receding famine: During this phase, the consumption of fruits, vegetables, and animal protein increases, and starchy staples become less important in the diet. Activity patterns start to shift, and inactivity and leisure become part of the lives of more people.
4. Degenerative diseases: The diet is high in total fat, cholesterol, sugar, and other refined carbohydrates; low in polyunsaturated fatty acids and fiber; and often accompanied by an increasingly sedentary life. This results in increased prevalence of obesity and contributes to degenerative diseases.
5. Behavioral change: The diet resembles more the dietary pattern of hunter-gatherer societies (phase 1) rather than that of societies characterized by degenerative diseases (phase 4). Compared to the diet in phase 4, it is characterized by the increased intake of fruits and vegetables, complex carbohydrates, and reduced intake of refined foods, meats, and dairy products. This dietary pattern likely emerges because of an increasing desire to prolong health and prevent degenerative diseases. It is associated with a new understanding of physical activity and fitness for promoting good health.

starts decreasing at about I$12,500 for women and I$17,000 for men. Webb and Block (2012) estimate that every 10 percent increase in per capita GDP is accompanied by a 3.2 percent decrease in the prevalence rate of stunting among children under five years of age, as well as by a 4.4 percent increase in the prevalence rate of obesity in the same age group. Thus, countries emerging from poverty typically experience rising rates of overnutrition along with declining rates of undernutrition, with overnutrition rising faster than undernutrition declines.

In the wake of rapid economic growth and transformation together with urbanization and technological advance (particularly in transportation and communications) in recent decades, the nutrition transition has progressed quite rapidly in some middle-income countries such as Egypt, Mexico, and China (Popkin et al. 2012; Rivera et al. 2002, 2004; Shetty 2013). The adoption of diets low in fiber and high in fat, sugar, and animal protein and of Western eating habits (such as convenience foods and fast foods), combined with an increasingly sedentary lifestyle that lacks physical exercise, has pushed up overnutrition rates (Mistry and Puthussery 2015; Ng and Popkin 2012). Drewnowski and Popkin (1997) show that an average country's national income level correlates positively with the share of energy from fats and sugar in the average diet and negatively with the average share of dietary energy from carbohydrates (mainly provided by staple foods).

Over recent decades, the costs of diets high in dietary fats and sugar have plummeted relative to household income, so fatty and sugary diets have become much more available to the poor. For example, in 1962, an average diet containing 20 percent of energy from fats was typical for a country with a GNP per capita of US$1,475, whereas the same diet was associated with a GNP per capita of only US$750 in 1990 (Drewnowski and Popkin 1997; Popkin 2002a). Urbanization has also contributed to improved accessibility of calorie-laden diets and rising rates of overnutrition (Drewnowski and Popkin 1997; Mendez, Monteiro, and Popkin 2005).

The consumption of refined grains, fats, animal products, sugar, and processed food is much higher in urban areas compared to rural areas, which can be explained by higher urban market penetration of these foods and lower prices in urban areas—at least, in real terms (Popkin 1999). In addition, people's physical work load and hence their energy expenditure for income generation has fallen substantially, thanks to technological advances. For example, the level of occupational physical activity among adults 18–55 years of age in China dropped by 46 percent for women and 35 percent for men between 1991 and 2006 (Ng, Norton, and Popkin 2009).

At the same time, physical exercise to burn surplus energy and body fat is uncommon among many developing countries' populations, especially among females. In the MENA region, the highest proportions of physically inactive people live in Egypt, Saudi Arabia, Iran, and the smaller Gulf States (Musaiger and Al-Hazzaa 2012). For example, 70 percent of the Egyptian adult population has less than 10 minutes of physical activity per day, compared to 31 percent in Syria. The physically inactive population accounts for 68 percent in Saudi Arabia, 67 percent in Iran, and 65 percent in Kuwait. In Saudi Arabia, 74 percent of women are physically inactive, compared to 61 percent of men. The gender gap is even wider in Iran, where 76 percent of the female adult population and 59 percent of the male adult population are physically inactive (Musaiger and Al-Hazzaa 2012).[2] A comparative study of 129 Egyptian adolescent females finds that the groups of overweight and obese girls spent significantly longer hours watching TV than the group of normal-weight girls (Youssef et al. 2010).

As a consequence, the risk of obesity and related NCDs such as type 2 diabetes, coronary heart disease, stroke, hypertension, and some cancers have sharply increased in the developing world. Globally, the prevalence of obesity among adults (20 years of age and older) nearly doubled between 1980 and 2008, reaching 14 percent among women and 10 percent among men (Finucane et al. 2011; Stevens et al. 2012). Contrary to popular belief, most deaths due to NCDs occur in low- and middle-income countries rather than in high-income countries. For example, low- and middle-income countries exhibit more than 80 percent of all cardiovascular and diabetes deaths (which is in part because they lack prevention and treatment capacities) (WHO 2011).

The MENA and LAC regions have experienced the fastest growth in mean BMI among adults since 1980, reaching rates similar to those of North America. The mean BMI of women (20 years of age and older) increased by 1.1 kilograms per square meter (kg/m^2) per decade and that of men (20 years of age and older) by 0.9 kg/m^2 per decade in the MENA region. The mean BMI growth among women and men averaged 1.3 kg/m^2 and 1.0 kg/m^2 per decade, respectively, in Central Latin America and 1.4 kg/m^2 and 0.8 kg/m^2 per decade in Southern Latin America, compared to 1.2 kg/m^2 and 1.1 kg/m^2 per decade in North America (Finucane et al. 2011).[3] Accordingly, the preva-

---

2 Musaiger and Al-Hazzaa (2012) do not report gender-specific prevalence rates of physical inactivity for Egypt.

3 "Central Latin America" includes Colombia, Costa Rica, El Salvador, Guatemala, Honduras, Mexico, Nicaragua, Panama, and Venezuela. "Southern Latin America" includes Argentina, Chile, and Uruguay.

lence rates of NCDs and resulting mortality rates in several MENA and LAC countries have become major public health concerns.

In the MENA region, Egypt has one of the highest rates of mortality from cardiovascular diseases and diabetes among women, with 384 deaths per 100,000 women (under age 70), and a moderately high rate among men, with 427 deaths per 100,000 men (under age 70) (WHO 2011). In comparison, Brazil (226 female deaths and 304 male deaths), China (260 female deaths and 312 male deaths), Mexico (217 female deaths and 258 male deaths), and the United States (122 female deaths and 191 male deaths) have lower cardiovascular disease and diabetes mortality rates. Deaths related to NCDs have been projected to increase worldwide by 15 percent between 2010 and 2020, with the greatest increases in the MENA region, Africa south of the Sahara, and Southeast Asia, all exceeding 20 percent (WHO 2011).

Trends in Food and Macronutrient Availability in Egypt

Between 1970 and 2011, total food consumption in Egypt—approximated by per capita food availability—increased, especially for sources of carbohydrates and animal protein.[4] The per capita availability of calories increased from about 2,270 kilocalories per day (kcal/d) in 1970 to about 3,560 kcal/d in 2011—an increase of 57 percent (Table 3.1). The per capita availability of total protein even increased by 67 percent and that of fat by 39 percent. These increases in macronutrient availability came along with a total increase in the per capita availability of cereals of 48 percent, of sugars of 97 percent, and of meat and fish of 253 percent.

Data from FAO's Food Balance Sheets (FBS) indicate three major shifts in Egyptians' food and macronutrient availability since 1970. The period of the first shift runs through the early 1980s (Figure 3.1). It is characterized by a rapid increase in total per capita calorie and fat availability. The increase in total calorie availability was mainly due to increased availability of cereals, sugars, and edible fats and oils, suggesting little diet diversification into nonstaple foods overall. The available calories from cereals, sugars, and vegetable

4 Due to a lack of sufficiently long time-series data on household food consumption (computable from household surveys), this section is based on food and macronutrient availability data as reported in the Food Balance Sheets (FBS) database (FAOSTAT 2014). Accordingly, a country's per capita supply of food that is available for human consumption—hereafter "food availability"—is calculated as the residual of the total quantity of foodstuffs produced and imported minus the total quantity exported, used for livestock feed and seed, put to manufacture for food and nonfood uses, and lost during storage and transportation. The total quantity of foodstuffs is then adjusted for any changes in stocks. Quantities of available per capita food were converted into levels of calorie, protein, and fat availability by applying appropriate food composition factors for all primary and processed products (FAOSTAT 2014).

TABLE 3.1 Per capita food and macronutrient availability in Egypt, and changes over time

	1970	1981	1994	2011	1970–1981 (%)	1981–1994 (%)	1994–2011 (%)	1970–2011 (%)
Food groups								
Cereals (g/d)	466	605	691	691	30	14	0	48
Meat & fish (g/d)	40	63	80	143	56	27	78	253
Milk & dairy products (g/d)	92	101	107	177	10	6	65	94
Vegetables (g/d)	344	398	388	565	16	−2	46	64
Sugars (g/d)	42	76	79	83	80	3	6	97
Edible fats & oils (g/d)	23	38	24	24	64	−36	1	6
Macronutrients								
Calories (kcal/d)	2,272	3,002	3,259	3,557	32	9	9	57
from cereals, sugars, vegetable oils (kcal/d)	1,818	2,462	2,651	2,668	35	8	1	47
Protein (g/d)	61.3	75.6	88.5	102.6	23	17	16	67
Fat (g/d)	46.0	66.8	55.5	64.1	45	−17	16	39

Source: Authors' calculation based on data from FAOSTAT (2014).

Note: g/d = grams per day; kcal/d = kilocalories per day.

Food availabilities are expressed in primary equivalences (hence including processed commodities). The food group "cereals" corresponds to the food group "cereals—excluding beer" in the Food Balance Sheets (FAOSTAT 2014); "meat & fish" corresponds to "meat" plus "offals," "fats, animals, raw," and "fish, seafood"; "milk & dairy products" corresponds to "milk—excluding butter"; "vegetables" corresponds to "vegetables"; "sugars" corresponds to "sugar & sweeteners"; and "edible fats and oils" corresponds to "butter, ghee" plus "vegetable oils."

oils increased by 35 percent per capita between 1970 and 1981, while total per capita calorie availability increased by 32 percent (Table 3.1). The per capita availability of cereals increased by 30 percent, that of edible fats and oils by 64 percent, and that of sugars by a vast 80 percent. In addition, the per capita availability of meat and fish increased by 56 percent—from a low level in 1970; most of the increase occurred within a few years around 1980 (Figure 3.1).

The period of the second shift runs from the early 1980s to the mid-1990s. It is characterized by a slowdown of the rapid increase in per capita calorie availability in the 1970s, stagnation of the increases in per capita availability of sugars and of meat and fish (for most of the period), and a decrease in the per capita availability of edible fats and oils back to the level in 1970 (Figure 3.1). Along with the decrease in the per capita availability of edible fats and oils, the per capita availability of dietary fat decreased—although more moderately (Table 3.1). The per capita availability of cereals continued to increase, with a total increase of 14 percent between 1981 and 1994, and the per capita availability of vegetables remained roughly constant.

FIGURE 3.1 Trends in food and calorie availability in Egypt, 1970–2011

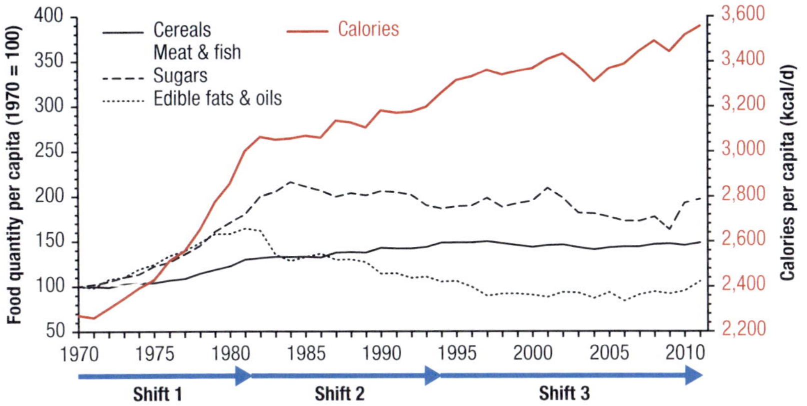

Source: Authors' representation based on data from FAOSTAT (2014).

Note: kcal/d = kilocalories per day.

Food availabilities are expressed in primary equivalences (including processed commodities). The food group "cereals" corresponds to the food group "cereals—excluding beer" in the Food Balance Sheets (FAOSTAT 2014); "meat & fish" corresponds to "meat" plus "offals," "fats, animals, raw," and "fish, seafood"; "milk & dairy products" corresponds to "milk—excluding butter"; "vegetables" corresponds to "vegetables"; "sugars" corresponds to "sugar & sweeteners"; and "edible fats and oils" corresponds to "butter, ghee" plus "vegetable oils."

The third shift occurred in the period since the mid-1990s (to 2011) and is mainly characterized by rapidly increasing per capita availability of animal-source foods, meat and fish in particular (Table 3.1; Figure 3.1). Despite this overall rapid increase, the per capita availability of meat and fish in 2001–2002, 2008, and 2011 dropped below the level of the preceding year, which may reflect the impact of recent crises (Ahmed 2014; Negro-Calduch et al. 2013; see below). Per capita meat and fish availability in 2011 still exceeded the (low) level in 1970 by more than 250 percent and the level in 1994 by 78 percent. Over the period 1994–2011, the per capita availability of cereals stabilized at around 148 percent of the 1970 level. The per capita availability of sugars fluctuated around 197 percent of the 1970 level, with little increase between 1994 and 2011. After its drop to the 1970 level in 1994, the per capita availability of edible fats and oils stabilized at just below that level (until 2010). During the period of the third shift, the per capita availability of vegetables increased at a rate that is more than double the rate during the period of the first shift. Yet this increase is still much below the increase in per capita availability of animal-source foods between 1994 and 2011.

Altogether, these trends during the third shift suggest that the average Egyptian diet has just started to move toward more micronutrient-rich foods since the mid-1990s. It appears that—under the current conditions—there is still a long way to go until the majority of the Egyptian population enters the fifth phase of the nutrition transition, characterized by a rising behavioral change in diet and lifestyle: along with increasing per capita availability of animal-source foods, the per capita availabilities of protein, fat, and even calories (although at a lower rate than those of protein and fat) increased between 1994 and 2011 (Table 3.1).

Granted, the precise values of food and macronutrient availability provided by the FBS should be treated with some caution, given data gaps in the underlying statistics and well-known methodological limitations (Gabbert and Weikard 2001; Nubé 2001; Smith 1998; Svedberg 1999, 2002). For example, the per capita calorie availability from the FBS seems to significantly overstate the average per capita calorie consumption as derived from household surveys. Based on data from the National Food Consumption Survey conducted by the Egyptian National Nutrition Institute, Galal (2002) finds that the average per capita calorie consumption in 1998 was about 2,620 kcal/d, which is more than 700 kcal/d below the FBS value (≈3,340 kcal/d). Lower survey-based consumption values may be largely due to food waste occurring within the household, which is not accounted for in the FBS (FAOSTAT 2014).[5]

Nevertheless, the trends in Egypt's food consumption patterns and total calorie consumption implied by the FBS data seem to be plausible and are consistent with results from survey-based food consumption and nutrition data. For example, considering the period from 1980 to 2013, Ng et al. (2014) find the largest increase globally in the national prevalence rate of obesity among women 20–49 years of age for Egypt. Moreover, our data from the DHSs between 2000 and 2008 (MOH, El-Zanaty and Associates, and Macro International 2008; MOHP, NPC, and ORC Macro 2000; MOHP et al. 2003; MOHP et al. 2005) suggest that the prevalence rates of overweight and obesity among women in the same age group have stabilized in the 2000s.[6]

Economic Crises and Poverty in Egypt

When we search for drivers of Egypt's nutritional challenges and especially the high prevalence of chronic child undernutrition, (income) poverty may appear as an obvious potential key factor. Globally, chronic child undernutrition is

5 Within the household, food waste occurs during storage, in meal preparation, and as plate-waste. Some food is also misused by feeding it to domestic animals.

6 See Tables A.1 and A.2 in the Appendix.

closely associated with household poverty (Brooks-Gunn and Duncan 1997; Black et al. 2008; Grantham-McGregor et al. 2007; Smith and Haddad 2000). In Egypt, the national poverty rate steadily increased between 2000 and 2011 (see below), as did the national prevalence rate of child stunting, at least between 2005 and 2011. Increasing child stunting prevalence has contributed to both the extreme double burden of malnutrition and the exceptional growth-nutrition disconnect. The steady increase in poverty and therewith household food insecurity has been widely attributed to a succession of economic crises (e.g., Ahmed 2014; Breisinger et al. 2013; WFP 2013), which hence have been deemed as key drivers of increasing child stunting rates as well (e.g., WFP 2013).

Since the late 1990s, Egypt has experienced at least four major economic crises, which seem to be reflected in the sudden slowdowns of increasing food and macronutrient availabilities (as discussed above). First, a series of economic shocks in the period 1997–2001 (including the Luxor terrorist attack in November 1997, the 2000–2001 economic recession in the European Union, and the September 11 terrorist attacks in the United States in 2001) slashed foreign currency earnings and prompted the government to gradually devalue the EGP from May 2000 onward and to finally adopt a free exchange rate floating system in January 2003 (Bolbol, Fatheldin, and Omran 2005). Second, the avian influenza outbreak in 2006 and the resulting mass culling of poultry affected a large proportion of small-scale farmers, who raised chicken for their own consumption and as source of household income (Ahmed 2014; Negro-Calduch 2013; Kavle et al. 2015a). Third, the global food, fuel, and financial crises of 2007–2009 increased domestic food and fuel prices and lowered foreign currency inflows substantially, given Egypt's heavy reliance on food and fuel imports and revenues from tourism, the Suez Canal, and petroleum exports (Ahmed 2014; Ianchovichina, Loening, and Wood 2014; Table 3.2). Globally, Egypt is the largest importer of wheat—the primary staple food. The three-year average import dependency ratio in 2007–2009 was about 41 percent for cereals, 38 percent for sugars, and 73 percent for edible fats and oils (Table 3.2). Fourth, the political instability in the wake of the 2011 revolution further aggravated Egypt's macroeconomic problems (Ahmed 2014; Breisinger et al. 2013; Dahi 2012).

Association between Poverty and Chronic Child Undernutrition

Despite these crises, Egypt's GDP grew at an annual average rate of 4.6 percent—2.7 percent on a per capita basis—between 2000 and 2011 (Table 3.2). However, poverty steadily increased by 0.8 percentage points

TABLE 3.2 Key macroeconomic indicators for Egypt, 2000–2011

	2000	2001	2002	2003	2004
GDP growth (%)[a]					
Overall	5.4	3.5	2.4	3.2	4.1
Per capita	3.5	1.7	0.5	1.3	2.2
Balance of payments (million US$)[b]					
Current account balance	−33	614	1,943	3,418	2,911
Trade balance	−9,363	−7,517	−6,615	−7,834	−10,359
Exports	7,078	7,121	8,205	10,453	13,833
Petroleum	2,632	2,381	3,161	3,910	5,299
Share (%)	—	—	—	37.4	38.3
Food	—	—	—	597	792
Share (%)	—	—	—	15.3	14.9
Imports	16,441	14,637	14,820	18,286	24,193
Petroleum	—	—	—	2,550	3,975
Share (%)	—	—	—	13.9	16.4
Food	—	—	—	3,208	3,421
Share (%)	—	—	—	17.5	14.1
Services, net	5,588	3,878	4,949	7,318	7,842
Receipts	11,696	9,618	10,441	12,981	15,030
Tourism	4,317	3,423	3,796	5,475	6,430
Share (%)	36.9	35.6	36.4	42.2	42.8
Suez Canal	1,843	1,820	2,236	2,848	3,307
Share (%)	15.8	18.9	21.4	21.9	22.0
Transfers	3,742	4,252	3,609	3,934	5,428
Remittances, net	2,973	3,109	2,946	3,046	4,372
Food import dependency ratio (%)[c]					
Cereals	35.4	36.8	36.9	31.3	27.6
Meat & fish	26.6	23.6	18.0	15.6	17.1
Milk & dairy products	8.1	7.2	5.5	5.8	6.2
Vegetables	0.0	0.1	0.1	0.1	0.1
Sugars	22.5	28.0	33.2	28.0	40.2
Edible fats & oils	79.2	71.3	61.7	55.5	79.4

Source: Authors' calculation based on data from the following sources: [a] World Bank (2014); [b] Central Bank of Egypt (2014); [c] FAOSTAT (2014).

Note: — = data not available; GDP = gross domestic product.

The annual values of the balance of payments accounts refer to the first half of the specified calendar years and the preceding half years.

The import dependency ratio is calculated as import quantity as a percentage share of total domestic supply quantity. The total domestic supply quantity is calculated as the sum of domestic production quantity and import quantity minus export quantity. Food availabilities are expressed in primary equivalences (including processed commodities).

2005	2006	2007	2008	2009	2010	2011	Annual average
4.5	6.8	7.1	7.2	4.7	5.1	1.8	4.6
2.6	4.9	5.2	5.3	2.9	3.3	0.1	2.7
1,752	2,269	888	−4,424	−4,318	−6,088	−10,146	
−11,986	−16,291	−23,415	−25,173	−25,120	−27,103	−34,139	
18,455	22,018	29,356	25,169	23,873	26,993	25,072	
10,222	10,108	14,473	11,005	10,259	12,136	11,225	
55.4	45.9	49.3	43.7	43.0	45.0	44.8	44.7
587	944	1,151	1,092	1,343	1,422	1,234	
5.7	9.3	8.0	9.9	13.1	11.7	11.0	11.0
30,441	38,308	52,771	50,342	48,993	54,096	59,211	
5,359	4,128	9,561	7,032	5,161	9,262	11,775	
17.6	10.8	18.1	14.0	10.5	17.1	19.9	15.4
2,951	4,153	6,207	5,898	6,791	9,494	10,983	
9.7	10.8	11.8	11.7	13.9	17.6	18.5	14.0
8,191	11,498	14,966	12,502	10,339	7,878	5,585	
17,438	20,456	27,211	23,801	23,563	21,873	20,872	
7,235	8,183	10,827	10,488	11,591	10,589	9,419	
41.5	40.0	39.8	44.1	49.2	48.4	45.1	41.8
3,559	4,170	5,155	4,721	4,517	5,053	5,208	
20.4	20.4	18.9	19.8	19.2	23.1	25.0	20.6
5,547	7,061	9,338	8,247	10,463	13,137	18,408	
4,975	6,261	8,377	7,632	9,509	12,384	17,776	
36.2	38.2	43.1	37.2	42.1	49.4	46.3	38.4
19.9	21.5	22.6	15.9	16.1	23.0	17.6	19.8
6.9	5.4	5.8	9.4	8.9	13.0	24.1	8.9
0.1	0.2	0.1	0.2	0.2	0.4	0.5	0.2
37.7	39.6	35.8	44.8	33.1	37.1	43.1	35.3
78.5	80.5	62.3	82.4	74.2	87.0	84.0	74.7

The food group "cereals" corresponds to the food group "cereals—excluding beer" in the Food Balance Sheets (FAOSTAT 2014); "meat & fish" corresponds to "meat" plus "offals," "fats, animals, raw," and "fish, seafood"; "milk & dairy products" corresponds to "milk—excluding butter"; "vegetables" corresponds to "vegetables"; "sugars" corresponds to "sugar & sweeteners"; and "edible fats and oils" corresponds to "butter, ghee" plus "vegetable oils."

The import dependency ratios of the food groups "meat & fish" and "edible fats & oils" are calculated as weighted averages of the import dependency ratios of their subgroups, using the relative shares in the domestic supply quantity as weights.

annually, from a low rate of 16.7 percent in 2000 (Table 3.3). The prevalence rate of child stunting increased by 0.6 percentage points annually, from 24.6 percent in 2000 (Table 2.2). The national poverty rate hence rose faster than the national prevalence rate of child stunting (by 50 percent compared to 34 percent).

Nevertheless, poverty remained less prevalent than child stunting in 2011. Unlike in Egypt, poverty is more prevalent than child stunting in most developing countries, according to data from World Bank (2014). Income inequality in Egypt declined from 2000 to 2011 (Table 3.3), which is unusual given rising poverty going along with high economic growth. With a Gini coefficient of about 0.34 in 2000, Egypt's income inequality was already quite low by regional and international standards, which appears to be at odds with Egyptians' perception of income inequality (Verme et al. 2014).[7] Yet Egypt and other MENA countries had low incidences of poverty and income inequality, at least throughout the 1980s and 1990s, due to high remittances from international migration and high public-sector (government) employment partially as a means of social protection (Adams and Page 2003; Hassine 2012). In addition, the Egyptian government considerably expanded food subsidies throughout the 2000s to mitigate the impacts of the economic crises on the poor (see below).

Government policies may also partly explain differences in subnational trends and patterns between poverty incidence and child stunting prevalence. Similar to the prevalence of child stunting, poverty rose faster in urban areas than in rural areas, although the urban-rural gap has been less pronounced. Between 2000 and 2011, the poverty rate increased by 66 percent in urban areas and 47 percent in rural areas; the child stunting rate increased by 81 percent in urban areas and only 13 percent in rural areas. In urban areas, the prevalence rate of child stunting hence increased over-proportionately relative to the poverty rate. Accordingly, income inequality in urban areas declined from 2000 to 2011, whereas it remained roughly constant in rural areas (Table 3.3). Nonetheless, income inequality in Egypt has been lower in rural areas than in urban areas. This is consistent with other developing countries in the MENA region (Adams and Page 2003) but different from developing countries in other world regions such as China (Chang 2002; Yang 1999) and many African countries south of the Sahara (Sahn and Stifel 2003).

---

7 A comprehensive study of Egypt's inequality (Verme et al. 2014) finds that the HIECS expenditure data—which underlie the official poverty and inequality estimates—are of good quality, and alternative measurements of inequality yield similar estimates to the official ones, presented in this book.

TABLE 3.3 Poverty and income inequality and annual average change in poverty, 2000–2011

	2000	2005	2009	2011	2013	2000–2011 (percentage points)
Poverty rate (%)						
Total	16.7	19.6	21.6	25.2	26.3	0.8
Urban	9.2	10.1	11.0	15.3	17.6	0.6
Rural	22.1	26.8	28.9	32.3	32.4	0.9
Poverty rate (%), by region and residential area						
Metropolitan	5.1	5.7	6.9	9.6	15.7	0.4
Lower Egypt	10.3	14.5	14.2	15.1	15.9	0.4
Urban	6.2	9.0	7.3	10.3	11.7	0.4
Rural	11.8	16.7	16.7	17.0	17.4	0.5
Upper Egypt	29.7	32.5	36.9	44.5	42.6	1.3
Urban	19.3	18.6	21.3	29.4	26.7	0.9
Rural	34.2	39.1	43.7	51.5	49.4	1.6
Income inequality (Gini coefficient)						
Total	0.344	0.323	0.307	0.316	0.298	
Urban	0.368	0.349	0.336	0.349	0.326	
Rural	0.233	0.233	0.224	0.236	0.236	

Source: Provided by Heba El-Laithy, based on data from CAPMAS and WFP (2011).

Note: Following the official definition, poverty and income inequality are derived from household expenditure data.

There were also several differences between the regional prevalence of child stunting and poverty that were persistent, at least between 2000 and 2011 (Table 2.1 and Table 3.3). The gap between Lower Egypt and Upper Egypt was much less pronounced for the prevalence of child stunting than for poverty. While poverty was less prevalent in the Metropolitan areas than in Lower and Upper Egypt and far below the national average, the prevalence of child stunting in the Metropolitan areas was higher than in Lower Egypt and much closer to the national average. The relatively low poverty rates in Lower Egypt and the Metropolitan areas were likely due to a concentration of government investments in these regions that pulled up the local economies, as well as insufficient social protection in lagging areas in Upper Egypt (World Bank 2007).

Finally, and most importantly, child stunting was common among both the poor and the rich. And, as discussed above, the gap between the poorest and the richest quintiles in child stunting prevalence diminished throughout the 2000s, so the prevalence rate among the poorest and richest was relatively similar in 2011 (Figure 2.6). Correlation analyses based on the 2011 HIECS data (CAPMAS and WFP 2011) reveal that children's HAZs are only very weakly correlated with household income indicators. The correlation coefficients for reported per capita income and per capita total expenditure, when transformed into logarithms, take values of below 0.045 across the total, urban, and rural samples. These coefficients are even statistically insignificant at the 10 percent level for the urban sample, and the coefficient for per capita income is statistically insignificant for the rural sample.[8] Correlation analyses based on data from the 2000, 2003, 2005, and 2008 DHSs (MOH, El-Zanaty and Associates, and Macro International 2008; MOHP, NPC, and ORC Macro 2000; MOHP et al. 2003; MOHP et al. 2005) confirm the low association found in the 2011 HIECS data. Overall, the 2005 DHS data show the highest—though still low—correlation coefficients between child HAZ and household wealth (measured by an asset wealth index), which amount to 0.133 for the total sample, 0.113 for the urban sample, and 0.111 for the rural sample.

Thus, although the increase in the prevalence of child stunting between 2000 and 2011 was accompanied by an increase in poverty at the national and—to a lesser extent—the subnational levels, low child HAZ has been only weakly associated with low household income at the individual level. This finding suggests that there were other factors—in addition to household poverty—that contributed to a high and growing prevalence of child stunting between 2000 and 2011. It may also imply that the social protection policies in place had at least fewer mitigating effects on child stunting than on poverty.

Household Food Insecurity and Coping Strategies

Along with rising poverty, Egypt experienced deteriorating household food security due to losses in household purchasing power in the course of the succession of economic crises. Between 2009 and 2011, the proportion of Egyptians who were income poor and had poor food consumption (in terms of inadequate dietary diversity, calorie deficiency, or both) increased from 14.0 percent to 17.2 percent, according to a study based on HIECS data and published by the World Food Programme (WFP 2013). It is believed that the expansion of the food subsidies in response to the economic crises in the 2000s were critical in protecting many people from even larger losses in purchasing power (Al-Shawarby and El-Laithy 2010; Breisinger et al. 2013; WFP

8 The coefficients are statistically insignificant when using household income and expenditure per capita in linear terms.

2013). Using estimates from a mixed demand model for policy simulations, Ramadan and Thomas (2011) find that cereal price increases at a rate similar to the ones experienced in 2007–2008 (by about 50 percent) would decrease total food expenditure by 10.5 percent among the lowest income quartile in rural areas and by 9.2 percent among the lowest income quartile in urban areas if there were no Baladi bread and flour subsidies. The averted losses for the total rural and urban populations would be 8.7 percent and 6.9 percent of total food expenditure, respectively.

The WFP study reports that 74.7 percent of the households who experienced an economic shock in the two years prior to the survey in 2011 stated that the most significant shock was a rise in food prices, with increases of 77.0 percent in rural areas and 72.1 percent in urban areas. To cope with this loss in purchasing power, households adopted coping strategies that may have had negative effects on nutrition in the longer term. The reported dominant strategies included more reliance on less expensive and less preferred foods (88.4 percent among poor households and 81.6 percent among non-poor households), reduction in the daily consumption of meat and fish (72.4 percent among poor households and 67.4 percent among non-poor households), and reduction in meal portions (41.7 percent among poor households and 43.8 percent among non-poor households) (WFP 2013). As a consequence, household dietary diversity declined as reliance on cheap calorie-rich foods—especially among the poor—heightened. The proportion of households with poor dietary diversity increased from 33.3 percent in 2009 to 35.1 percent in 2011 (WFP 2013).

Decreased dietary diversity, reduced meat and fish consumption, reduced vegetable and fruit consumption, and increased consumption of sugary foods were also found in the 2008 DHS data, compared to the 2005 DHS data (Kavle et al. 2015a). Kavle et al. (2015a) relate these changes in the diets of young children and their mothers to the 2006 avian influenza outbreak and the following food and fuel price crisis. They argue that the observed increase in the prevalence of child stunting in Lower Egypt between 2005 and 2008 can partly be explained by a decline in dietary diversity, and particularly by sugary foods being substituted for more nutritious foods. Sugary foods were increasingly available and easily affordable during this period, thanks in part to the expansion of food subsidies (see below).

Thus, economic shocks and increasing food insecurity do not necessarily lead to reduced calorie intake and declining overweight and obesity because households tend to reduce their consumption of relatively expensive, micronutrient-rich foods first. For example, evidence from the 1998

Indonesian economic crisis suggests that affected people may largely maintain and partly even increase their consumption of basic staple foods and calorie intake levels, despite considerable losses in household purchasing power (Headey, Ecker, and Trinh Tan 2014). There is also evidence from high- and middle-income countries that shows that overweight and obesity can even be positively associated with household food insecurity, especially among beneficiaries of food assistance and social welfare programs (Dinour, Bergen, and Yeh 2007; Kuku, Garasky, and Gundersen 2012; Mohd Shariff and Khor 2005).

Food Subsidies and Nutritional Implications

Egypt has a long history of food subsidies. Food subsidies have been a main pillar of the Egyptian social safety net along with fuel subsidies and relatively minor social benefits. The high prevalence of chronic child undernutrition, as well as the high prevalence of overnutrition among children and women, implies that the food subsidy system was ineffective in reducing at least these forms of malnutrition. Moreover, in combination with the general phenomenon of the nutrition transition, the design of the food subsidy system and its modifications over time may have contributed to preventing common nutritional progress and even aggravating Egypt's two nutritional challenges (as we will explain in the following).

In Egypt, food subsidies have been a popular political instrument, particularly to mitigate the expected impacts of high food prices during economic crises. Although the food subsidies may have helped to raise the purchasing power of poor people and to prevent more rapid rises in poverty in recent years, they may have incentivized overconsumption of calorie-rich foods and favored shifts toward less balanced diets (diets having less diversity and bioavailable micronutrient contents). Both may have had adverse nutritional effects.

The long-standing, continuous existence of the food subsidy system at a large scale may have led to an internalization of calorie-rich and unbalanced diets into common food habits. Certainly, the food subsidy system was never designed to tackle malnutrition, but interventions in food markets—and their modifications—naturally have critical implications for people's food consumption preferences and hence their nutritional status. In other words, food subsidies and their reforms are unlikely to be neutral with regard to nutritional outcomes.

Past discussions on reforming the Egyptian food subsidy system were focused on implications for the fiscal budget and poverty reduction/prevention. However, nutritional concerns—at least related to overnutrition—and the consequences for public health and related economic costs seem to have never played a notable role, either in the political or in the public debate. This section therefore draws particular attention to the potential nutritional implications of Egypt's food subsidy system. Especially after the revolution in 2011, reforming the food subsidy system was deemed politically challenging due to the potential economic and social impacts conjectured. It was believed that many Egyptians consider food (and fuel) subsidies as the only notable social benefits they receive from the government, and most of them perceive the subsidies as their legitimate civil right (Ghoneim 2013; Sachs 2012). Nonetheless, critical modifications of the food subsidy system were undertaken (and the fuel subsidies were cut back) recently—quietly and without sparking notable civil unrest (probably because of the presence of a new strong government backed by a large majority of the population, and because of people's desire for stability in the aftermath of the 2011 revolution).

History of the Egyptian Food Subsidy System until May 2014

Started in 1941, Egypt's food subsidy system is one of the oldest food subsidy systems still in existence in the world. It provides food at subsidized prices to the vast majority of the population. Despite several modifications, the subsidization of Baladi bread, cooking oil, and sugar has been the centerpiece of the system continuously since 1945. Until May 2014, the food subsidy system consisted of two separate programs—the Baladi bread (and flour) program and the ration card program.

Baladi bread subsidies were introduced in 1941 under the reign of King Farouk I as universal consumer subsidies (Ahmed et al. 2001). To maintain the subsidies, the government since then has intervened in wheat marketing by controlling the supply chain through purchasing domestic wheat at prices often above the world market price; transacting the bulk of wheat imports; handling most of wheat transportation and storage; selling wheat to processors at fixed prices (below the world market price); operating flour mills, bakeries, and, most of all, Baladi bread outlets; providing fuel subsidies to private wheat processors; fixing the price of Baladi bread; and issuing compulsory regulations meant to ensure Baladi bread's quality. These quality regulations relate to issues such as loaf size, flour extraction rates, and, more recently, iron fortification amounts (Alderman, von Braun, and Sakr 1982; Coelli 2010).

In 1945, near the end of World War II, the government of King Farouk I also introduced the ration card–based subsidies. The program was designed as a temporary measure with the purpose of ensuring the supply of necessary goods to the whole population and therewith helping people to cope with the scarcity and inflation resulting from the war (Ahmed et al. 2001; Ali and Adams 1996; WFP 2008). Household rations were issued for basic foods, including cooking oil, sugar, and tea, and for some nonfood necessities such as kerosene and coarse cotton textiles (Ahmed et al. 2001). Until May 2014, beneficiaries received fixed quotas of food items—noted on the ration card—at fixed prices (determined by the government). The difference between the subsidized price and the market price has been covered by the public budget—before and after the 2014 reform (see the next section). Both the Baladi bread (and flour) program and the ration card program have been the responsibility of the Ministry of Supply and Internal Trade (MSIT, as it is termed today), and since 2005 they have been managed by the General Authority for Supply Commodities.

After World War II, the ration card program remained in place as a policy instrument for promoting social equity and political stability and for mitigating adverse effects of economic reforms and structural adjustments. Under the rule of President Gamal Abdel Nasser (1956–1970), a social contract between the government and the people was concluded that explicitly stated the government's mandate to ensure a basic food supply to all Egyptians (Ahmed et al. 2001). Under the early rule of President Anwar Sadat (1970–1981), the ration card program was expanded by subsidizing additional foods, including beans, lentils, rice, yellow maize, chicken, frozen meat, and frozen fish, adding up to a total of 18 food items (Ahmed et al. 2001; Ali and Adams 1996). The expansion was associated with significant increases in the supply of animal products and sugar and a sharp rise in the availability of calories, marking the first aforementioned shift in Egypt's food supply patterns (Figure 3.1).

However, the food subsidies quickly became fiscally unsustainable in the wake of rising international food prices in the early 1970s. The fiscal burden peaked in 1975/1976, when food subsidies accounted for 16.9 percent of total public expenditures and 9.4 percent of national GDP (Alderman, von Braun, and Sakr 1982). In 1977, the government attempted to cut back on the total costs of food subsidies through reducing subsidies for some food items (including Fino bread and Fino bread flour, rice, sugar, and tea), which sparked heavy, violent riots (Alderman 1986; Ahmed et al. 2001). Thereupon, the reform attempt was rescinded hastily, and the subsidy system was even further expanded. The government increased the value of the existing subsidies and introduced the distribution of bread flour in rural areas for baking bread at home (Ahmed et al. 2001).[9] In the 1980s and early 1990s, food

9 Accordingly, we term the program after this point "bread and flour program."

FIGURE 3.2 Costs of the Egyptian food subsidy system

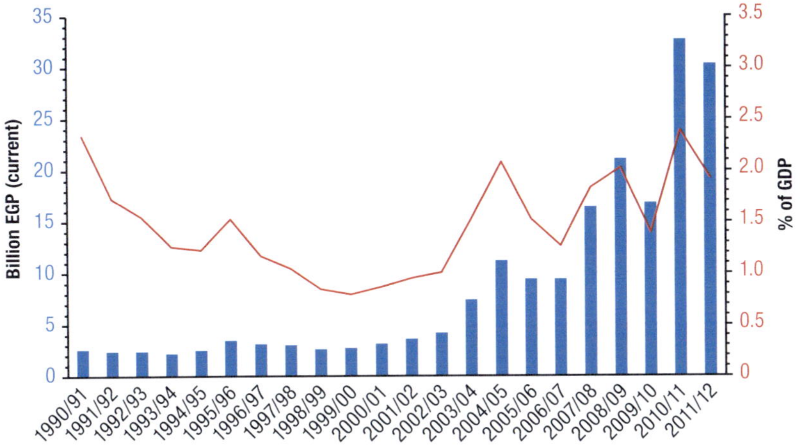

Source: Authors' representation based on data from MOF (2014); Central Bank of Egypt (2014); and World Bank (2014).
Note: EGP = Egyptian pounds; GDP = gross domestic product.
Years listed are Egyptian fiscal years. Egypt's fiscal year starts on July 1 and concludes on June 30.

subsidies were cut back quietly, gradually, and moderately through a series of reforms under the rule of President Hosni Mubarak (1981–2011). The costs of the food subsidy system were kept under EGP 3.5 billion between 1990/1991 and 2001/2002 and steadily decreased relative to Egypt's GDP, except for the spike in 1995/1996 (Figure 3.2).

The ration card program underwent a major structural reform in 1981 by the introduction of a targeting mechanism. A main aspect of the structural reform was that all ration-card-holding households were divided into two categories according to their income status, and subsidy rates were issued accordingly. Poor households received green cards that enabled them to purchase food rations at full-subsidy rates, and better-off households received red cards that enabled them to purchase rations of sugar, cooking oil, rice, and tea at reduced-subsidy rates (Adams 2000; Ahmed et al. 2001; Gutner 2002). Green ration cardholders were also eligible for additional quotas of those four items at the reduced-subsidy rates. This dual system persisted until the food, fuel, and financial crisis in 2007–2009.

The reform of the Baladi bread subsidy began three years later and was carried out with minimal publicity. In 1984, the price of Baladi bread was increased from 1 to 2 Egyptian piasters (EGP 0.02), and the price was increased again to 5 Egyptian piasters (EGP 0.05) in 1989 (Al-Shawarby and

El-Laithy 2010). The mandatory loaf size was reduced in two steps, from 168 grams (g) to 160 g in 1984 and to 130 g in 1991; the 1991 mandatory loaf size officially still applies today. The price of Baladi bread has also been fixed since 1989 and has led to a mounting burden for the public budget. In real terms, the price of Baladi bread dropped 5.9-fold between 1989 and 2011 (taking the reduction of loaf size into account).

Other reforms to the food subsidy system in the late 1980s and 1990s included the gradual reduction of the number of beneficiaries under the ration card program by abolishing the automatic inclusion of newborns on the household ration cards and removing persons who died or moved abroad; gradual reduction of both the quotas of subsidized foods and the subsidy rates under the ration card program; and phasing out of subsidies for some food items such as Fino bread and its flour, chicken, meat, fish, and tea in 1991–1992 and Shami bread and its flour in 1996 (Adams 2000; Ahmed et al. 2001; Gutner 2002; Trego 2011). The gradual reform process was successful in fiscal terms. The costs of the food subsidies declined from around 15 percent of total government expenditures in 1980 to 6 percent in 2000 without sparking major civil unrest, probably partly because of tight state control (Trego 2011). Moreover, the rapid rise in the (over)supply of calories throughout the 1970s was slowed down considerably (Figure 3.1), possibly through creating a disincentive for food wastage (considering that the calories available for human consumption were far above reported calorie consumption).

In the 2000s, the government increasingly focused on better controlling the fiscal costs by improving efficiency through better targeting mechanisms and reducing leakages and losses along the supply chains (WFP 2008). The rapidly growing costs of the Baladi bread and flour program attracted particular reform attention. Al-Shawarby and El-Laithy (2010) and Coelli (2010) attributed large potential for optimizing the Baladi bread and flour subsidies to improving wheat trade and storage practices, utilizing economies of scale in mills and bakeries, better geographic targeting toward the residential areas of the needy population, and moving the subsidies to the end of the bread supply chain so as to eliminate incentives to leak flour to the black market.

Although the government managed to reduce leakages in the Baladi bread chain from 41 percent of total output in 2004/2005 to 31 percent in 2008/2009 (Al-Shawarby and El-Laithy 2010), the costs of the program surged in the 2000s, and particularly during the food, fuel, and financial crises of 2007–2009, partly due to high prices for imported wheat (Figure 3.2). The national government also phased out the national Baladi flour subsidy, although some governors managed to achieve continuation of the subsidy in their governorates. To improve the efficiency of the ration card program, the government considered implementing proxy means tests to monitor and evaluate the eligibility of ration cardholders; the tests' intended implementation was expected to reduce administrative costs, too. Electronic smart cards have, starting in 2005, gradually replaced the existing ration card booklets (Al-Shawarby and El-Laithy 2010). However, the government did not succeed in improving the cost-effectiveness of the ration card program. Leakages actually increased from 27 percent to 31 percent for cooking oil, increased from 19 percent to 20 percent for sugar, and stagnated at 11 percent for rice between 2004/2005 and 2008/2009 (Al-Shawarby and El-Laithy 2010). To the best of our knowledge, proxy means tests were never implemented—at least not to revoke ration cards from households in noncompliance with eligibility criteria.

In the course of the recent crises, reforming the food subsidy system has been proven to be difficult due to Egyptians' economic situation and the political sensitivity of such reforms, so urgently needed structural changes were abandoned. Instead, the government often used food (and fuel) subsidies to mitigate adverse household welfare effects and calm civil unrest, particularly during the food, fuel, and financial crises of 2007–2009 and the political uprising in 2011 and thereafter (Breisinger, Ecker, and Al-Riffai 2011; Bush 2010). High economic growth in the 2000s and resulting tax revenues enabled Egypt's government to be somewhat generous in public spending. Since 2003, the government has gradually rolled back the fiscally successful reforms made to the ration card program in the 1980s and 1990s. Sparked by rising inflation after the EGP devaluation, violent riots prompted the government to increase the quotas for rice, sugar, and cooking oil in mid-March 2004 and to reduce the subsidy prices a few days later. In addition, the ration card program was broadened by adding subsidized macaroni, beans, lentils, and ghee, which, however, were again removed from the ration card in April 2006 (Al-Shawarby and El-Laithy 2010).

Starting in mid-2007, the government expanded the coverage of the ration card program to include vulnerable households: the ration card program was opened to all households that received benefits from the national social insurance program in June 2007; persons born between 1988 and 2005 and living in households with existing ration cards were added to the ration cards in January 2008; and in 2009 the ration card program was progressively opened to specific household categories, including single women with dependents, pensioners, and temporary (low-income) workers and unemployed people (Al-Shawarby and El-Laithy 2010; Hannusch 2008).

In June 2008, the dual ration card system was phased out, and all holders of reduced-subsidy ration cards received full-subsidy ration cards. Moreover, the subsidy prices of the additional quotas were adjusted downward to match the subsidy prices of the regular quotas in three steps, namely in May 2008, August 2008, and July 2010. As a consequence of these expansions, the costs of the ration card program shot up, exceeding EGP 15 billion in 2010/2011. For the first time after 1991/1992, the costs of the ration card program in 2010/2011 exceeded the costs of the Baladi bread and flour program, which made up the bulk of the food subsidies in the second half of the 2000s, with a maximum share of 93 percent in 2007/2008 (Figure 3.3).

In 2011, the government issued a large number of new household ration cards, expanding the coverage of the ration card program considerably. The number of beneficiary households increased by almost 5.0 million (41.4 percent), from 11.9 million in July 2010 to 16.9 million in November 2011 (MSS 2010; MSIT 2014a). In return, the government reduced the number of registered beneficiary individuals among the existing beneficiary households (likely by removing some "ghost" household members from the ration cards), although to a much lower extent. The total number of individual beneficiaries increased by almost 2.9 million people, from 63.4 million in July 2010 to 66.3 million in November 2011 (MSS 2010; MSIT 2014a). Hence, the beneficiary population increased by 4.6 percent in 2011, which, in fact, marks a lower annual increase than during the period 2004–2010, when the number of beneficiaries increased at an annual average rate of 8.2 percent. However, the number of household ration cards increased by only 2.4 percent annually between 2004 and 2010 (MSS 2010; MSIT 2014a). It implies that, during this period, the ration card program was expanded more rapidly among existing beneficiary households—by including additional household members—than new beneficiary households were admitted to the program. The 2011 increase in the coverage of the ration card program is not (fully) reflected in our 2011 HIECS data (CAPMAS and WFP 2011), because most of it occurred after the survey's data collection period. The econometric analysis in the next chapter therefore reflects the situation before this program expansion.

The Recent Reform of the Egyptian Food Subsidy System (June 2014 to May 2015)

Since the end of the recent revolution—marked by the adoption of a new constitution in January 2014 and the election of President Abdel Fattah El-Sisi in May 2014—Egypt's food subsidy system has undergone fundamental

FIGURE 3.3 Costs of the bread and flour subsidy program and the ration card program

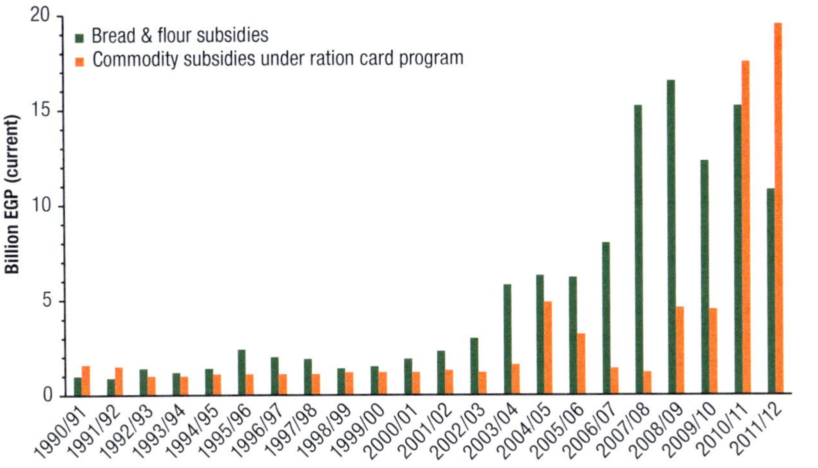

Source: Authors' representation based on data from CAPMAS (2013).
Note: EGP = Egyptian pounds.
Years listed are Egyptian fiscal years. Egypt's fiscal year starts on July 1 and concludes on June 30.

changes, and further critical modifications have been announced. The reform of the food subsidy system was issued by Ministerial Decree in June 2014 and includes five key changes:[10]

First, the new subsidy system is administered through electronic smart cards, with one per household. These smart cards are needed for accessing all subsidized products—including Baladi bread. The switch from paper-based (booklet) ration cards to smart cards is expected to be completed soon, as announced in early April 2015. The costs of the new smart cards are EGP 2, of which half has to be paid by the beneficiary household.

Second, the quota-based ration card program was phased out and replaced by a voucher-based program. Each beneficiary household receives a monthly cash allotment on the smart card, which can be redeemed for any (prepackaged) quantity of the subsidized commodities. This allows beneficiaries to better align the benefits with their needs compared to the old ration card program, where each household received fixed quotas of a few subsidized food items (cooking oil, sugar, rice, and black tea). Still, the allotment amount per

10 MSIT announces modifications to the food subsidy system on its website or its Facebook page (which are the main sources for this subsection).

household depends on the number of registered household members, similar to the quotas that were granted previously. The allotted monthly amount is EGP 15 per registered person, plus EGP 7 per registered person for the month of Ramadan. Unused amounts cannot be carried over to the following month.

Third, the basket of subsidized commodities expanded substantially, and the beneficiary contribution increased considerably. Since the introduction of the new subsidy system, the specific selection of subsidized commodities has changed twice. Many of the currently subsidized commodities were already included in the expanded ration card program of the 1970s (and thereafter)—which, however, quickly became fiscally unsustainable. As of January 2015, the basket of subsidized foods includes pasta, flour, beans, lentils, milk, various white cheeses, and frozen beef, chicken, and fish, in addition to—as under the pre-June 2014 subsidy system—sugar, (several types of) cooking oil, and rice.[11] It also includes nonfood necessities such as soap, washing machine detergent, and cleanser. Several of these commodities are offered in different package sizes. At the end of 2015, MSIT stated that it intended to increase the number of subsidized commodities to 100.

When purchasing the subsidized commodities, the beneficiaries need to contribute a small cash copayment out of pocket in addition to the amount that is deducted from the smart card. This out-of-pocket copayment does not exceed 10 percent of the card deduction for all commodities and is less than 5 percent of the deduction for most commodities. The prices of the subsidized commodities—including the amount deductible from the ration card and the beneficiary copayment—remain fixed at below-free-market prices but are amended as deemed necessary by MSIT. The prices of the traditional subsidized food items went up significantly, albeit from very low levels. At the time of the implementation of the new system in June 2014, the kilogram-price (including the amount deducted from the smart card and the beneficiary copayment) for subsidized sugar increased from EGP 1.25 to EGP 4.40—or by 252 percent; for subsidized cooking oil from EGP 3 to EGP 7.35—or by 145 percent; for subsidized rice from EGP 1.5 to EGP 2.4—or by 60 percent; and for subsidized black tea from EGP 13 to EGP 15 (for the largest package size)—or by 15 percent. Hence, the subsidy amount per registered person fell by EGP 10.9 (from EGP 25.9 to EGP 15) for a household with four or fewer registered household members during a regular month.[12] This change is esti-

11 See Table A.9 in the Appendix.

12 The subsidy amount per registered person before the reform is calculated based on the allotted quotas under the old system.

mated to reduce the annual costs of the ration card program by EGP 123.9 (US$17.35) per beneficiary—or, by about 40 percent—if other conditions remain the same. The subsidy prices were raised further between June 2014 and May 2015.

Fourth, Baladi bread subsidies are no longer universal, and bread purchases are no longer unrestricted. In August 2014, MSIT announced that Baladi bread has to be purchased on smart cards (or temporarily on specific bread distribution cards until the introduction of smart cards was completed). Hence, it restricted the access to smart-card holders and thereby ended the era of universal bread subsidies in Egypt—73 years after its introduction. For each registered household member, beneficiary households receive a quota of 150 bread loaves per month. The daily purchase is restricted to a maximum of 40 loaves per registered person (with a minimum number of 5 loaves per purchase). Unused "bread points" on the smart card can be used, within the first 10 days of the following month, for purchases of other subsidized commodities. The Baladi bread price at the outlets remains fixed at EGP 0.05 per loaf. Since February 2015, the bread points can also be used for purchases of Fino bread, which was already part of the subsidy system in the 1970s and 1980s (and removed in the early 1990s). Fino bread sells at EGP 0.25 per package of 5 loaves (equivalent to the Baladi bread loaf price). The entire bread quota of 150 loaves per month can be distributed between Baladi and Fino bread as desired. In some parts of rural Egypt, the bread points can also be used for purchasing Baladi bread flour for baking bread at home. The monthly flour quota is restricted to a maximum of 10 kg per registered person.

Fifth, the bread subsidy was moved to the end of the production chain to reduce leakage—as proposed by Al-Shawarby and El-Laithy (2010), among others. Specifically, the fixed flour price for bakeries was lifted and flour purchase quotas for bakeries were removed so that bakers could purchase any amount of flour at market prices. The state covers the production costs of Baladi bread and transfers an agreed cost price, plus a profit margin per each bread loaf sold, to the baker's bank account on a daily basis. Existing regulations on Baladi bread production remain in place (e.g., 130 g per bread loaf, 1,160 loaves from one 100 kg flour bag). Specific regulations on Fino bread production have not been published as of June 2015.

Thus, these fundamental changes to the food subsidy system imply the end of the dual subsidy system of a separate bread (and flour) program and food ration program and mark a shift toward a more flexible voucher-based system with better means of government control. With the introduction of the new system, the government increased the beneficiary population, possibly to also admit households that have benefited from the Baladi bread program but were excluded from the ration card program, such as many of the poor households. The total number of active ration cards reached 18.2 million by the end of December 2014—an increase of 7.7 percent from the number of cards in November 2011. The electronic system also allows the government to easily exclude households through voiding their smart card, to remove "ghost" household members or illegitimate beneficiaries, and to add newly registered newborns. The total beneficiary population reached 70 million in December 2014—80 percent of the total population, including 6 million newly registered children born between 2006 and 2011. More recently, the government has made efforts to reduce the number of beneficiaries. For example, with the support of popular Egyptian actors, MSIT has run a campaign that encourages households with incomes high enough not to rely on subsidized foods to return their cards voluntarily. MSIT also has run awareness campaigns to educate people about the modalities of the new system, its intended purpose, and related people's rights.

This reform was implemented after the collection of the HIECS data that underlie the analysis of this study. While the empirical analysis in the following chapter reflects the situation before the 2014–2015 reform, its findings do provide important insights and lessons that may help in shaping future food assistance policies in Egypt and other countries.

Characteristics of the Egyptian Food Subsidy System (under Study)

Until June 2014, Egypt's food subsidies were issued through two separate programs—the Baladi bread and flour program and the food ration program.[13] The Baladi bread and flour subsidy was a universal subsidy, so the benefits were available to everybody (in unrestricted amounts), in principle. Baladi bread was available to all consumers at specific bread outlets for EGP 0.05 per loaf. It was distributed on a first-come, first-served basis, and there were no

13 The bread and flour program included several different types of breads in the past, including Baladi, Tabaki, Fino, and Shami breads. At the time of 2010–2011 HIECS data collection (CAPMAS and WFP 2011), the production of Tabaki bread was semi-subsidized. However, Tabaki bread made up approximately only 15 percent of the total annual production quantity of subsidized bread (ECES 2010). The production of Tabaki bread was subsidized mainly through subsidizing energy costs of Tabaki bread bakeries and providing half-subsidized Tabaki bread flour to the bakeries. Hence, the subsidy amount per loaf was much lower for Tabaki bread than Baladi bread. Tabaki bread was sold in the free market at prices of EGP 0.10 for a small loaf of 85 g (Mansour 2012)—that is, more than twice the price of Baladi bread. Because of the relatively low supply of Tabaki bread, its distribution through the free market, and the relatively low subsidy rate for Tabaki bread production, this study omits the Tabaki bread subsidy.

regulations on the maximum number of Baladi bread loaves handed out per person. However, the geographic location of the Baladi bread outlets—with a higher concentration in poor neighborhoods—may have served to some extent as a self-targeting mechanism of the Baladi bread subsidy. Further, often long queues at the outlets and perceptions of the bread as having an inferior taste and texture may have discouraged some households—for example, those with high incomes and time constraints—to regularly consuming Baladi bread.

Since maintaining a high spatial coverage of Baladi bread bakeries and outlets for supplying the local population in remote areas is costly, the government also subsidized flour for baking Baladi bread at home. Principally all consumers without restrictions could purchase subsidized Baladi bread flour directly from warehouses, usually in a 25 kg sack (at a price of EGP 0.55 per kg). With the exception of the four metropolitan governorates (Cairo, Alexandria, Port Said, and Suez), consumer warehouses for Baladi bread flour were located in all governorates until the mid-1990s (Ahmed et al. 2001). Then the government started progressively to close consumer warehouses in parts of the country with high coverage of Baladi bread bakeries and outlets, so at the time of the 2011 HIECS data collection, only households in some governorates in Upper Egypt consumed subsidized Baladi bread flour.

Unlike the Baladi bread and flour subsidies, the food subsidies under the ration card program were restricted to households with valid ration cards. Each beneficiary household received fixed-quantity quotas of highly subsidized foods that were determined based on the number of family members registered on the card. From April 2006 to May 2014, ration cardholders were eligible to purchase high quantities of specific rice, sugar, cooking oil, and black tea at very low prices (see below).

The principal goal of the food subsidy system was to ensure affordability of a basic diet for all Egyptians by controlling the price of the main staple food—(Baladi) bread—and for the needy by controlling the prices of key basic food items such as rice, sugar, and cooking oil, particularly during times of economic hardship. As discussed above, the food subsidy system is considered to have large poverty-mitigation effects. However, the food subsidy system has also long been heavily criticized for its inefficiencies (e.g., Ahmed et al. 2001; Ahmed and Bouis 2002; Alderman, von Braun, and Sakr 1982; Alderman and von Braun 1984; Al-Shawarby and El-Laithy 2010; Löfgren and El-Said 2001; Kennedy and Alderman 1987).

From a national food security perspective, the main problem with the Baladi bread and flour program was the vast diversion away from intended uses, including waste throughout the supply chain (in storage, transportation, processing, and marketing) and within households (using bread as animal or fish feed and selling flour and bread on the black market) (Coelli 2010; ECES 2010; Al-Shawarby and El-Laithy 2010). The main problem with the food ration program was the poor targeting of the people in need (Ghoneim 2013; Al-Shawarby and El-Laithy 2010). Using data from 2008/2009, Al-Shawarby and El-Laithy (2010) estimate that up to 73 percent of the food subsidy costs could be saved by eliminating leakages and narrowing the coverage.

The coverage of Egypt's subsidy system has indeed been broad. Our 2011 HIECS data (CAPMAS and WFP 2011) suggest that 84.1 percent of all Egyptian households consumed Baladi bread, flour, or both over a 15-day recall period, while 75.0 percent purchased only Baladi bread, 3.7 percent purchased only Baladi flour, and 5.5 percent purchased both Baladi bread and flour.[14] Among poor households, 90.4 percent consumed Baladi bread or Baladi flour or both, compared to 82.7 percent among the non-poor households. Thus, the effectiveness of the self-targeting mechanisms appears to have been rather low, and the program seems to have even excluded some of the needy population, given that 9.7 percent of the poor seem to have had no access to the subsidized bread or flour. According to our 2011 HIECS data (CAPMAS and WFP 2011), 68.4 percent of all households had ration cards, and almost all of them (98.1 percent) also purchased subsidized oil, sugar, rice, or tea with the cards during the 15-day recall period between January and June 2011. The coverage estimated from the 2011 HIECS data is consistent with the coverage available from official sources, according to which 11.9 million households—an estimated 66.7 percent of all households—had ration cards in late 2010.[15] The number of ration cards considerably increased in 2011, reaching 16.9 million in November. Moreover, according to our 2011 HIECS data, 12.7 percent of all households who did not have a ration card consumed subsidized rice, sugar, cooking oil, or black tea, which they might have bought on the black market.

14 The Central Agency for Public Mobilization and Statistics (CAPMAS) of Egypt granted us access to data from 11,802 households of the 2010–2011 HIECS (CAPMAS and WFP 2011). They account for 48.7 percent of the total sample size (24,224 households), were all surveyed in the first half of 2011, and are considered to be representative (at the presented levels) by CAPMAS. Nonetheless, the (nutrition-unrelated) estimates presented in this report may slightly deviate from estimates presented in official reports consulting the full sample.

15 The percentage coverage of 66.7 percent is calculated from the number of ration cards reported by MSS (2010) (11.932 million in mid-2010), total population estimates reported by CAPMAS (2014) (79.618 million at the end of 2010), and average household size derived from our 2011 HIECS data (4.452 persons) (CAPMAS and WFP 2011).

TABLE 3.4 Allocation of food ration cards by income quintile and poverty status in Egypt

	Income quintile					Poverty status		
	Quintile 1 (poorest)	Quintile 2	Quintile 3	Quintile 4	Quintile 5 (richest)	Poor	Non-poor	Total
Households holding ration cards (%)								
Total	72.2	71.7	67.7	67.9	62.4	79.6	65.8	**68.4**
Urban	61.7	60.3	61.4	62.5	54.2	72.2	58.4	**59.9**
Rural	75.1	77.1	75.0	74.6	76.4	82.6	73.4	**75.7**
Family members registered on household ration card as proportion of actual household members (%)								
Total	90.4	101.2	114.2	127.4	166.9	98.8	124.4	**119.0**
Urban	93.8	112.4	118.2	144.3	181.9	99.3	134.2	**129.6**
Rural	89.0	95.6	106.7	117.3	149.5	98.6	116.4	**111.7**

Source: Authors' calculation based on data from CAPMAS and WFP (2011).

The ration card program suffered from a considerable misallocation of the subsidies, which primarily benefited rich urban households with ration cards (Table 3.4). According to our 2011 HIECS data, 20.4 percent of poor households had no ration cards and hence were excluded from the benefits of the program. In contrast, 65.8 percent of non-poor households had ration cards. Granted, the proportion of households with ration cards was somewhat higher overall among poorer income quintiles than richer income quintiles and among the rural population than the urban population. Nevertheless, richer households and urban households with ration cards had access to larger per capita amounts of subsidized foods because they had more family members registered on the ration card (given that the quotas are allocated based on the number of registered persons). In fact, among the middle- and higher-income quintiles in both urban and rural areas, there were more family members registered on the household ration cards than actually lived in the households. This illegitimacy is higher among higher-income households. Accordingly, urban households in the highest income quintile with ration cards are eligible for food rations (at full-subsidy rates) that amount, on average, to more than 180 percent of the actual legitimate quotas. On the contrary, not all members of urban households in the lowest income quintile and of rural households in the two lowest income quintiles with ration cards are registered. This misallocation likely resulted from a lack of oversight and enforcement of eligibility criteria such that, for example, young adults who left their parental households, as well as persons who died, stayed on the households' ration cards. Also, households may have been deliberately engaged in overreporting of household members.

Dietary Incentives and Nutritional Implications of the Egyptian Food Subsidy System

Since the introduction of the ration card program in 1945, the food items that have been continuously subsidized at high rates are sugar and cooking oil, in addition to (Baladi) bread. White rice and bread flour in rural areas have been subsidized since the 1970s. All these foods are rich sources of carbohydrates. Until May 2014, micronutrient-rich foods were rarely subsidized in Egypt, with the exception of pulses, meats, and fish in the 1970s and pulses occasionally thereafter. Vitamin-rich vegetables and fruits, however, were never subsidized. Hence, it has been argued that the (old) food subsidy system incentivized beneficiaries to consume an unhealthy diet that is too rich in calories and insufficient in micronutrients and therewith contributed to today's high prevalence of overweight/obesity, micronutrient deficiencies, and related NCDs (Asfaw 2006, 2007a, 2007b; Austin, Hill, and Fawzi 2013; Galal 2002; Kilpi et al. 2013; Musaiger 2011; Thow et al. 2010). Given that micronutrient deficiencies and inadequate child feeding practices are among the main causes of child stunting (Branca and Ferrari 2002; Rivera et al. 2003; Walker et al. 2007), the food subsidy system may have also contributed to the high and growing prevalence of child stunting, as the food subsidy system was gradually expanded in the 2000s. Hence, the food subsidy system may be a driver of both the double burden of malnutrition and the growth-nutrition disconnect.

The potential direct effects of the food subsidy system on malnutrition may occur through two interlinked dietary effects. Both effects emerge from the system's market intervention for lowering the prices of calorie-rich and micronutrient-poor/empty foods such as bread (and bread flour), cooking oil, sugar, and rice.

The first effect is that both the Baladi bread and flour program and the food ration program lowered the costs of becoming overweight/obese through incentivizing overconsumption of cheap, calorie-rich foods. The price of Baladi bread has been fixed at EGP 0.05 since 1989. Hence, in real terms, the Baladi bread price has declined substantially over time. In 2011, the Baladi bread price was below 20 percent of the 1989 price (taking the reduction of loaf size from 160 g to 130 g in 1990 into account). While the price of Baladi bread in 1990 was 3.2 US cents per loaf, it was only 0.8 US cents per loaf in 2011. The foods on the ration card have been highly subsidized, too. Our estimates based on the 2011 HIECS data (CAPMAS and WFP 2011) suggest

TABLE 3.5 Monthly quotas and prices of foods subsidized under the ration card program in Egypt

	Cooking oil	Sugar	Black tea	Rice
Quota per registered person (kg)	0.50	1.00	0.05	n.a.
Additional quota per registered person (kg), with maximum allowance of 4 persons	1.00	1.00	n.a.	2.00
Subsidy price (EGP/kg)	3.00	1.25	13.00	1.50
Average market price (EGP/kg)	8.00	5.50	31.25	3.50
Average subsidy rate (%)	62.5	77.3	58.4	57.1

Source: Authors' presentation based on data from MSS (2012) and CAPMAS and WFP (2011).

Note: EGP = Egyptian pound; kg = kilogram; n.a. = not applicable.

The average market price is the median price reported for market purchases in our 2011 HIECS data (CAPMAS and WFP 2011). The true market price of the subsidized foods may be slightly lower because of the lower quality of the subsidized foods compared to the respective free-market foods.

that the average subsidy amount accounted for 57 percent to 77 percent of the free-market price, with sugar having the highest subsidy rate (Table 3.5).

From a nutrition point of view, the quotas for the subsidized foods were too high when compared to common recommendations for healthy diets. For example, an average four-person household with all members registered for food rations was eligible to receive 6 kg of cooking oil, 8 kg of sugar, and 8 kg of rice per month (Table 3.5) as well as 3.1 loaves of Baladi bread (weighing 130 g) per person per day (according to official 2011 production guidelines for supplying the entire population; MSIT 2014c). If the household fully utilized these quotas, the subsidized foods provided the household with about 1,960 kcal per capita per day. This calorie allotment exceeds the minimum requirements of the average Egyptian four-person household by 6.4 percentage points if its members have low physical activity levels (the allotment equals 87.7 percent of the minimum requirements if household members have moderate physical activity levels). Of these calories, about 1,250 kcal (68.1 percent) come from the subsidized cereals (Baladi bread and rice), about 440 kcal (24.1 percent) from cooking oil (which admittedly may not be all ingested when used for frying), and about 260 kcal (13.4 percent) from sugar (in addition to the consumption of other sugary products such as soft drinks, sweets, honey, and dried fruits). Such cheap calories may incentivize overconsumption and give rise to weight gains, as explained in the next subsection in detail.

Our 2011 HIECS data also suggest that the subsidized food quantities at least met—or even exceeded—the demand of the vast majority of the beneficiary households in the ration card program. Only 7.7 percent of the beneficiary households who consumed subsidized cooking oil purchased additional quantities of free-market cooking oil. For sugar and rice, 9.6 percent and 22.6 percent, respectively, of households receiving subsidized quotas of these goods purchased additional quantities on the free market. This holds even though the quality of the subsidized products is considered to be inferior compared to the nonsubsidized substitutes sold in the free market and despite the fact that not all household members are registered on the ration card in 27.7 percent of all beneficiary households.

The second effect emerges from consumer preferences for foods based on relative prices and substitution of foods in response to relative price changes. Through subsidizing only calorie-rich and micronutrient-poor/empty foods, Egypt's old food subsidy system lowered the costs to a household of a low-diversified, unbalanced diet relative to a diversified diet that is well balanced over food groups and provides essential micronutrients in sufficient amounts. As the prices of the subsidized foods were fixed, and the prices of free-market foods increased particularly rapidly during economic crises, the resulting loss in real incomes encouraged households to shift their diet toward more calorie-rich and micronutrient-poor foods. As food prices in the free market stay high, households tend to stick to unbalanced diets, increasing the risk of micronutrient deficiencies. The underlying consumer behavior is explained in the next subsection.

Persistent large cost differences between micronutrient-rich and micronutrient-poor diets may entail permanent changes in consumer food preferences. Unlike a lack of dietary energy, micronutrient deficiencies do not create a feeling of hunger, and mild deficiencies show no obvious symptoms, so micronutrient deficiencies are often not detected by the individual or family members. With growing income, households may allocate only small shares of the additional budget to diversify their diet and may use most of it for increasing consumption of foods with low nutritive value but high consumer satisfaction, such as fast food and soft drinks (or for satisfying nonfood needs). The food consumption patterns of households with young children in Egypt are explored in the last subsection.

For Egypt, Asfaw (2007b) finds that the odds of being overweight are 80.8 percent higher for micronutrient-deficient mothers than for non-deficient mothers (keeping all other variables constant). In addition, data on child feeding practices from the 2005 and 2008 DHS confirm that many young Egyptian children receive an inadequate diet and that diets have worsened (MOH, El-Zanaty and Associates, and Macro International 2008; MOHP, NPC, and ORC Macro 2000; MOHP et al. 2003; MOHP et al. 2005). In 2008, only 40.6 percent of nonbreastfed children in the age group

6–23 months and 27.8 percent of children in the same age group who had ever been breastfed consumed fruits or vegetables rich in vitamin A during the 24 hours prior to the survey, compared to 48.4 percent and 37.0 percent in 2005 (El-Zanaty and Way 2006, 2009). In contrast, sugary food was given to 55.8 percent of the nonbreastfed children and 41.6 percent of the breastfed children in 2008, and to 39.6 percent and 26.5 percent of nonbreastfed and breastfed children, respectively, in 2005.

Indeed, the prevalence of micronutrient malnutrition is high in Egypt and has increased. For example, anemia, which is predominantly caused by dietary iron deficiency in Egypt (as malaria—the other main cause of anemia globally—is not prevalent), increased considerably in the first half decade of the 2000s. Egypt showed prevalence rates among preschool children that mark anemia as a severe public health problem according to international standards set by the World Health Organization (WHO). The 2005 DHS data suggest that 39.6 percent of all nonpregnant women 20–49 years of age and even 48.6 percent of all children ages 6–59 months are anemic.[16]

The Mechanism of Food Subsidy Effects on Nutrition in Egypt

Consumer theory offers an explanation for the mechanism through which the Egyptian food subsidy system potentially affects beneficiaries' nutrition. It suggests that food subsidies influence consumers' food choice through two separable effects of price changes—income and substitution effects (Timmer, Falcon, and Pearson 1983). First, the reduction in the prices of subsidized foods causes real purchasing power to increase when household incomes stay constant. This increase in real incomes will cause consumption of most commodities—including food—to increase (with the exception of inferior goods). Second, even if the increase in real incomes were to be offset by real income losses due, for example, to food price shocks, the change in relative prices would still cause consumers to adjust the composition of their commodity bundle toward higher consumption of the foods that have become relatively cheaper if consumers' demand for these foods is not fully satisfied. In a country with food subsidies, this means an increased consumption of subsidized foods (if subsidy quotas allow) if other conditions remain the same.

16 The latest available data that are nationally representative are from the DHS in 2005 (MOH, El-Zanaty and Associates, and Macro International 2008; MOHP, NPC, and ORC Macro 2000; MOHP et al. 2003; MOHP et al. 2005). For anemia prevalence rates, see Table A.10 in the Appendix. The calculated annual increases between 2000 and 2005 in the prevalence rates among nonpregnant women of 2.4 percentage points and among children of 3.7 percentage points appear to be too high, however, and therefore may leave some doubts about the accuracy of the anemia measurements in the 2000 DHS, 2005 DHS, or both.

The choice of the commodity bundle for consumption is constrained by household income—and thus by household ability to compensate food price shocks. According to consumer theory, a consumer chooses the composition of the bundle of food and nonfood commodities so as to maximize her total consumption utility subject to a budget constraint or so as to minimize her expenditures to achieve a certain level of consumption utility, assuming given commodity prices.

For the effects of food subsidies on household diets, substitution effects are of particular relevance when households experience—during food price crises, for example—real income losses and large price differences between subsidized and nonsubsidized foods. More specifically, when foods are normal (non-inferior) goods and food budget shares and prices are constant, applying food subsidies already incentivizes increased consumption of the subsidized foods by reducing their prices. The (positive) substitution effect resulting from the relative price changes reinforces the (positive) income effect resulting from reducing the costs of the consumption basket. Further, if now prices of only nonsubsidized foods increase, they become even more expensive than the subsidized foods. As a result, consumers have an incentive to substitute nonsubsidized foods with similar (but probably less preferred) subsidized foods: for example, consumers may substitute subsidized Baladi bread and rice (if subsidy quotas allow) for pasta and nonsubsidized types of rice. Yet, the (negative) income effect resulting from the increase in prices of nonsubsidized foods forces budget-constrained consumers to switch consumption to a commodity bundle that provides them with less utility. Rational consumers will choose the composition of this new commodity bundle so as to maximize total consumption utility. Regarding food consumption, this may entail reduced consumption of or abstention from some food items. Consumers tend to first reduce or relinquish the consumption of relatively superior foods such as animal-source products. For foods with price-elastic demand, consumers will over-proportionately reduce consumption in response to the price increase. They may use the resulting gain in real incomes for increasing consumption of cheaper—possibly subsidized—foods of another type, yielding an additional substitution effect. For example, Kavle et al. (2015a) argue that the increase in the consumption of sugary foods among children in Lower Egypt between 2005 and 2008 may have been the result of substituting these foods primarily for meat and fish in the course of the 2006 avian influenza outbreak and the following food and fuel price crisis. Increasing food subsidies may compensate for negative income effects resulting from price increases of nonsubsidized foods, but they do not prevent substitution effects to occur—instead they amplify them. Ramadan and Thomas (2011) find that a reduction in the price of subsidized sugar by 1 percent would increase sugar consumption by 0.12 percent and reduce meat and fish consumption by 0.39 percent.[17]

Given that these principles of consumer theory hold, the kinds of foods that are subsidized and hence their content of absorbable nutrients relative to that of nonsubsidized foods matter for the nutritional effects of food subsidies. As discussed above, Egypt's past food subsidy system provided subsidies only for foods that are dense in carbohydrates or fats and scarce/empty in absorbable micronutrients, which incentivizes overconsumption of cheap calories and unbalanced diets. Certainly, individual household preferences determine which foods will be included in household diets and thereby may alter the food subsidy effects at the household level. Moreover, the intrahousehold distribution of the available food affects the nutritional status of household members.

Ultimately, it is the nutrient intake relative to individual physiological requirements that determines individual nutritional outcomes. For adequate nutrition, the consumption of those nutrients that a person (most) lacks is decisive, while the overconsumption of some (macro)nutrients has adverse nutrition and health consequences. For example, low child HAZ and child stunting is often caused by insufficient consumption of absorbable micronutrients, especially zinc (Brown, Wuehler, and Peerson 2001; IZiNCG 2004), which are available in meat and fish, legumes, and some vegetables in high amounts and readily absorbable forms. Excess consumption of carbohydrates and fats—cheaply available from the subsidized foods—does not improve child growth but causes unhealthy weight gains and increases the risk of overweight/obesity and related NCDs in children and adults. Using a simple reduced-form regression model and data from the 1997 EIHS, Asfaw (2006) finds that a 1 percent decrease in the price of Baladi bread is associated with an increase in the average BMI of Egyptian mothers by 0.12 percent if other conditions remain the same. A 1 percent decrease in the price of subsidized sugar is associated with a 0.16 percent increase in mothers' BMI, whereas a 1 percent decrease in the price of fruits is associated with a 0.12 percent decrease in mothers' BMI (Asfaw 2006). Although the econometric model underlying these estimates does not permit causal interpretation of the relationship between food subsidies and nutritional outcomes, the results are

17 Ramadan and Thomas (2011) use a mixed demand model estimation based on data from the Egyptian Integrated Household Survey (EIHS) in 1997, when ration card quotas for sugar were smaller and prices of subsidized sugar higher than in 2011.

consistent with findings from developed countries, which show that high body weight and the prevalence of overweight/obesity are associated with low-priced calorie-rich foods (e.g., Bleich et al. 2008; Chou, Grossman, and Saffer 2004; Duffey et al. 2010).

Evidence on the causal effects of food subsidies on nutrient consumption and nutritional outcomes is very limited for developing countries and so far is missing for Egypt. Notable exceptions are Jensen and Miller (2011), who analyze the effects of a randomized program of staple food subsidies in China, and Kochar (2005) and Tarozzi (2005), who analyze the effects of India's food subsidy program. Unlike in Egypt, overconsumption of calories does not appear to be a considerable problem for the sample populations of all three studies; on the contrary, shortages of calorie-rich foods might have been a common threat to household food security for these studies' sample populations.

For poor households in two provinces of China, Jensen and Miller (2011), using experimental data they collected in 2006, find no positive and statistically significant effects of wheat and rice subsidies on the consumption of calories, protein, minerals, and vitamins. In fact, the wheat and rice subsidies may have had adverse nutritional effects for some households. The elasticity estimates are negative for all nutrients, though they are very small and statistically insignificant. Kochar (2005) finds that wheat and rice subsidies provided through the Indian Public Distribution System (PDS) had a statistically significant but quite small positive effect on household calorie consumption in rural areas of major PDS-beneficiary states in central and northern India between 1993 and 1999–2000. The estimated elasticity is 0.07. Tarozzi (2005) finds no statistically significant effect of rice subsidies on children's weight (relative to their age) in Andhra Pradesh, using health survey data from 1992–1993. However, as Kochar (2005) shows, the limited effect of India's food subsidy program is primarily due to low household take-up rates and low purchases of subsidized foods among these households. In Egypt, by contrast, the household take-up rate of the Baladi bread and flour program is high, and the household take-up rate of the ration card program is almost total, as shown above.

Food Consumption of Subsidized and Nonsubsidized Foods in Egyptian Families

Food consumption patterns provide an indication of the composition of household diets and therefore household preferences for more or less nutritious foods. The food expenditure and consumption section of the 2010–2011 HIECS (CAPMAS and WFP 2011) reports household expenditures for almost 300 food items—including subsidized foods and their nonsubsidized substitutes—consumed over a period of 15 days.[18] These HIECS data allow for calculating average food budget shares and estimating Engel curves, which describe how food expenditures change with increasing household incomes. Because this study is concerned with malnutrition among young children and their mothers, the samples that underlie the food budget shares and Engel curves presented in the following include only households in our 2011 HIECS dataset with children ages 6–59 months—referred to as "families." The analysis is conducted for urban and rural areas separately, given that there are substantial urban-rural differences in people's living conditions and food sourcing and the design and coverage of the food subsidy programs. The samples are identical to the household sample datasets that are used in the main empirical analysis presented in the next chapter.[19]

Food consumption patterns suggest that urban families spend on average significantly higher per capita amounts—but lower shares of their incomes—on food than do rural families (Table 3.6). Except in the case of subsidized foods, urban-rural differences in (absolute) food expenditures are partly due to differences in food prices, which are higher in urban areas than in rural areas, as the HIECS data suggest. Despite their higher absolute expenditure on food, urban families allocate on average 38.7 percent of their household income to food consumption, compared to 42.4 percent for rural families. Also, the variation in food budget shares among urban families is about twice as high as that among rural families. Urban and rural families devote the largest shares of their food budgets to the consumption of meat and fish. Meat and fish consumption accounts for more than 30 percent of both urban and rural food budgets, on average. Urban and rural families devote much lower food budget shares to the consumption of cereals (13.0 percent and 16.0 percent, respectively) and vegetables (around 12 percent for both urban and rural families). Among the considered food groups, the largest differences in food budget shares between urban and rural families exist for cereal consumption and the consumption of milk and dairy products. Urban families use considerably lower shares of their food budgets for the consumption

18 For foods households produce themselves and for food gifts, the 2010–2011 HIECS reports interviewees' estimated values. It also provides data on consumed quantities but only for some food items that are usually nonprocessed. Quantities are unavailable for 19.9 percent of all consumed food items in our 2011 HIECS dataset (CAPMAS and WFP 2011), which includes basic food items such as all types of bread and baked products, milk, and several other animal-source foods. Therefore, reliable, quantity-based food consumption patterns cannot be produced.

19 See the "Survey Data and Estimation Variables" subsection in the next chapter.

of cereals (by 3.0 percentage points) and higher shares for the consumption of milk and dairy products (by 3.4 percentage points). Compared to rural families, urban families also devote slightly larger shares of their food budgets to the consumption of meat and fish (by 0.7 percentage points) but slightly smaller shares to the consumption of vegetables (by 0.8 percentage points) and edible fats and oils (by 0.6 percentage points). Urban and rural families devote similar shares of their budgets to the consumption of sugars (3.7 percent) and legumes (1.8–1.9 percent).

Given that the prices of subsidized foods are identical in urban and rural areas, the food consumption patterns imply that urban and rural families consume similar per capita quantities, on average, of Baladi bread, flour, or both (Table 3.6). Urban families with ration cards consume significantly more of the foods that are subsidized under the ration card program than do rural families with ration cards. This is consistent with our finding that the per capita quotas are higher among urban ration cardholders (Table 3.4). To be specific, urban families with ration cards consume somewhat more subsidized rice and cooking oil and less subsidized sugar than rural families with ration cards. The lower consumption of subsidized sugar among urban families with ration cards might reflect their preferences for nonsubsidized, more refined sugar, because the average per capita consumption among urban families is higher than that among rural families (and sugar prices show no significant difference).

The subsidized foods make up large shares in food group expenditures (Table 3.6). Their shares in food group consumption if measured in food quantities or calories can be expected to be still larger. Consumers of subsidized foods would be making considerably higher expenditures for purchasing the same quantities or calorie amounts of these foods if there were no subsidies. In expenditure terms, Baladi bread and flour make up around 24 percent of the cereal consumption in urban and rural families, on average. Rice accounts for 32.7 percent of cereal consumption in urban families, and 29.7 percent in rural families. Among ration cardholders, most of the rice is subsidized rice, while the share of subsidized rice is higher in urban families than in rural families (by 4.3 percentage points). Most sugar and vegetable oil consumed by families with ration cards is subsidized. Subsidized sugar makes up around 72 percent of the sugar expenditure in both urban and rural areas, and subsidized cooking oil makes up 82.4 percent and 91.5 percent of vegetable oil expenditures in urban and rural areas, respectively. The share of subsidized cooking oil in all edible fats and oils consumed is significantly higher among urban families with ration cards than among rural families with ration cards (36.9 percent and 30.9 percent, respectively). Taken together,

TABLE 3.6 Per capita income and food consumption in urban and rural Egyptian families

	Urban		Rural		Difference (t-test)		
	Mean	Std. dev.	Mean	Std. dev.	Mean[c]		Std. err.
Income (EGP)	**230.3**	**166.7**	**172.2**	**81.0**	**58.1**	***	**5.29**
Food consumption (EGP)	**82.6**	**45.5**	**68.7**	**23.8**	**13.9**	***	**1.46**
Share of income (%)	38.7	10.7	42.4	10.5	−3.7	***	0.40
Cereals (EGP)	10.1	5.3	10.8	5.0	−0.7	***	0.19
Share of food consumption (%)	13.0	4.8	16.0	5.5	−3.0	***	0.19
Baladi bread & flour (EGP)	1.9	1.3	1.9	1.4	0.0		0.05
Share of cereal consumption (%)	24.0	18.7	24.1	21.5	−0.1		0.74
Rice (EGP)	3.3	2.5	3.5	3.3	−0.2	**	0.11
Share of cereal consumption (%)	32.7	17.6	29.7	19.5	3.0	***	0.69
Subsidized rice (EGP)[a]	0.9	0.7	0.7	0.7	0.2	***	0.04
Share of rice consumption (%)	59.0	44.9	54.7	45.6	4.3	*	2.50
Vegetables (EGP)	9.0	4.3	8.4	3.6	0.6	***	0.15
Share of food consumption (%)	11.7	4.1	12.4	3.8	−0.8	***	0.15
Legumes (EGP)	1.3	1.5	1.2	1.2	0.1	*	0.05
Share of food consumption (%)	1.8	2.0	1.9	1.8	−0.1		0.07
Meat & fish (EGP)	27.4	18.2	21.9	9.5	5.4	***	0.58
Share of food consumption (%)	32.5	8.5	31.8	7.9	0.7	**	0.31
Milk & dairy products (EGP)	10.2	8.6	5.8	4.2	4.4	***	0.27
Share of food consumption (%)	11.5	6.0	8.1	4.4	3.4	***	0.20
Sugars (EGP)[b]	3.0	2.3	2.5	2.0	0.5	***	0.08
Share of food consumption (%)	3.7	2.4	3.7	2.6	0.0		0.09
Sugar (EGP)	2.5	1.8	2.2	1.8	0.3	***	0.07
Share of sugars consumption (%)	87.4	20.4	87.2	20.0	0.2		0.76
Subsidized sugar (EGP)[a]	0.8	0.4	0.9	0.4	−0.1	***	0.02
Share of sugar consumption (%)	71.9	34.4	72.6	32.1	−0.8		1.87
Edible fats & oils (EGP)	6.0	3.7	5.5	3.1	0.5	***	0.13
Share of food consumption (%)	7.5	3.4	8.1	3.7	−0.6	***	0.13
Vegetable oils (EGP)	3.2	2.4	2.0	1.5	1.2	***	0.08
Share of fats & oils consumption (%)	54.5	23.3	41.1	24.5	13.4	***	0.89
Subsidized cooking oil (EGP)[a]	1.3	0.7	1.2	0.6	0.1	**	0.04
Share of vegetable oils consumption (%)	82.4	31.9	91.5	23.0	−9.2	***	1.64

(continued)

FIGURE 3.6 **Per capita income and food consumption in urban and rural Egyptian families, 2011 (continued)**

	Urban		Rural		Difference (t-test)		
	Mean	Std. dev.	Mean	Std. dev.	Mean[c]		Std. err.
Rice, sugar, vegetable oils (EGP)	9.0	4.9	7.7	4.7	1.3	***	0.18
Share of food consumption (%)	11.5	5.2	11.0	5.4	0.4	**	0.20
Subsidized rice, sugar, cooking oil (EGP)[a]	2.9	1.4	2.7	1.1	0.2	**	0.07
Share of rice, sugar, oil consumption (%)	64.9	34.4	63.1	34.0	1.8		1.90

Source: Authors' calculation based on data from CAPMAS and WFP (2011).

Note: EGP = Egyptian pound.

The full urban and rural samples include 1,130 and 1,911 households, respectively. Reported per capita income and consumption expenditures refer to a time period of 15 days.

[a] The values refer to ration cardholders. The urban and rural sample includes 453 and 1,171 households, respectively.

[b] Sugars include sugar, honey, and molasses.

[c] ***, **, * Mean difference is statistically significant at the 1 percent, 5 percent, and 10 percent level, respectively. The t-tests are performed by accounting for unequal variances in the urban and rural samples.

the consumption of subsidized foods under the ration card program is significantly higher in absolute terms among urban beneficiary families than rural beneficiary families, while the share of subsidized rice, sugar, and cooking oil in the consumption of all rice, sugar, and vegetable oil is not significantly different between urban and rural beneficiary families.

Food consumption patterns change with increasing household incomes, because consumers make their food choices subject to budget constraints. Hence, food consumption differences between poor and non-poor Egyptians are likely. Egypt's food subsidy system has been deemed to be self-targeted to the poor—especially in urban areas—through subsidizing foods that are inferior goods (e.g., Adams 2000; Ali and Adams 1996; Al-Shawarby and El-Laithy 2010). Consumer theory suggests that inferior goods are consumed more (in both relative and absolute terms) by low-income than high-income households. Accordingly, it is believed that the Egyptian food subsidy system achieves inferiority through subsidizing only basic foods and product differentiation of the subsidized foods. Engel curves provide evidence on the validity of this assumption and on how much households spend on particular foods at different income levels.

Engel curves estimated based on the 2011 HIECS data (CAPMAS and WFP 2011) suggest that only Baladi bread (and flour) is an inferior food among families in both urban and rural areas. The per capita expenditures

FIGURE 3.4 Engel curves for total food consumption, consumption of cereals, and consumption of Baladi bread and flour in Egyptian families

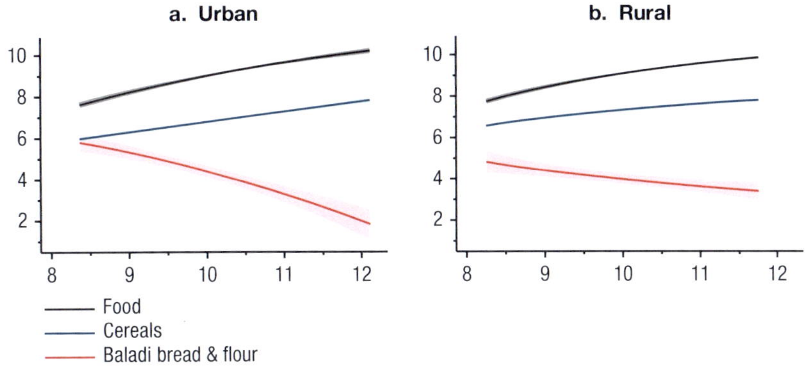

Source: Authors' estimation based on data from CAPMAS and WFP (2011).

Note: Household income and expenditure values are expressed on a per capita basis, refer to a period of 15 days, are reported in Egyptian piasters, and are transformed into logarithms. The y-axis indicates household expenditure levels (in logarithms), and the x-axis indicates household income levels (in logarithms).

The Engel curves are estimated using fractional polynomial regressions of degree 1 and a robust estimator of variance. To control for possible spatial and temporal price differences, the regressions include binary variables indicating household location by governorate (aggregate) and the survey month. The presented curves connect the predicted expenditure values for reported household incomes (controlling for spatial and temporal price differences). The shaded areas around the curves mark the 95 percent confidence interval.

The urban and rural samples include 1,130 and 1,911 households, respectively. In the urban sample, the R-squared—indicating the overall statistical fit of the estimated regression model—is 0.689 for total food consumption, 0.407 for cereal consumption, and 0.104 for Baladi bread and flour consumption. In the rural sample, the R-squared is 0.626, 0.373, and 0.099, respectively.

for Baladi bread and flour are significantly lower among high-income families than low-income families, especially in urban areas (Figure 3.4). In contrast, the per capita expenditures for all food items subsidized under the ration card program are significantly higher among high-income beneficiary families than low-income beneficiary families in both urban and rural areas (Figure 3.5). Looking at the ration card foods separately, the per capita expenditures for subsidized rice and cooking oil are significantly higher, in urban areas, among high-income families with ration cards than among low-income families with ration cards (Figure 3.6, Figure 3.7, and Figure 3.8). Per capita expenditures also tend to be higher among high-income beneficiary families for subsidized rice and cooking oil in rural areas and subsidized sugar in urban and rural areas, although the regression coefficient of the income variable is statistically insignificant at the 10 percent level (Figures 3.6–3.8). Thus, the estimated Engel curves do not support the assumption of inferiority of any food

(text continued on page 78)

FIGURE 3.5 Engel curves for total food consumption; consumption of rice, sugar, and vegetable oils; and consumption of subsidized rice, sugar, and cooking oil in Egyptian families

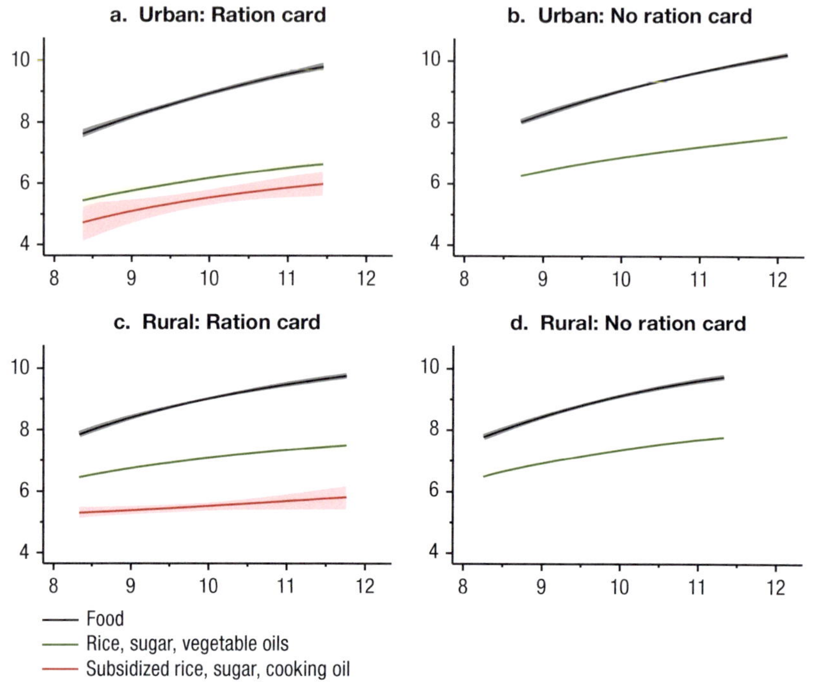

Source: Authors' estimation based on data from CAPMAS and WFP (2011).

Note: Household income and expenditure values are expressed on a per capita basis, refer to a period of 15 days, are reported in Egyptian piasters, and are transformed into logarithms. The y-axis indicates household expenditure levels (in logarithms), and the x-axis indicates household income levels (in logarithms).

The Engel curves are estimated using fractional polynomial regressions of degree 1 and a robust estimator of variance. To control for possible spatial and temporal price differences, the regressions include binary variables indicating household location by governorate (aggregate) and the survey month. The presented curves connect the predicted expenditure values for reported household incomes (controlling for spatial and temporal price differences). The shaded areas around the curves mark the 95 percent confidence interval.

The urban and rural samples of ration cardholders include 453 and 1,171 households, respectively. The urban and rural samples of non-cardholders include 677 and 740 households, respectively. In the urban sample of ration cardholders, the R-squared is 0.644 for total food consumption; 0.426 for consumption of rice, sugar, and vegetable oil; and 0.076 for consumption of subsidized rice, sugar, and cooking oil. In the urban sample of non-cardholders, the R-squared is 0.705 for total food consumption and 0.340 for consumption of rice, sugar, and vegetable oil. In the rural sample of ration cardholders, the R-squared is 0.610, 0.609, and 0.059, respectively. In the rural sample of non-cardholders, the R-squared is 0.658 and 0.487, respectively.

FIGURE 3.6 Engel curves for consumption of cereals, rice, and subsidized rice in Egyptian families

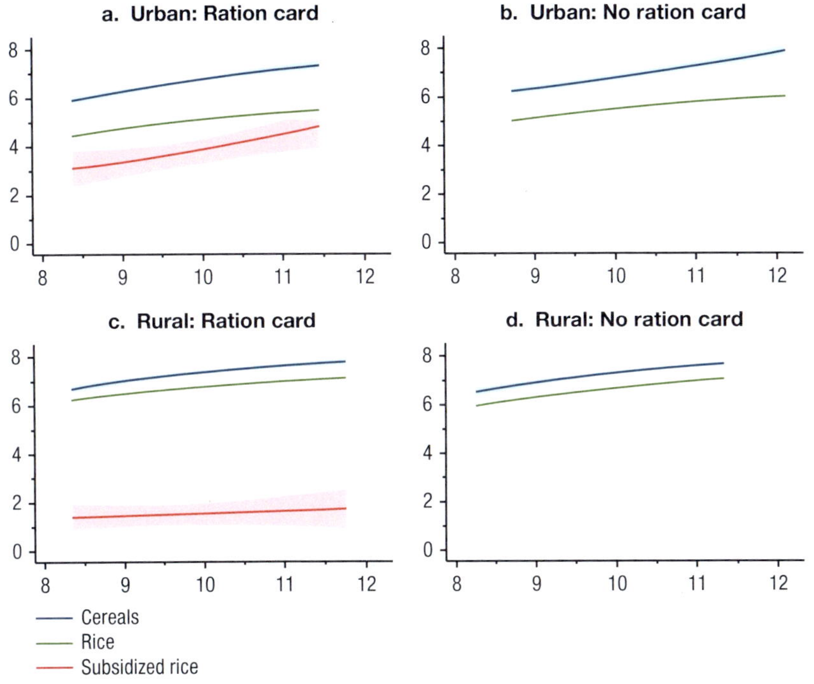

Source: Authors' estimation based on data from CAPMAS and WFP (2011).

Note: Household income and expenditure values are expressed on a per capita basis, refer to a period of 15 days, are reported in Egyptian piasters, and are transformed into logarithms. The y-axis indicates household expenditure levels (in logarithms), and the x-axis indicates household income levels (in logarithms).

The Engel curves are estimated using fractional polynomial regressions of degree 1 and a robust estimator of variance. To control for possible spatial and temporal price differences, the regressions include binary variables indicating household location by governorate (aggregate) and the survey month. The presented curves connect the predicted expenditure values for reported household incomes (controlling for spatial and temporal price differences). The shaded areas around the curves mark the 95 percent confidence interval.

The urban and rural samples of ration cardholders include 453 and 1,171 households, respectively. The urban and rural samples of non-cardholders include 677 and 740 households, respectively. In the urban sample of ration cardholders, the R-squared is 0.421 for cereal consumption, 0.518 for rice consumption, and 0.145 for subsidized rice consumption. In the urban sample of non-cardholders, the R-squared is 0.406 for cereal consumption and 0.512 for rice consumption. In the rural sample of ration cardholders, the R-squared is 0.406, 0.705, and 0.297, respectively. In the rural sample of non-cardholders, the R-squared is 0.341 and 0.594, respectively.

FIGURE 3.7 Engel curves for consumption of sugars, sugar, and subsidized sugar in Egyptian families

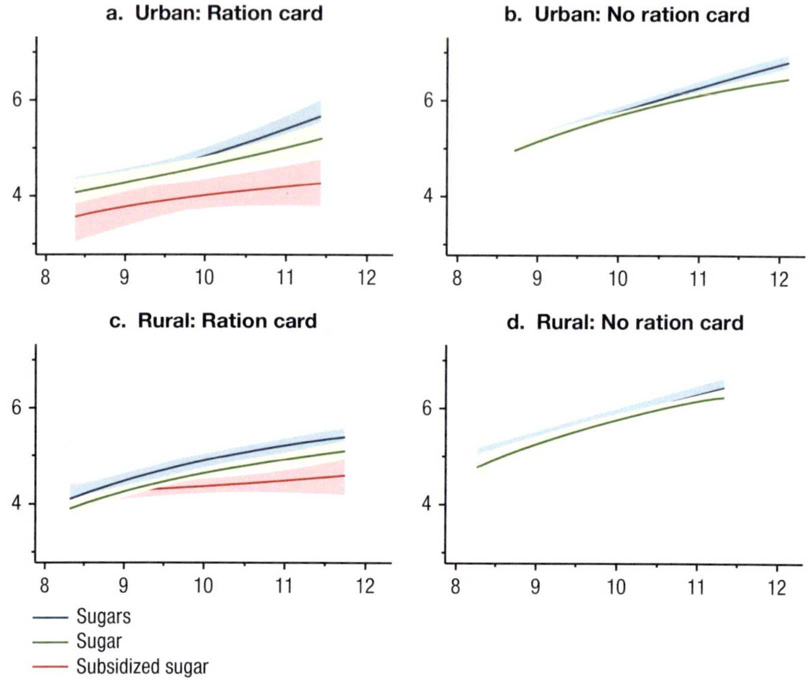

Source: Authors' estimation based on data from CAPMAS and WFP (2011).

Note: Sugars include sugar, honey, and molasses.

Household income and expenditure values are expressed on a per capita basis, refer to a period of 15 days, are reported in Egyptian piasters, and are transformed into logarithms. The y-axis indicates household expenditure levels (in logarithms), and the x-axis indicates household income levels (in logarithms).

The Engel curves are estimated using fractional polynomial regressions of degree 1 and a robust estimator of variance. To control for possible spatial and temporal price differences, the regressions include binary variables indicating household location by governorate (aggregate) and the survey month. The presented curves connect the predicted expenditure values for reported household incomes (controlling for spatial and temporal price differences). The shaded areas around the curves mark the 95 percent confidence interval.

The urban and rural samples of ration cardholders include 453 and 1,171 households, respectively. The urban and rural samples of non-cardholders include 677 and 740 households, respectively. In the urban sample of ration cardholders, the R-squared is 0.156 for consumption of sugars, 0.149 for sugar consumption, and 0.055 for subsidized sugar consumption. In the urban sample of non-cardholders, the R-squared is 0.235 for consumption of sugars and 0.197 for sugar consumption. In the rural sample of ration cardholders, the R-squared is 0.143, 0.226, and 0.041, respectively. In the rural sample of non-cardholders, the R-squared is 0.148 and 0.149, respectively.

FIGURE 3.8 Engel curves for consumption of edible fats and oils, vegetable oils, and subsidized cooking oil in Egyptian families

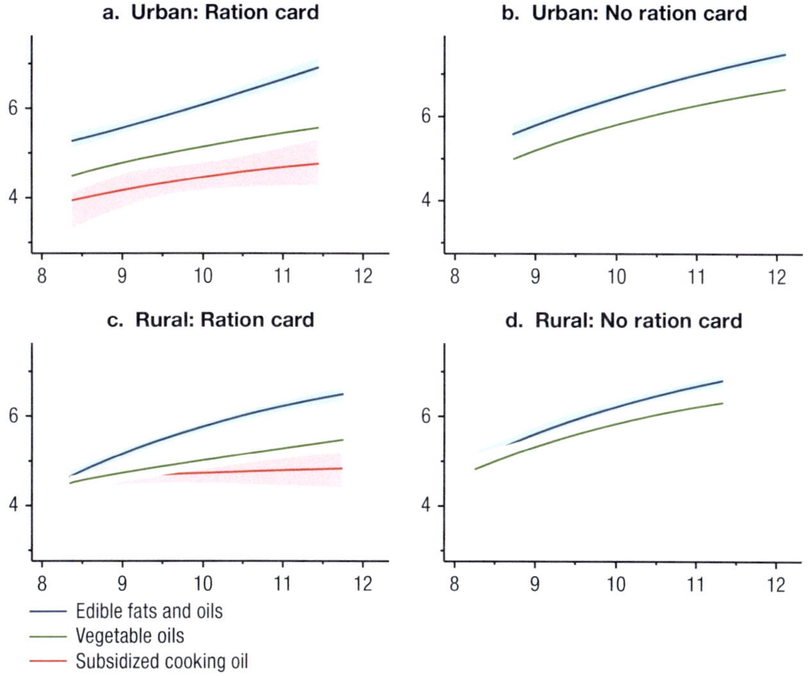

Source: Authors' estimation based on data from CAPMAS and WFP (2011).

Note: Household income and expenditure values are expressed on a per capita basis, refer to a period of 15 days, are reported in Egyptian piasters, and are transformed into logarithms. The y-axis indicates household expenditure levels (in logarithms), and the x-axis indicates household income levels (in logarithms).

The Engel curves are estimated using fractional polynomial regressions of degree 1 and a robust estimator of variance. To control for possible spatial and temporal price differences, the regressions include binary variables indicating household location by governorate (aggregate) and the survey month. The presented curves connect the predicted expenditure values for reported household incomes (controlling for spatial and temporal price differences). The shaded areas around the curves mark the 95 percent confidence interval.

The urban and rural samples of ration cardholders include 453 and 1,171 households, respectively. The urban and rural samples of non-cardholders include 677 and 740 households, respectively. In the urban sample of ration cardholders, the R-squared is 0.349 for consumption of edible fats and oils, 0.219 for consumption of vegetable oils, and 0.080 for subsidized cooking oil consumption. In the urban sample of non-cardholders, the R-squared is 0.328 for consumption of edible fats and oils and 0.235 for consumption of vegetable oils. In the rural sample of ration cardholders, the R-squared is 0.295, 0.193, and 0.104, respectively. In the rural sample of non-cardholders, the R-squared is 0.263 and 0.311, respectively.

FIGURE 3.9 Engel curves for consumption of vegetables and legumes in Egyptian families

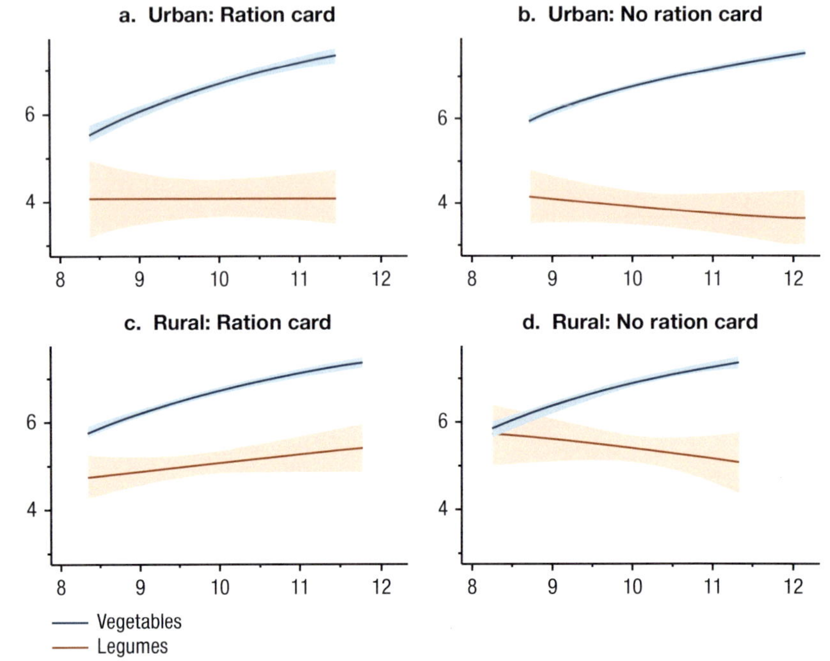

Source: Authors' estimation based on data from CAPMAS and WFP (2011).

Note: Household income and expenditure values are expressed on a per capita basis, refer to a period of 15 days, are reported in Egyptian piasters, and are transformed into logarithms. The y-axis indicates household expenditure levels (in logarithms), and the x-axis indicates household income levels (in logarithms).

The Engel curves are estimated using fractional polynomial regressions of degree 1 and a robust estimator of variance. To control for possible spatial and temporal price differences, the regressions include binary variables indicating household location by governorate (aggregate) and the survey month. The presented curves connect the predicted expenditure values for reported household incomes (controlling for spatial and temporal price differences). The shaded areas around the curves mark the 95 percent confidence interval.

The urban and rural samples of ration cardholders include 453 and 1,171 households, respectively. The urban and rural samples of non-cardholders include 677 and 740 households, respectively. In the urban sample of ration cardholders, the R-squared is 0.425 for consumption of vegetables and 0.191 for consumption of legumes. In the urban sample of non-cardholders, the R-squared is 0.427 for consumption of vegetables and 0.109 for consumption of legumes. In the rural sample of ration cardholders, the R-squared is 0.375 and 0.226, respectively. In the rural sample of non-cardholders, the R-squared is 0.376 and 0.168, respectively.

FIGURE 3.10 Engel curves for consumption of meat and fish and milk and dairy products in Egyptian families

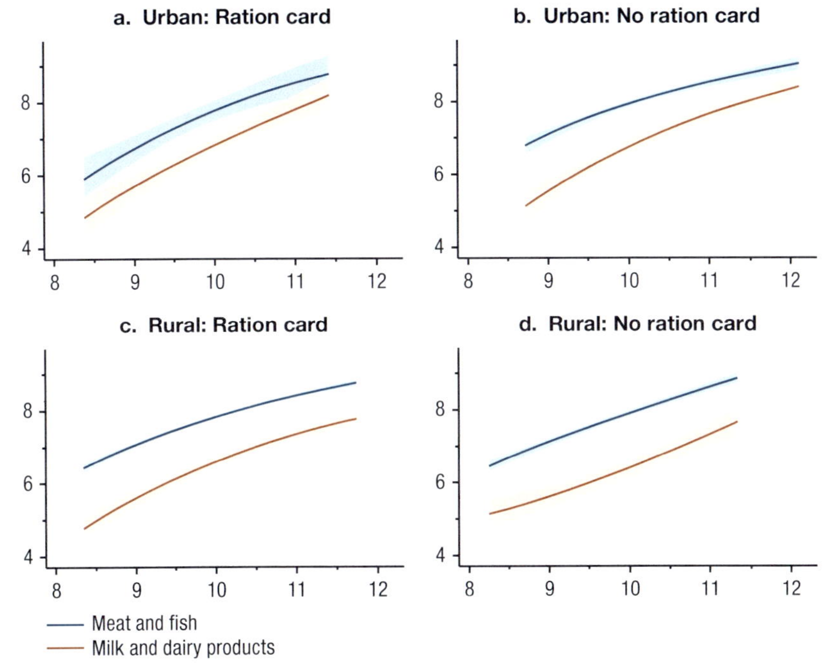

Source: Authors' estimation based on data from CAPMAS and WFP (2011).

Note: Household income and expenditure values are expressed on a per capita basis, refer to a period of 15 days, are reported in Egyptian piasters, and are transformed into logarithms. The y-axis indicates household expenditure levels (in logarithms), and the x-axis indicates household income levels (in logarithms).

The Engel curves are estimated using fractional polynomial regressions of degree 1 and a robust estimator of variance. To control for possible spatial and temporal price differences, the regressions include binary variables indicating household location by governorate (aggregate) and the survey month. The presented curves connect the predicted expenditure values for reported household incomes (controlling for spatial and temporal price differences). The shaded areas around the curves mark the 95 percent confidence interval.

The urban and rural samples of ration cardholders include 453 and 1,171 households, respectively. The urban and rural samples of non-cardholders include 677 and 740 households, respectively. In the urban sample of ration cardholders, the R-squared is 0.227 for meat and fish consumption and 0.261 for consumption of milk and dairy products. In the urban sample of non-cardholders, the R-squared is 0.372 for meat and fish consumption and 0.310 for consumption of milk and dairy products. In the rural sample of ration cardholders, the R-squared is 0.384 and 0.342, respectively. In the rural sample of non-cardholders, the R-squared is 0.311 and 0.230, respectively.

subsidized under the ration card program—at least for households with children ages 6–59 months.

The estimated Engel curves also reveal no (clear) differences between families with and without ration cards regarding how their food expenditures change with increasing income (Figures 3.5–3.10). Per capita food expenditure, as well as per capita expenditures for all (considered) food groups, increases almost linearly among both urban and rural families with increasing per capita income. Thus, there is no tendency toward satisfaction of food demands at high income levels—not even in the case of basic foods such as cereals, sugars, and edible fats and oils. Nevertheless, there are obvious differences between food group expenditures in their income elasticity, as the slopes of the estimated Engel curves suggest. Consumption of milk and dairy products is most responsive to income changes, followed by meat and fish consumption; cereal consumption is the least responsive. Consumption of sugars, edible fats and oils, and vegetables are moderately responsive to income changes, and the income elasticities for these food group expenditures appear to be similar. The estimated Engel curves for legume consumption yield coefficients for the income variable that are statistically insignificant at the 10 percent level and therefore do not permit interpretation.

Finally, it should be noted that the estimated Engel curves and the consumption patterns of beneficiary and nonbeneficiary families do not allow for drawing conclusions on the (nutritional) effects of Egypt's food subsidies. The results may be driven by covariates that are systematically correlated with (non)participation in the food subsidy system or the received subsidy amounts and that are not controlled for. Such a systematic correlation can lead to biased estimates. This methodological problem will be addressed in the main empirical analysis, in the next chapter.

Nutrition-Beneficial Investments in Egypt

Besides insufficient and inadequate food intake, ill health—and specifically parasitic and diarrheal diseases—is a cause of chronic undernutrition, particularly among children (Black et al. 2008; Katona and Katona-Apte 2008; Stephenson, Latham, and Ottesen 2000; UNICEF 1990). Hence, an increasing disease burden as well as decreasing prevention and treatment of under- and overnutrition during the 2000s may have driven Egypt's double burden of malnutrition and growth-nutrition disconnect. Poor health conditions and lack of awareness thereof may be a consequence of underinvestment in nutrition-sensitive infrastructure and public services as well as in primary healthcare, including maternal and child health and nutrition interventions. The possible underinvestment may be due to the declining fiscal space in the public budget, which, in turn, may be due to the rising costs of the food subsidy system to some extent. Then, the Egyptian food subsidy system would have another—indirect—effect on nutritional outcomes, in addition to the hypothesized direct, diet-related effects. This indirect effect would arise from the allocation of the available public budget to the food subsidy system, which cannot be used for alternative and more nutrition-beneficial investments. Because the main empirical analysis presented in the next chapter is concerned only with the potential direct nutritional effects, the following two subsections only briefly review key areas of possible underinvestment that lead to conditions that could contribute to Egypt's nutritional challenges, particularly chronic child undernutrition.

Nutrition-Sensitive Infrastructure and Public Services

Globally, many of the parasitic and diarrheal diseases that reduce food absorption and cause nutrient loss—including intestinal helminthiasis, schistosomiasis, and bacterial infections—enter the human body through ingestion of contaminated drinking water and food or direct contact with feces (Stephenson, Latham, and Ottesen 2000). Thus, living in conditions with poor access to safe drinking water and clean sanitation and in an environment with malfunctioning sewage systems and garbage removal increases the prevalence of infectious diseases and thus chronic undernutrition—especially among children. Children are often more directly exposed to these conditions (when crawling, exploring edibility of objects, and playing outdoors, for example) and have weaker immune systems during the first months of their lives.

Yet DHS data suggest that the coverage of improved sources of drinking water and sanitation facilities is high in Egypt—both in urban and rural areas (Table 3.7). The coverage increased steadily throughout the 2000s and more rapidly in rural areas, albeit from a lower rate. In 2008, 94.8 percent of all households received their drinking water from a tap piped inside their dwelling or building, with 98.8 percent of households in urban areas and 91.0 percent of households in rural areas receiving water in this way. These rates are quite similar to our rates calculated from the 2011 HIECS data (CAPMAS and WFP 2011). According to our calculations, 95.8 percent of all households, 99.0 percent of urban households, and 93.1 percent of rural households receive their drinking water from the tap. Throughout Egypt, the tap water is taken (almost exclusively) from the Nile and usually treated to reduce the risk of infection with waterborne diseases.

TABLE 3.7 Proportion of households in Egypt with improved drinking-water sources and sanitation facilities

	2000	2005	2008
Piped drinking water (%)			
Total	87.4	93.3	94.8
Urban	99.0	98.8	98.8
Rural	75.9	88.3	91.0
Flush toilet (%)			
Total	94.4	97.8	99.2
Urban	99.2	99.7	99.8
Rural	89.7	96.0	98.6

Source: ICF International (2014), based on DHS data.

Almost all households in urban and rural areas use flush toilets (Table 3.7). In 2008, modern flush toilets (which are directly connected to the drinking-water system, unlike tank or bucket flush toilets) were used by 48.5 percent of all households, 77.1 percent of urban households, and 21.8 percent of rural households. Again, these rates are very consistent with our rates calculated from the 2011 HIECS data, according to which 52.0 percent of all households, 79.0 percent of urban households, and 28.4 percent of rural households use modern flush toilets. In addition, most households are connected to a waste water system. According to the 2008 DHS, 89.8 percent of urban households and 37.0 percent of rural households are connected to the public sewer; 5.4 percent of urban households and 28.5 percent of rural households are connected to a vault; and 4.3 percent of urban households and 28.4 percent of rural households are connected to a septic system (El-Zanaty and Way 2009).

Thus, the risk of infection from inappropriate drinking water sources and sanitation within people's housing may be low. However, these statistics provide no information on the quality of the drinking water and waste water system and therefore on the risk of infection outside the home. For example, the waste water system includes open surface canals near houses that may leak into irrigation canals. As a result, humans may be regularly exposed to feces, and feces can easily enter the food chain. Especially in rural areas, some children swim in possibly contaminated canals, and domestic animals drink water from these canals.

Another source of pathogens is openly rotting waste and trash that comes in contact either with humans directly or with animals for human

TABLE 3.8 Proportion of households by method of waste/trash disposal in Egypt

	2005			2008		
	Urban	Rural	Total	Urban	Rural	Total
Collected from home (%)	53.6	26.4	39.5	46.5	28.2	37.0
Collected from street container (%)	32.8	4.4	18.0	34.4	3.5	18.4
Dumped into street or empty plot (%)	9.9	25.9	18.3	16.4	31.2	24.1
Dumped into canal or drainage (%)	1.3	18.3	10.1	0.8	16.4	8.9
Burned (%)	1.9	18.9	10.8	1.4	15.5	8.7
Fed to animals (%)	0.3	5.9	3.2	0.2	4.6	2.5

Source: El-Zanaty and Way (2006, 2009).

consumption. Waste disposal is suboptimal in Egypt overall, and proper waste disposal is considerably less common in rural areas than in urban areas (Table 3.8). The quality of the system did not markedly improve or—depending on the indicator used—may even have declined between 2005 and 2008 (for which comparable data in the 2000s are available). According to the DHS data, waste/trash was collected from 53.6 percent of urban households in 2005 and from 46.5 percent of urban households in 2008 (MOH, El-Zanaty and Associates, and Macro International 2008; MOHP, NPC, and ORC Macro 2000; MOHP et al. 2003; MOHP et al. 2005). In rural areas, the coverage slightly increased from a low 26.4 percent to 28.2 percent over the same time period. The proportion of urban households whose trash/waste was collected from street containers slightly increased from 32.8 percent to 34.4 percent, and the proportion of rural households who dumped their waste/trash into water canals and drainage slightly decreased from 18.3 percent to 16.4 percent.

Still, a larger proportion of households in both urban and rural areas dumped their waste/trash into the street or any empty plot. Waste/trash piles, as well as the heaps around street containers, sometimes serve to feed domestic animals. Between 2005 and 2008, this proportion increased more rapidly in urban areas than in rural areas, from 9.9 percent to 16.4 percent in urban areas compared to from 25.9 percent to 31.2 percent in rural areas. The comparability of these DHS-based rates with our rates calculated from the 2011 HIECS data (CAPMAS and WFP 2011) is somewhat limited because of different formulations of the survey questions. Nonetheless, the HIECS data suggest that 67.5 percent of all households, 58.9 percent of urban households, and 74.9 percent of rural households openly dump their waste/trash into street containers into the street and empty spots, or use another unsafe disposal method.

Overall, there is no strong indication that Egypt's growing growth-nutrition disconnect and double burden of malnutrition during the 2000s was driven by deteriorating infrastructure and public services.

Primary Healthcare and Nutrition Interventions

A well-functioning primary healthcare system can significantly reduce malnutrition through prevention and treatment of nutritional deficiencies, overweight/obesity, and related diseases. With the exception of nutrition education in public educational institutions and food fortification programs, public investments in most nutrition-related interventions are under the responsibility of the health sector. In Egypt, total health expenditure (including public and private expenditures) as a share of GDP declined from 6.1 percent in 2002 to 4.9 percent in 2011—a similar share to that in 1997 (World Bank 2014). However, total health expenditure in value terms steadily increased through the 2000s, from I$337 per capita in 2000 to I$520 per capita in 2011 (at constant 2011 prices).[20] The largest share of total health expenditure has been private expenditure—a possible indication of a healthcare system that does not meet most people's health needs. Between 2000 and 2011, household out-of-pocket expenditure accounted for somewhere between 55 percent and 61 percent of total health expenditure (World Bank 2014). The share of out-of-pocket expenditure in total health expenditure in Egypt is considerably above the global average (32.1 percent in 2011), the developing-country average (36.5 percent), and the Arab country average (44.0 percent).

Information on the allocation of Egypt's healthcare budget to nutrition-relevant primary healthcare services and their cost-effectiveness is lacking. Evidence from cross-country studies points to generally very low cost-effectiveness in primary healthcare across the developing world. Filmer and Pritchett (1999) demonstrate this low cost-effectiveness by comparing the cost of medical interventions to avert child mortality with actual public spending per child death averted. The estimated costs of common medical interventions to avert the largest causes of child mortality in developing

---

20 The exceptions to this general increase in health expenditure were slight decreases in 2003 and 2004 and a drop in 2010—likely as a consequence of the EGP devaluation in early 2003 and the 2009 global financial crisis, respectively.

countries fall into the range of I$10 to I$4,000 per child (Filmer and Pritchett 1999). However, using the national prevalence rates of child and infant mortality as indicators for capturing the effect of primary healthcare service delivery, Filmer and Pritchett (1999) estimate that the actual public spending per child death averted is I$50,000–100,000 for a developing country at average income levels. According to the authors, this cost ineffectiveness is mainly caused by ineffective health budget allocation and healthcare service delivery. In a follow-up study, Filmer, Hammer, and Pritchett (2000) show that, in most developing countries, government funds are largely concentrated in some inexpensive (curative) healthcare services, where they tend to crowd out functional private services, and that most developing countries lack adequate provision of other, potentially more effective basic healthcare services. The other main shortcoming of the healthcare system in many developing countries is the lack of institutional capacity in service delivery and especially the inability to monitor and control the behavior of public employees (Filmer, Hammer, and Pritchett 2000).

Although estimates of the cost-effectiveness of Egypt's primary healthcare service are unavailable, findings from health sector evaluation studies point to conditions that are consistent with those analyzed by Filmer and coauthors. For example, the Readat Refiat (community health worker; literally, "village pioneer" in Arabic) program is the frontline program of the public sector's primary healthcare system in rural areas. A main purpose of the community health worker program is to counsel expecting mothers on maternal and child health issues and refer them to health units, if needed. The program—with a total workforce of 14,280 permanent staff (in 2012)—is ill functioning, especially in terms of staff development and program performance evaluation, pays insufficient attention to maternal and child nutrition, and completely ignores issues related to overweight/obesity and associated diseases (Abdelmegeid et al. 2015).

Obviously, the first step in addressing NCDs is to make the affected individuals aware of their conditions. The Egypt Health Issues Survey (HIS) 2015 reveals that many Egyptians are unaware that they have high blood pressure. Among HIS respondents, 47 percent of women and 73 percent of men who were classified as hypertensive had never been told before by a healthcare provider that they had high blood pressure (MOHP, El-Zanaty and Associates, and ICF International 2015).

One of the most important determinants of individuals' nutritional status is feeding practices during their infancy. Suboptimal breastfeeding, especially nonexclusive breastfeeding in the first six months of life, is a leading risk factor of morbidity, possibly causing child growth retardation. It is estimated to be responsible for 10 percent of the disease burden in children younger than five years of age globally (Black et al. 2008). Although most Egyptian children are breastfed at some point, the initiation of breastfeeding and the methods of supplementary feeding are inadequate. Throughout the 2000s, the proportion of children in Egypt who had ever been breastfed was stable at around 95 percent, with no significant differences between urban and rural areas, according to DHS data (Table 3.9). However, only 78.0 percent of all newborns were put to the breast within the first day after birth and only 49.7 percent within one hour after birth in 2008. The proportion of breastfeeding initiation within the first hour after birth was significantly lower in urban areas than in rural areas (which may be partly explained by the higher proportion of urban births in hospitals and common after-birth care practices). The early initiation of breastfeeding declined considerably between 2000 and 2008 and at similar rates in urban and rural areas (Table 3.9). Prelacteal feeding has been common in Egypt. Almost half of the newborns received prelacteal feeds, and most of them were given sugar or glucose water, tea, or other inappropriate infusions (El-Zanaty and Way 2009).

Exclusive breastfeeding of infants has been far from universal in Egypt, and it slightly decreased during the 2000s (Table 3.9). According to DHS data, the proportion of children under six months of age who were exclusively breastfed declined from 56.2 percent in 2000 to 53.2 percent in 2008 (MOH, El-Zanaty and Associates, and Macro International 2008; MOHP, NPC, and ORC Macro 2000; MOHP et al. 2003; MOHP et al. 2005). The proportion of children ages 0–3 months who were given only breast milk remained constant between 2000 and 2008 while—on a positive note—the proportion of children who were given inappropriate liquids such as cow's milk, tea, and sugar water decreased substantially. Although just over one-half of all children under six months of age were exclusively breastfed in Egypt, the prevalence of exclusive breastfeeding was relatively high compared to global and regional averages. Our calculations based on the latest health survey data in 113 developing countries from 2005–2012 (World Bank 2014) suggest that the average exclusive breastfeeding rate is 37.3 percent, and Egypt actually belongs to the top 25 percent in this sample. The average rate across the 12 Arab countries with available data is only 24.2 percent.

Evidence on the effectiveness of large-scale nutritional interventions in Egypt is scarce, too. Several seminal publications in the nutrition literature, including articles in the 2008 and 2013 *Lancet* series on maternal and child undernutrition (Bhutta et al. 2008, 2013; Bryce et al. 2008) and others (e.g.,

TABLE 3.9 Prevalence of common infant-feeding practices in Egypt

	2000	2005	2008
Breastfeeding (%)			
Ever breastfed			
Total	95.5	95.1	96.1
Urban	94.9	94.2	95.9
Rural	95.9	95.6	96.2
Initiation of breastfeeding within one day after birth			
Total	87.5	73.3	78.0
Urban	86.1	75.8	79.5
Rural	88.3	71.9	77.1
Initiation of breastfeeding within one hour after birth			
Total	56.5	37.7	49.7
Urban	52.0	33.2	45.6
Rural	59.3	40.2	52.2
Supplementation (%)			
Exclusive breastfeeding among children under 6 months of age			
Total	56.2	—	53.2
Type of supplementation among children ages 0–3 months			
Only breast milk			
Total	68.5	—	68.2
Milk and other liquids (including tea, sugar water)			
Total	26.8	—	15.4

Source: ICF International (2014), based on Demographic and Health Surveys data.

Note: — = data not available.

All prevalence rates refer to children born in the three years preceding the surveys.

Horton et al. 2010), identify a set of specific interventions that have been proven to be highly cost-effective in reducing maternal and child malnutrition worldwide. These nutrition-specific interventions can be grouped into the following: interventions aimed at behavioral change, including promotion of breastfeeding and adequate complementary feeding; micronutrient and deworming interventions, including iron fortification of staple foods, vitamin A supplementation, and deworming campaigns; and complementary and therapeutic feeding interventions delivered through the healthcare system (Horton et al. 2010). In fact, some of these interventions were implemented, at least as trials, in Egypt.

The Government of Egypt in collaboration with WFP and the Global Alliance for Improved Nutrition implemented fortification programs for subsidized Baladi bread flour and cooking oil. Fortification of the flour provided to bakeries for Baladi bread was piloted at large scale over a period of five years, and its fortification with folate was tested (Elhakim et al. 2012; Hefni and Witthöft 2011). Fortification of the subsidized cooking oil with vitamin A was tested, too. However, the results of the effectiveness evaluation of the Baladi flour fortification programs are still unpublished, and serious quality problems were found for the oil fortification program, limiting the success of the program (Laillou et al. 2012).

Moreover, the coverage of the national vitamin A supplementation program for young children is much lower in Egypt than in most other developing countries (ICF International 2014). According to the DHS reports, approximately only 3 in 10 children ages 9–23 months received a vitamin A capsule in the six-month period before the survey interview in both 2005 and 2008 (El-Zanaty and Way 2006, 2009). In addition to reducing vitamin-A-deficiency-caused visual problems and blindness, vitamin A supplements can reduce the severity of measles and diarrheal infections and the rates of child mortality and morbidity caused by these diseases (Beaton et al. 1994; Black et al. 2008; Mayo-Wilson et al. 2011; Villamor and Fawzi 2000). Yet there is no conclusive evidence that vitamin A supplementation reduces the prevalence of child stunting (Rivera et al. 2003).

Similar to our findings on nutrition-sensitive infrastructure and public services, our review of key nutrition-relevant primary healthcare services and nutrition interventions does not show an obvious indication of their deterioration during the 2000s, which could explain the increasing double burden of malnutrition and the widening growth-nutrition disconnect over this decade. Moreover, a very recent longitudinal cohort study on infant malnutrition in 10 Egyptian villages (5 in Lower Egypt and 5 in Upper Egypt) suggests that the causes of child malnutrition seem to be predominantly related to food intake rather than adverse health conditions (Kavle et al. 2016). The authors find that infants' length-for-age z-score decreased and weight-for-length z-score increased from 6 to 12 months of age, forming the double burden of malnutrition.[21] They also find that diarrhea, fever, and exposure to a

21 Six months of age is the recommended infant age for introducing complementary feeding with solid foods. Earlier introduction is a common cultural practice in Egypt (Kavle et al. 2016). Length-for-age z-scores and weight-for-length z-scores (terms used during infancy) correspond to height-for-age z-scores and weight-for-height z-scores during childhood (when children's body height is measured in a standing position instead of a recumbent position).

community-level nutrition education and rehabilitation program were not associated with any growth outcome during infancy. The authors therefore conclude that improving diet quality and reducing reliance on energy-dense foods is needed to address both stunting and overweight in countries like Egypt that are facing the nutrition transition. Nevertheless, poor health conditions, lack of their awareness, and insufficient prevention and treatment of malnutrition are certainly factors that may have contributed to the persistence of Egypt's nutritional challenges.

Chapter 4

ANALYZING THE NUTRITIONAL EFFECTS OF THE EGYPTIAN FOOD SUBSIDY SYSTEM

The main hypothesis of this study is that Egypt's large food subsidy system has been ineffective in reducing undernutrition and may have contributed to the sustenance and even aggravation of both the double burden of malnutrition and the growth-nutrition disconnect. Accordingly, Egypt's exceptionalism in the global comparison with respect to these nutritional challenges may be partly driven by the country's food subsidy system, in combination with the three other drivers (the rapid nutrition transition, the succession of economic crises, and the persistent lack of nutrition-beneficial investments). Over time, the long-standing and expanding food subsidy system may have contributed to both nutritional challenges through two major effects. First, given its design until May 2014, the food subsidy system incentivized overconsumption of cheap, calorie-rich foods and unbalanced diets, which may have led to rapid increases in overweight and obesity and to slow or stagnant reduction of chronic child undernutrition. Second, given its heavy and growing burden to the public budget, the food subsidy system may have bound funds, which hence have been unavailable for more nutrition-beneficial investments, thereby maintaining and aggravating malnutrition indirectly. Thus, slow or stagnant reduction or even an increase of undernutrition may have contributed to a growing double burden of malnutrition if overnutrition rose faster than undernutrition declined, and to an aggravating growth-nutrition disconnect if it were accompanied by high economic growth.

In this chapter, we use impact evaluation methods and cross-sectional household survey data to explore whether the food subsidies affect child and maternal nutrition and the double burden of malnutrition in Egypt, as hypothesized. The results can provide evidence on the potential direct effect of the food subsidy system—the first of the aforementioned effects. The lack of suitable time-series data does not allow us to analyze the effects of the food subsidy system on people's nutritional status over time or to estimate the nutritional effects of past reforms. Instead, our analysis aims at identifying causal relationships between food subsidies and nutritional outcomes across individuals and families. The existence of these relationships is fundamental for the hypothesized role of the food subsidy system as a driver of the double burden of malnutrition and the growth-nutrition disconnect.

We are particularly interested in the "dose-response relationship" between the acquired food subsidy levels and the nutritional status of the beneficiaries rather than only the nutritional effect of receiving any amount of food subsidies compared to receiving no food subsidies. We expect that the nutritional responses differ significantly between beneficiaries of high subsidy amounts and low subsidy amounts. Further, beneficiaries' nutritional status may become less or more responsive with increasing subsidy amounts, and an optimal subsidy level may exist; this suggests allowing the functional form of the dose-response relationship to be nonlinear and concave. Analyzing the hypothesized causal effects at different subsidy levels as well as relaxing the linearity assumption of the dose-response function may yield estimation results that have more accurate—and thus more useful—policy implications compared to an analysis that compares the causal effect only in a with-and-without-subsidies case or in a more-or-less-subsidies case.

Methodology and Data

Identification Strategy

Until May 2014, Egypt's food subsidies were issued through two separate programs with different eligibility criteria and different subsidy allotment criteria. The Baladi bread and flour subsidies were, in principle, accessible to every citizen in unrestricted amounts. In contrast, the subsidies under the ration card program were restricted to households with valid ration cards, and the quotas for subsidized rice, sugar, and cooking oil (and black tea) were allotted based on the number of household members registered on the ration card. Given these differences, we analyze the nutritional effects of the Baladi bread and flour program and the ration card program separately.

The nutritional effects of the subsidies under both programs cannot be simply assessed through an examination of the relationship between observed food subsidies and nutritional outcomes. Our analysis faces a common problem of observational studies for causal effects (Rosenbaum and Rubin 1983). When we estimate the effect of a treatment (such as the food subsidies) on an outcome (such as people's nutritional status) using observational data, a selection bias is likely, due to the nonrandom assignment of the treatment. A selection bias occurs when observed and unobserved characteristics of individuals are associated with the probability of receiving the treatment—or the received amount of the treatment—and with the outcome. For example, an eligibility criterion for receiving a ration card in Egypt has been poverty, so low-income households are more likely to have ration cards than high-income households; low-income households also have less purchasing power for acquiring an expensive, well-balanced diet, which increases the risk of malnutrition among their household members. Similarly, Baladi bread outlets are geographically targeted to low-income neighborhoods, and Baladi flour was handed out only in some governorates in Upper Egypt at the time of the survey underlying our analysis.

The typical solution to the selection bias problem in the literature of experimental design is a randomized control trial (RCT), where random assignment to treatment balances observed and unobserved characteristics of individuals across treatment and comparison groups. Given that only one treatment level can be observed for each individual at a time, individuals of the comparison group who are similar to the treated individuals in everything but the treatment received are used as proxies for the counterfactual in RCTs. The randomization of treatment is generally impossible in observational studies, such as when evaluating social policies, because they are usually designed to be targeted at specific groups of individuals.

The second-best option is to mimic randomized assignment to treatment and comparison groups. As in many other observational studies, our choice of an impact evaluation method is constrained by data availability. Given that the 2010–2011 HIECS (CAPMAS and WFP 2011) is so far the only household survey that makes evaluating the nutritional effects of the Egyptian food subsidy system possible (Box 4.1), we are left with approaches that do not necessarily require a baseline or panel survey. Such quasi-experimental approaches include regression discontinuity design (RDD), instrumental variable (IV), and matching methods.

The RDD method can be used only for programs that have a continuous eligibility index with a clearly defined cutoff score to determine who is eligible and who is not (Gertler et al. 2011). Egypt's food subsidy programs do not meet this necessary condition, as our discussion of the food subsidy system in the previous chapter shows. Apart from that, the RDD method yields estimates of the program impact around the cutoff score—measuring local average treatment effects, which cannot necessarily be generalized to individuals with eligibility scores further away from the cutoff, such as high compliers. Considering the context of our study, we are less interested in such partial treatment effects.

An IV approach involves finding an instrument that is highly correlated with program participation but that is not correlated with the outcome—other than through program participation. We were unable to find such a credible instrument, mainly because (observed) household characteristics that determine participation in the food subsidy programs are naturally associated with nutrition, and thus the outcome variable, too. Even if there is an instrument that satisfies the exclusion restriction, it is likely not a good instrument, given the imperfect targeting of Egypt's food subsidies, especially of the ration card program. Because it has to account for unobserved heterogeneity, the instrument is very unlikely to be perfectly correlated with program participation, so only a subset of participants would be picked up by the instrument and resulting IV effect (Khandker, Koowal, and Samad 2010). Thus, at best we were able to estimate partial treatment effects, which, again, are of less interest in the context of this study.

Matching methods are suited for evaluating programs for which the rules of treatment assignment are less clear, but they require strong assumptions. We therefore decided to choose a matching approach and will demonstrate that the assumptions underlying our estimation model's specifications are reasonable. Matching methods use statistical techniques to construct a comparison group based on observed characteristics. Hence, they rely on the assumption that there is no unobserved, systematic difference between treatment and comparison groups that is associated with the outcome. We will detail and formalize this so-called "unconfoundedness assumption" in the next subsection. Because, by definition, it is impossible to statistically test for a selection bias stemming from unobservables, we note beforehand that the possibility of such a potential bias exists. Our strategy therefore is to minimize the probability of a potential selection bias as much as possible and to statistically assess how well the observed covariates explain program participation.

The propensity score matching (PSM) methodology offers a way to balance measured covariates across treatment and comparison groups, which helps to isolate the treatment effect. PSM also deals with the "curse of dimensionality" by compressing all relevant covariates into a single score—another attractive feature for our analysis. PSM was introduced by Rosenbaum and Rubin (1983) and has become a popular approach to estimate causal effects for cases of binary treatment, as in the case of program impact evaluations focusing on the effects of participation in the program compared to nonparticipation. However, many studies are rather concerned with the causal effects of a certain "dose" of a treatment—such as a received subsidy amount—relative to a lower or a higher "dose." Hirano and Imbens (2004) extended the

PSM methodology with binary treatment to cases where treatment is continuous. The generalization of the standard propensity score is referred to as the generalized propensity score (GPS), and the respective estimation function is known as the "dose-response function." In our analysis, we apply PSM methods with both binary and continuous treatments, which are explained in the next subsection.

Because receiving food subsidies under the ration card program is conditional on having a valid ration card, we first analyze whether participation in the ration card program has a causal effect on nutritional outcomes. For that, we apply the PSM method with binary treatment using samples of beneficiary and nonbeneficiary individuals/households. Then in order to go beyond the average treatment effect, we apply the PSM method with continuous treatment using samples restricted to individuals from households with ration cards, and adopt a quadratic specification of the dose-response function. In this second set of estimations, we hence analyze whether different amounts of received food subsidies cause different nutritional outcomes, while we allow the dose-response functions to take nonlinear and concave forms. However, for analyzing the causal effects of Baladi bread and flour subsidies on nutritional outcomes, we apply only the PSM method with continuous treatment, using samples of reported participating and nonparticipating individuals/households. The reason is that—unlike the ration card program—the access to subsidized Baladi bread and flour was de jure unrestricted at the time of the survey underlying our analysis. For both the ration card program and the Baladi bread and flour program, the amount of the allotted and utilized food subsidies depends on a set of household characteristics, which are also likely to determine the selection of households for the ration card program. The household characteristics included in the estimation models are described in the subsection after next.

We analyze the causal effects of the participation in the ration card program, the food subsidy amounts under the ration card program, and the food subsidy amounts under the Baladi bread and flour program on a large set of nutrition outcome indicators. They include indicators of chronic child undernutrition, child and maternal overnutrition, and the double burden of malnutrition at the individual and the family levels. For analyzing the effects on child undernutrition and child and maternal overnutrition, we use a continuous and a binary indicator each. Estimates for continuous indicators provide information about the effects across the nutrition spectrum, while estimates for binary indicators provide information about the probability of under- or overnutrition. Accordingly, child nutrition indicators are child HAZ and child stunting (the respective binary indicator identifying chronic child undernutrition) as well as child BMIZ and child overweight (the respective binary indicator identifying child overnutrition). Similarly, maternal nutrition indicators are mother's BMI and maternal overweight—the respective binary indicator identifying maternal overnutrition. The binary indicator of the double burden of malnutrition at the individual level is child stunting and child overweight at the same time. The binary indicator of the double burden of malnutrition at the family level is child stunting in combination with maternal overweight. For complementarity, we also include a binary indicator of child overweight in combination with maternal overweight, as it may provide information about whether food subsidies contribute to overweight among children and their mothers from the same households at the same time.

Low child HAZ and child stunting is often caused by insufficient intake of absorbable micronutrients, especially zinc (Brown, Wuehler, and Peerson 2001; IZiNCG 2004). Dietary diversity is a strong predictor of micronutrient adequacy in children in developing countries, is associated with child HAZ, and is strongly associated with the micronutrient density of the diet (Ruel, Harris, and Cunningham 2013). Dietary diversity is typically measured by the number of different food groups consumed over a specified reference period (usually a maximum of seven days). The regular consumption of some food groups such as vegetables, legumes, meat and fish, and milk and dairy products is particularly important for nutrient adequacy. Several food items within these food groups are rich sources of absorbable zinc and other nutrients essential for children's physical growth. In order to explore whether unbalanced diets lacking diversity and frequency of nutritious foods qualify as a likely pathway through which food subsidies adversely affect child nutrition and hence drive the double burden of malnutrition—as hypothesized—we analyze the causal effects of the food subsidy programs on respective diet quality indicators. As dietary diversity indicator, we use a common food group count measurement—that is, the household dietary diversity score (HDDS). We complement it with measurements of the consumption frequency of four key food groups (vegetables, legumes, meat and fish, and milk and dairy products) over a one-week recall period. The indicators are described below.

We conduct our analysis of the causal effects of food subsidies on nutrition and diet quality outcomes for Egypt's urban and rural areas separately. Given that there are considerable urban-rural differences in the design and coverage of the food subsidy programs and in families' food consumption patterns (as discussed in the previous chapter), we expect that there are also structural differences between urban and rural individuals in nutritional responses to received food subsidies. Moreover, the separate analysis may allow us to draw more specific conclusions from the estimation results.

Estimation Framework

Every impact evaluation study has to overcome the basic problem of evaluation and thereby to deal with the possibility of selection bias. The basic problem is essentially a missing data problem. For assessing the effects of a policy or a program, we would like to know the difference in an outcome indicator with and without the policy or program—that is, the "treatment." However, we cannot observe both outcomes for the same individual at the same time. Comparing the mean outcomes of treated and untreated individuals is inappropriate, since the characteristics of treated and untreated individuals likely differ, even in the absence of treatment. This is because a policy or program is usually designed to target a specific group of individuals. Hence, in observational data, treatment assignment is not random. This can lead to a selection bias, where observed and unobserved characteristics of individuals are associated with the probability of receiving treatment and the outcome.

The matching approach is a possible solution to deal with the potential selection bias in observational data (Caliendo and Kopeinig 2008). The principal idea is to identify a group of untreated individuals who are similar to the treated individuals in all relevant pre-treatment characteristics so that they can serve as proxies for the counterfactual. Then, differences in outcomes between treated and untreated individuals can be attributed to the treatment. The underlying identifying assumption, as mentioned above, is known as "unconfoundedness" (Rosenbaum and Rubin 1983), "selection on observables" (Heckman and Robb 1985), or "conditional independence" (Lechner 2002). However, conditioning on all relevant covariates is limited in the case of a high-dimensional vector. As variables are added to the matching process, it becomes increasingly difficult to find exact matches of individuals with similar characteristics in both the treatment and comparison groups. Rosenbaum and Rubin (1983) suggest using propensity scores to deal with this "curse of dimensionality."

PROPENSITY SCORE MATCHING WITH BINARY TREATMENT

Following Rosenbaum and Rubin (1983), we are interested in estimating the causal effect of a binary treatment on a binary or continuous outcome. Let the treatment, T_i, equal 1 if individual i receives the treatment and 0 otherwise. The two potential outcomes are then $Y_i(1)$ and $Y_i(0)$ for each individual, i, where $i = 1, \ldots, N$ and N is the sample size. If $Y_i(1)$ and $Y_i(0)$ were observable, the treatment effect on individual i would be directly observable as:

$$\tau_i = Y_i(1) - Y_i(0). \tag{1}$$

Since for each individual only one outcome is observable, estimating the individual treatment effect τ_i is impossible, and we have to concentrate on average treatment effects for groups of individuals. Two average treatment effects can be estimated. The first effect is the average treatment effect (ATE) on the total population:

$$\tau_{ATE} = E[Y(1) - Y(0)]. \tag{2}$$

The parameter gives the expected change in outcome if individuals in the population were randomly assigned to the treatment. The ATE is of little policy interest in general as well as of minor relevance in the context of our study, because it averages over individuals who might never be subject to treatment. The second, more prominent, average treatment effect is the average treatment effect on the treated (ATT):

$$\tau_{ATT} = E[Y(1) - Y(0) \mid T = 1] = E[Y(1) \mid T = 1] - E[Y(0) \mid T = 1]. \tag{3}$$

The parameter gives the expected change in outcome due to treatment for those individuals who were actually treated. Since the counterfactual mean for those being treated, $E[Y(0) \mid T = 1]$, cannot be observed, we need to identify an appropriate substitute for it. As noted above, using the mean outcome of untreated individuals, $E[Y(0) \mid T = 0]$, to estimate the ATT is usually no solution, because it is very likely that characteristics that determine the selection for receiving treatment also determine the outcome variable. Hence, even in the absence of treatment, the outcomes of individuals in the treatment and comparison groups would differ, leading to a selection bias. For the ATT, it can be noted as:

$$\begin{aligned} &E[Y(1) \mid T = 1] - E[Y(0) \mid T = 0] = \\ &\tau_{ATT} + E[Y(0) \mid T = 1] - E[Y(0) \mid T = 0], \end{aligned} \tag{4}$$

where the difference between τ_{ATT} and the term on the left-hand side of equation (4) is the selection bias. The parameter of the ATT is correctly estimated only if:

$$E[Y(0) \mid T = 1] - E[Y(0) \mid T = 0] = 0. \tag{5}$$

With observational data, some identifying assumptions are required to solve the selection problem, noted in equation (4). The unconfoundedness assumption implies that systematic differences in outcomes between treated and untreated individuals with the same values for all relevant covariates can be attributed to the treatment. It ensures that the selection for receiving treatment satisfies some form of exogeneity. The unconfoundedness assumption can be written as:

$$Y(0), Y(1) \perp T \mid X, \tag{6a}$$

meaning that the potential outcomes $Y(0)$ and $Y(1)$ are independent of treatment assignment T, given a vector of covariates X (that is, conditional independence). It implies that all variables that influence treatment assignment and potential outcomes simultaneously have to be observed, putting high requirements on data quality (Caliendo and Kopeinig 2008). Thus, unconfoundedness is technically a strong assumption.

Besides unconfoundedness, another required assumption is the "common support" or "overlap" condition. It can be written as:

$$0 < pr\,(T = 1 \mid X) < 1, \tag{7a}$$

meaning that individuals with the covariates X have a positive probability of receiving treatment. The common support condition implies that there must be both treated and untreated individuals with each value of X, so that there is, for each treated individual, at least one untreated individual with the same characteristics. It rules out the phenomenon of perfect predictability of T given X. Rosenbaum and Rubin (1983) refer to the unconfoundedness and common support conditions together as "strong ignorability." Under strong ignorability, the ATE (equation 2) and ATT (equation 3) can be determined for all values of X.

Since we are only interested in estimating the ATT, we can relax the assumptions as follows:

$$Y(0) \perp T \mid X \tag{6b}$$

and

$$pr\,(T = 1 \mid X) < 1. \tag{7b}$$

These assumptions of unconfoundedness for untreated individuals (equation 6b) and weak overlap (equation 7b) are sufficient for identification of equation (3), because the moments of the distribution of $Y(1)$ for the treated are directly estimable (Imbens 2004).

Conditioning on all relevant covariates is limited in the case of a high-dimensional vector X. For example, if X has m covariates and all are binary variables, the total number of possible matches is 2^m. To deal with this "curse of dimensionality," Rosenbaum and Rubin (1983) suggest using balancing scores. A balancing score, $b(X)$, is a function of the observed covariates, X, such that the conditional distribution of X given $b(X)$ is the same for treated ($T = 1$) and untreated ($T = 0$) individuals. That is:

$$X \perp T \mid b(X), \tag{8}$$

Rosenbaum and Rubin (1983) show that, if potential outcomes ($Y(0)$, $Y(1)$) are independent of treatment assignment conditional on covariates, X (equation 6a), they are also independent of treatment assignment conditional on a balancing score, $b(X)$. A possible balancing score is the propensity score. The propensity score is the probability for an individual to receive the treatment given a vector of observed covariates, X:

$$P(X) = pr(T = 1 \mid X). \tag{9}$$

Imbens (2004) shows that, if the unconfoundedness assumption holds, all biases due to observable covariates can be removed by conditioning solely on the propensity score. The condition of unconfoundedness given the propensity score can be noted as:

$$Y(0), Y(1) \perp T \mid P(X), \tag{10a}$$

and for estimating the ATT:

$$Y(0) \perp T \mid P(X). \tag{10b}$$

Given that the unconfoundedness assumption holds and that there is overlap between the treatment and comparison groups for all covariates, X, the PSM estimator for the ATT can be generally written as:

$$\tau_{ATT}^{PSM} = E_{(P(X) \mid T=1)}\{E[Y(1) \mid T = 1, P(X)] - E[Y(0) \mid T = 0, P(X)]. \tag{11}$$

Thus, the PSM estimator is the mean difference in outcomes of treated and untreated individuals over the common support area, appropriately weighted by the propensity score distribution for the treated.

When implementing PSM, three choices have to be made. The first one concerns the model to be used for the estimation of the propensity score, the second one concerns the covariates to be included in this model, and the third one concerns the algorithm for matching treated and untreated individuals.

First, when estimating the probability of treatment versus nontreatment, logit and probit models usually produce similar results (Caliendo and Kopeinig 2008). We chose the logit distribution because it has more density mass in the bounds, which tends to result in better fits of the data when sample sizes are large and extreme independent variable levels are present. Other than that, results from logit and probit models were found to be indistinguishable (Chambers and Cox 1967). It should also be noted that the role of the propensity score is only to reduce the dimensions of the conditioning covariates; as such, the propensity score has no behavioral assumption attached to it (Dehejia and Wahba 2002).

Second, our choice of the variables to be included in the propensity score model was guided by evidence from the food and health economics literature and our deep understanding of the Egyptian food subsidy system but limited by data availability and quality. In the next subsection, we discuss data issues and explain in detail the variables we included.

Third, we applied the *psmatch2.ado* routine developed by Leuven and Sianesi (2003) for application in Stata. We had to choose between several matching methods, including one-to-one (nearest neighbor or within caliper; with or without replacement), *k*-nearest neighbors, radius, kernel, local linear regression, spline-smoothing, and Mahalanobis matching. The choice of the matching algorithm involves trade-offs between bias and efficiency, especially in small samples (Caliendo and Kopeinig 2008). We chose the (Epanechnikov) kernel matching estimator, because—unlike nearest neighbor or radius matching estimators, for instance—it uses weighted averages of (nearly) all individuals in the comparison group for constructing the counterfactual outcome and therewith achieves low variance, because more information is used. Kernel matching can be seen as a weighted regression on an intercept with weight given by the kernel weights that vary with the point of evaluation (Smith and Todd 2005). The weights depend on the distance between each individual of the comparison group and the treated individual for which the counterfactual is being constructed. The average places higher weights on untreated individuals that are close to the treated individual in terms of the propensity score, and lower weights to more distant untreated individuals (if weights from a symmetric, non-negative, unimodal kernel such as the Epanechnikov kernel—the default kernel estimator in the *psmatch2.ado* routine—are used). The estimated intercept gives the estimate of the counterfactual mean. Applying kernel matching requires choosing the bandwidth parameter that involves finding a compromise between a small variance and an unbiased estimate of the true density function (Caliendo and Kopeinig 2008). Choosing a high bandwidth value yields a smoother density function, thus leading to a better fit and a decreasing variance between the estimated and true underlying density function. On the contrary, large bandwidth may smooth away underlying features, leading to a biased estimate. We chose the default bandwidth of 0.06, which may optimize the trade-off between variance and bias (Heckman, Ichimura, and Todd 1997, 1998).

A drawback of nonparametric methods is that possibly individuals are used that are bad matches. Therefore, the proper imposition of the common support condition is critical. For estimating the ATT, it is sufficient that any combination of characteristics found in the treatment group may also be observed in the comparison group, whereas, for estimating the ATE, it is additionally required that any combination of characteristics seen in the comparison group may also be observed in the treatment group (Bryson, Dorsett, and Purdon 2002). We imposed the common support condition by enabling the respective option available in the *psmatch2.ado* routine. It drops treated individuals whose propensity score is above the maximum and below the minimum propensity score of untreated individuals. The number of observations that are "on-support" relative to those that are "off-support" indicates the area of common support.[1]

Finally, we test for the balancing property of the treatment and comparison groups after matching by calling the Stata routine *pstest.ado*—developed by Leuven and Sianesi (2012)—directly after *psmatch2.ado*. For each variable included in the model, the *pstest.ado* routine reports the means of the treatment and comparison groups and a standardized percentage bias, which is calculated as proposed by Rosenbaum and Rubin (1985), and performs t-tests for equality of the means.[2] It also provides overall measures of covariate balance between the treatment and comparison groups, including the pseudo-R-squared score (Sianesi 2004); the value of the likelihood-ratio test of the joint insignificance of all the regressors (LR chi-squared); the mean and median bias; and the Rubin's B and R scores (Rubin 2001). The pseudo-R-squared score indicates how well the regressors, *X*, explain the probability of selection into the treatment group (Sianesi 2004). There should be no systematic differences in the distribution of covariates between treatment and comparison groups after matching, and thus the pseudo-R-squared score should be fairly low (Caliendo and Kopeinig 2008). The likelihood-ratio test of the joint insignificance of all the regressors in the logistic regression model should not reject the null hypothesis of joint insignificance. Rubin (2001)

---

1 We report the numbers of "on-support" and "off-support" observations in the "Estimation Results" subsection.

2 Performing t-tests-based comparisons after PSM is controversial, because the t-test makes often untenable assumptions—including normal distribution of the covariates in treatment and comparison groups—and is sensitive to sample sizes (Austin 2009).

recommends that B should be less than 25 and R should be between 0.5 and 2 for the groups to be considered as sufficiently balanced.

PROPENSITY SCORE MATCHING WITH CONTINUOUS TREATMENT

Hirano and Imbens (2004) extend Rosenbaum and Rubin's (1983) PSM methodology for binary treatments to cases where treatment is continuous. The generalization of the propensity score for binary treatment is known as the GPS. Hirano and Imbens (2004) show that the GPS has a balancing property similar to the binary propensity score. Under certain conditions, the GPS removes all biases associated with differences in the covariates. The estimation function that indicates the relationship between a specific (continuous) treatment level—the "dose"—and its average outcome—the "response"—is referred to as the "dose-response function."

PSM with continuous treatment has been applied much less than PSM with binary treatment, given its fairly recent introduction. Applications of GPS matching include evaluations of the effects of maternal time on child development in the United States (Carneiro and Rodrigues 2009), breastfeeding duration on childhood obesity in the United States (Jiang and Foster 2013), South Africa's Child Support Grant on child nutrition (Aguëro, Carter, and Woolard 2006), Ethiopia's Productive Safety Net Program and related transfers on agricultural productivity (Berhane et al. 2014; Hoddinott et al. 2012), public subsidies on corporate research and development investments in China (Dai and Cheng 2015), and firms' export levels on their sales growth in Germany (Fryges 2009).

In line with the notation for deriving the binary PSM approach, let T be a continuous set of potential treatments defined over the interval $[t_0, t_1]$, and $Y(t)$ a set of potential outcomes for $t \in$ T. For each individual, i, where $i = 1, \ldots, N$ and N is the sample size, we observe the actual treatment, T_i, the outcome corresponding to the treatment level received, $Y_i = Y_i(T_i)$, and a vector of treatment-unrelated covariates, X_i. We are interested in estimating the average dose-response function, $\mu(t) = E[Y_i(t)]$. For simplicity of notation, we omit the individual subscript i in the sequel.

Following Hirano and Imbens (2004), we assume that $\{Y(t)\}_{t \in \mathrm{T}}$, T, and X are defined on a common probability space; T is continuously distributed with respect to the Lebesgue measure on T; and $Y = Y(T)$ is a well-defined random variable. The unconfoundedness assumption for the case of binary treatment (equation 6a) can be generalized to the case of continuous treatment as:

$$Y(t) \perp T \mid X \text{ for all } t \in \mathrm{T}. \quad (12)$$

This assumption is referred to as weak unconfoundedness, because it requires conditional independence only at each value of the observed treatment, T, instead of joint independence of all potential outcomes, $\{Y(t)\}_{t \in t_0, t_1}$.

Next, Hirano and Imbens (2004) define the propensity function as the conditional density of the treatment given the covariates, as

$$f_{T|X}(t|x) = r(t,x). \tag{13}$$

Then, the GPS is

$$R = r(T,X). \tag{14}$$

The GPS has a balancing property similar to that of the binary propensity score; that is, within Strata with the value of $r(t,x)$, the probability that $T = t$ does not depend on the value of X:

$$X \perp 1\{T = t\}|r(t,X). \tag{15}$$

Hirano and Imbens (2004) prove that, if assignment to treatment is weakly unconfounded given X, then it is weakly unconfounded given the GPS:

$$f_T\{t|r(t,X),Y(t)\} = f_T\{t|r(t,X)\} \text{ for every } t \in \mathrm{T}. \tag{16}$$

Based on that, they also prove that the GPS can be used to remove any bias associated with differences in the covariates. Finally, the dose-response function can be obtained in two steps:

$$\beta(t,r) = E[Y(t)|r(t,X) = r] = E[Y|T = t,R = r] \text{ and} \tag{17}$$

$$\mu(t) = E[\beta(t,r(t,X))]. \tag{18}$$

In the first step of the practical implementation, the conditional expectation of the outcome, $\beta(t,r) = E[Y|T = t,R = r]$, is estimated as a function of two scalar variables—the treatment level, T, and the GPS, R. In the second step, the dose-response function, $\mu(t) = E[\beta(t,r(t,X))]$, is estimated by averaging the estimated conditional expectation, $\hat{\beta}(t,r(t,X))$, over the GPS at each treatment level of interest.

In most previous economic applications of the GPS (e.g., Aguëro, Carter, and Woolard 2006; Berhane et al. 2014; Hoddinott et al. 2012), the treatment, T—or its transformation, $h(T)$—is assumed to be normally distributed, conditional on the covariates, X. However, this assumption may not always hold, as in our case. The Kolmogorov-Smirnov test for normality yields decisive evidence against the condition of normal distribution of the treatment variable in all our estimation samples. Guardabascio and Ventura (2014) propose a flexible way to parametrically estimate the GPS when the treatment variable is not necessarily normally distributed. Hence, we applied the *glmdose .ado* routine developed by Guardabascio and Ventura (2014) for application in Stata.

Practically, the dose-response function is obtained in three steps (Guardabascio and Ventura 2014). First, the GPS is estimated for each individual given the received treatment level and the observed covariates (equation 14). Second, the conditional expectation of the individual outcome is estimated as a function of two scalar variables; these are the treatment level and the GPS (equation 17). Third, the dose-response function is estimated by averaging the estimated conditional expectation over the GPS at each treatment level of interest (equation 18). Guardabascio and Ventura's (2014) approach differs from previous approaches assuming normal distribution of the treatment variable (e.g., Bia and Mattei 2008) through the first step.

In detail, Guardabascio and Ventura (2014) replace the ordinary maximum likelihood estimator in the computation with the more flexible generalized linear model (GLM) estimator. By using the GLM estimator, the modeling differs from the ordinary regression by choosing the distribution of the treatment, T, from the exponential family—thus explicitly allowing nonnormal distributions—and by applying a non-identity transformation of the mean of the treatment that is linearly related to the explanatory variables, X:

$$f(T) = c(T,\phi)exp\left\{\frac{T\theta - a(\theta)}{\phi}\right\} \text{ and} \quad (19)$$

$$g[E(T)] = \gamma' X. \quad (20)$$

The *glmdose.ado* routine requires specifying the distribution form of $a(\theta)$ and the functional form of $g(.)$. The choice of $a(\theta)$—referred to as the family—is guided by the nature of the treatment variable, because it determines the actual probability function. We chose the binomial distribution, which appears to be a good approximation of the treatment distribution in our estimation samples, as graph charts suggest. Irrespective of the distribution chosen, it holds for the first and the second moment that

$$E(T) = \dot{a}(\theta) \text{ and } Var(T) = \phi\ddot{a}(\theta), \quad (21)$$

where the dots symbolize the first and the second derivative with respect to θ; and θ and ϕ are the canonical and the dispersion parameter, respectively. The choice of $g(.)$—referred to as the link function (which is monotonic and differentiable)—is suggested by the relationship between the treatment and the explanatory variables, as it determines how the mean is related to the covariates X. We chose the logit link function, which is the default for the binomial family. The GPS estimator can be generally written as

$$\hat{R} = r(T,X) = c(T,\hat{\phi})exp\left\{\frac{T\hat{\theta} - a(\hat{\theta})}{\hat{\phi}}\right\}, \tag{22}$$

where $\hat{\theta}$ and $\hat{\phi}$ are the parameters of the chosen conditional distribution of the treatment that were estimated in a preceding step given the covariates.

For implementing the dose-response model, the *glmdose.ado* routine requires several data operations and model specifications, which we conducted consistently for all estimations. For the estimations related to the ration card program, we dropped households without ration cards from the sample, given the conditionality of having a ration card for receiving the subsidies.[3] In line with Hirano and Imbens (2004) and others (e.g., Aguëro, Carter, and Woolard 2006; Fryges 2009), we transformed the treatment variable into a fractional variable (after dropping outlier observations), such that the received subsidy level of a particular household is expressed as a fraction of the maximum subsidy level in the estimation sample. For each estimation sample, we divided the range of the received subsidies into three intervals, each of an equal number of observations (that is, tertiles), indicating low, moderate, and high subsidy levels. Consistent with previous studies (e.g., Berhane et al. 2014; Hirano and Imbens 2004; Hoddinott et al. 2012), we specified that the GPS is evaluated at the mean of the treatment variable within each treatment interval and that the GPS values are divided into quintiles for each treatment interval. Accordingly, for each of the covariates, the routine evaluates the balance by testing whether the mean in one of the three treatment groups is different from the mean in the other two treatment groups combined and adjusts the unbalanced covariates distribution for the GPS so that the balancing property is satisfied at a significance level lower than 1 percent. After the adjustment, the routine estimates the GPS using the GLM estimator, given the specified (binomial) distribution family and the specified (logit) link function for the treatment variable. Technically, we hence estimate a

---

3 Nonetheless, all samples include households with zero observations in the treatment variables. The treatment variables are described in the next subsection in detail. In the samples used for estimating the effects of the ration card program, there are a few households who hold ration cards but did not report consuming subsidized rice, sugar, or cooking oil during the 15-day food consumption recall period. As noted in the subsection "Characteristics of the Egyptian Food Subsidy System (under Study)" in the previous chapter, almost all households who have ration cards also use them. Less than 4 percent of the households in all urban samples and less than 2 percent in all rural samples underlying the dose-response model estimations for the ration card program report zero consumption for the subsidized foods.

fractional-logit (dose-response) model—a common case in empirical economics (Guardabascio and Ventura 2014).

We chose a quadratic estimation form for the dose-response function, because it allows for possible nonlinearity and concavity in the relationship between food subsidies and nutritional outcomes. We adopted a functional form that has both the GPS score and the fractional treatment variable in linear and quadratic terms as well as a term capturing interaction between the two variables. We determined the use of bootstrapping to derive standard errors and confidence intervals, performing 768 bootstrap replications. To determine a sufficiently large number of bootstrap replications, we used the *bssize.ado* routine developed by Poi (2004) for application in Stata. The routine implements Andrews and Burchinsky's (2000) method for choosing the number of bootstrap replications. The calculated number is the initial estimate of the number of bootstrap replications needed to obtain bootstrap standard errors that do not deviate by more than 5 percent from the ideal bootstrapped values with a probability of 95 percent. For defining the bandwidth, we chose the default option of the *glmdose.ado* routine. It applies an automatic procedure that estimates the unknown terms in the optimal global bandwidth as described in Fan and Gijbels (1996). Finally, we specified that the routine estimates the average potential outcome at 50 treatment levels that are equally spaced over the range of the observed treatment—that is, in steps of 2 percentage points in the fractional treatment level. The routine produces a graph of the dose-response function based on these estimates, which we present in the estimation results subsection.

Survey Data and Estimation Variables

Our analysis of the causal effects of the Egyptian food subsidy system on nutritional outcomes uses data from the 2010–2011 round of the HIECS, conducted by Egypt's CAPMAS (CAPMAS and WFP 2011). This round provides us a unique opportunity to conduct such analysis, because it contained an additional module on household food security and the anthropometry of some household members. This module provides the data for the construction of all our nutrition and diet quality indicators. It was included upon request and with the support of WFP. No previous and—to date—no following round of the HIECS collected anthropometric measurements.

The basic HIECS is a large-scale, nationally representative household survey and includes a detailed household expenditure and consumption module that explicitly differentiates between subsidized food items and nonsubsidized food items. To the best of our knowledge, there is no other nationally

BOX 4.1 **Dilemma of the 2011 HIECS data: Household survey sampling**

The HIECS is a household survey that collects detailed data on household incomes, expenditures, and consumption. It is a very large household survey, compared to comparable surveys in other countries. The 2010–2011 round collected data for 24,224 households (CAPMAS and WFP 2011). The HIECS is designed to be subnationally representative at the household level for all regions (Metropolitan areas, Upper Egypt, Lower Egypt, and Frontier Governorates), all governorates (there were 29 at the time of the 2010–2011 round), and urban and rural areas within the regions and governorates. The HIECS is carried out regularly—usually every other year—over a one-year period per round. The household sampling is designed to also yield representative estimates on a quarterly basis. Until 2010–2011, the HIECS was a purely cross-sectional survey (while part of the 2012–2013 round was designed as a panel of the 2010–2011 round), so changes in household variables cannot be tracked over time and variations between households need to be exploited for analysis.

CAPMAS has used its own local field survey teams for conducting paper and pencil interviewing (PAPI) for the HIECS, while another team at the headquarters has been responsible for digitalizing and cleaning the data, checking their consistency, requesting household revisits (if needed), and creating key variables. By default, households were revisited when absent during the first visit for interview. This system has been well established over decades. Nonetheless, it may be more prone to data collection and entry errors than a modern, well-established computer-assisted personal interview (CAPI)-based system. Moreover, traditional PAPI systems yield sufficiently large digital datasets for rigorous consistency checks usually only after several weeks or even months, which limits the possibility of timely reinterviewing of households for implausible records. Like in many other large household surveys, a possible consequence is that the HIECS data

representative survey in any other country with large food subsidies that provides both anthropometric measurements and detailed quantitative food subsidy information for the same households. However, the 2011 HIECS data also have some limitations, some of which present challenges to our analysis. We had to overcome data dilemmas related to the household survey sampling (Box 4.1), the construction of nutrition and diet quality indicators (Box 4.2), and the identification of food subsidy benefits (Box 4.3).

may contain a few flawed observations. For the econometric estimations, we therefore drop households/individuals that show outlier values in household income or anthropometric measurements.

For the first time and with financial and technical support from WFP, the basic HIECS in 2010–2011 was complemented with a module on household food security and anthropometry for children, adolescents, and women of reproductive age. The food security and nutrition module was carried out with a subsample of the full HIECS sample. Only those households that were visited in 2011 for the basic HIECS (during the third and fourth quarters of the one-year data collection period) were selected for the food security and nutrition survey; 11,802 households (48.7 percent of the full sample) completed both the basic HIECS and the complementary food security and nutrition survey. In 2011, the HIECS was carried out from January to June 2011 but suspended for most of February because of the political uprisings. CAPMAS and WFP deem the subsample to be representative at least nationwide and for Egypt's three main regions—the Metropolitan areas, Upper Egypt, and Lower Egypt—as well as for urban and rural areas nationally and regionally. CAPMAS granted us access to all expenditure and consumption data and data for several agreed-upon income variables from the basic HIECS for those households that were also interviewed for the food security and nutrition module. Hence, our analysis is based on this subsample. Our estimates from the basic HIECS data may therefore slightly deviate from estimates presented in official reports consulting the full sample. For the econometric estimations, we dropped households (and individuals) located in the sparsely populated desert Frontier Governorates (Matrouh, New Valley, Red Sea, North Sinai, and South Sinai), amounting to less than 1.5 percent of all valid observations in each estimation sample. We dropped these observations because of perfect predictability, given the set of covariates (which include households' residence by governorate and characteristics).

ESTIMATION SAMPLES

All our estimations are based on three core datasets, which are (1) a child sample dataset, (2) a mother sample dataset, and (3) a household sample dataset. Because we ran the estimations for urban and rural areas separately, we split these core samples into urban and rural samples. All estimations of the effects on child nutrition employ the first datasets, all estimations of the effects on maternal nutrition employ the second datasets, and all estimations

BOX 4.2 Dilemma of the 2011 HIECS data: Nutrition and dietary diversity indicators

The data collection for the complementary food security and nutrition survey was carried out by CAPMAS field survey teams (CAPMAS and WFP 2011). According to WFP and CAPMAS staff involved in the supervision of the data collection, enumerators were trained and received support in measuring child anthropometry from experienced health professionals. Nevertheless, anecdotal evidence suggests that taking adequate anthropometric measurements for infants and very young children appeared to be challenging in some cases. It was the first time in 2011 that the basic HIECS was complemented with an anthropometry module. Hence, the quality of the anthropometry data—especially for infants and very young children—may be somewhat lower than in specialized surveys, which prompted us to drop individuals with biologically implausible measurements from the samples.

Anthropometric measurements were taken for all children and adolescents between ages six months and 19 years and all women 20–49 years of age, who were present in the interviewed households when visited. Our analysis focuses on children ages 6–59 months and their nonpregnant mothers 20–49 years of age with biologically plausible anthropometric measurements. Identification of the children's mothers was not straightforward, because the household roster of the HIECS does not allow for explicitly recording the biological mother or caretaker. However, there is only one woman of reproductive age living in most households, whom we assume to be the biological mother or main caretaker. Only 9.8 percent of all households have more than one woman 20–49 years of age with plausible anthropometric measurements and also a child ages 6–59 months with plausible anthropometric measurements. In those cases, we employ a sequential procedure using combined information on a woman's age, marital status, and relationship to the household head to identify the likely mother (or female caretaker). We give the highest probability to married women of common

of the effects on household diet quality employ the third datasets. The estimations of the effects on the double burden of malnutrition at the family level use subsamples of the first and the second datasets—precisely with those child-mother pairs, where plausible anthropometric measurements are available for both individuals.

The child sample datasets include one child per household, who is 6–59 months old and has plausible HAZ and BMIZ values. For computing child HAZ and BMIZ from the height/length, weight, age, sex, and childbearing age (that is, 20–28 years of age at the child's birth) who are the wives of the male household head and to women of common childbearing age who are the female household heads (who are often single mothers).

For deriving household food consumption and diet-related indicators, the 2011 HIECS data offer two principal sources. The first one is the food expenditure and consumption section of the basic HIECS. The second one is the food security section of the complementary food security and nutrition module. We use only data from the second source for computing our diet-related indicators for various reasons. The recall period of the food security section is 7 days, whereas it is 15 days for the food expenditure and consumption section. Seven days is a common—although already long—recall period for surveying dietary diversity. An even longer recall period is unsuitable for calculating established food-group-based dietary diversity indicators, because most households tend to consume foods from most considered food groups at least once over a long recall period. This is usually reflected in small cross-household variations of the indicators, which make them unsuited in (econometric) analysis. Choosing a dietary diversity indicator that counts the number of consumed food items instead of consumed food groups is not a real alternative because such an indicator does not provide information on whether households' diet is more diversified within one—perhaps relatively non-nutritious—food group or across food groups. Also, the food expenditure and consumption section does not allow us to calculate calorie and nutrient adequacy indicators because consumption quantities for processed foods—including bread, pasta, some dairy products, packed meat, and canned fish and vegetables—are not recorded. In contrast, the food security section provides data on the number of days a particular food group was consumed over the past 7 days. The listing of the food groups enables us to calculate the Household Dietary Diversity Score—a standard dietary diversity indicator. And the recorded number of days a particular food group is consumed allows us to explore the consumption frequency of key nutritious food groups in addition.

height measuring position records in the anthropometry section, we used the *zscore06.ado* routine, developed by Leroy (2011) for application in Stata. We dropped children with implausible anthropometric measurements from the samples, following standard WHO definitions of outlier measurements. Likely outliers are children who have a HAZ value below −6 or above +6 or a BMIZ value below −5 or above +5. If there were more than one child ages 6–59 months with plausible anthropometric measurements in the same

Text continues on page 112

BOX 4.3 Dilemma of the 2011 HIECS data: Food subsidy benefits

The main purpose of the basic HIECS is to provide data for measuring poverty, inequality, and consumer price indexes. Hence, it is very detailed in household income and expenditure accounts, but it naturally falls short of what would be the ideal set of variables for our specific analysis (which can only be obtained from a specialized and probably very costly survey). We therefore need to compromise on optimal data adequacy in some aspects and rely more on econometric tools to demonstrate analytical robustness of our results.

The basic HIECS provides two alternatives to identify the subsidies that households receive under the ration card program. First, it gives the (self-) reported number of persons registered on the ration card, which can be used to calculate the allotted quotas of subsidized rice, sugar, and cooking oil (and tea). Second, the household food expenditure and consumption section reports the consumed quantities for the subsidized food items.

We decided against the first alternative, because there is a considerable possibility that a significant proportion of households systematically underreport the actual number of persons registered on the ration card. Households that have more persons registered on the ration card than are actually living in the household may underreport, because it earns them an illegally—or at least immorally—high benefit. Hence, they may be concerned that the provided information to the government's statistics organization may be used against them. Our HIECS data (CAPMAS and WFP 2011) suggest that systematic underreporting is indeed likely. According to the survey data, 72.4 percent of the population were beneficiaries of the ration card program in 2011. However, GASC—the ministerial department in charge of the food subsidy system—reported that 79.6 percent of the population were beneficiaries at the beginning of 2011, and 81.3 percent at the end of that year (CAPMAS 2014; MSIT 2014a, 2014b). The estimated number of household ration cards in the HIECS data is similar to (and even slightly higher than) the number from official sources.

Further, there is no accurate way to check if the allotted quotas derived from the reported number of registered persons are consistent with the consumed quantities of the subsidized foods, in such a way that the consumed quantities should not exceed the quotas. The comparison is inaccurate because the food consumption recall period is 15 days and the quotas are allotted on a monthly basis; the subsidized foods are nonperishable and therefore can be stored and then consumed in amounts above the monthly quotas; and the 15-day recall period can cut across two months, making purchases of twice the monthly quotas per recall period possible. Nevertheless, the correlation between the calorie amount of the monthly quotas and the consumed calorie amount from the subsidized foods is high, with a coefficient of 0.518.

The variables to be included as covariates in the propensity score estimation models need to satisfy two principal conditions so that the models yield unbiased estimates. First, they should simultaneously influence the treatment variable and the outcome variable. Second, they should be unaffected by the treatment or the anticipation of it, which holds for variables that are fixed over time or measured before the treatment was received or its benefits are known. The limited availability of potentially deterministic variables in the HIECS data could interfere with the first condition, and the cross-sectional nature of the HIECS does not allow for verification of the second condition. Concerning the first condition, we would like to have had several specific variables that possibly better identify households' participation in the Baladi bread and flour program and the participation in and the received subsidy quotas under the ration card program.

For example, having georeferenced data on every household and on the Baladi bread outlet usually visited by the household, as well as the time spent queuing up for purchasing Baladi bread, would provide information on household transaction costs—a likely decisional factor of program participation and frequency of bread purchases. Related to the ration card program, we would like to have had copies of ration cards reporting the number of registered persons and quotas as well as information on when the household entered the program and on the eligibility criteria used to admit them to the program. Alternatively, more and more detailed information on certain household characteristics such as the year the household was established as well as (past) household affiliation with specific government and social institutions and organizations would have been desirable to check the characteristics' relevance for selection for the program. However, because such specific variables are unavailable from the HIECS data, we rely on proxy variables. To comply with the second condition as much as the data allow, we made several critical choices related to variable selection and specification. For example, for approximating household income levels, we used reported household income—instead of reported household expenditure (as used in the calculation of the official poverty estimates)—because reported household income is not influenced by the received food subsidies. Instead of using continuous variables for household income and household size, for instance, we used only categorical variables. Household income and household size are not fixed over a long period, ration cards seem not to have been revoked based on household incomes in the past, and household members have been continuously added to the cards of beneficiary households in past waves of program expansion. Household income quintiles and household size categories may be more time constant.

household, we randomly selected one child. We reduced the samples to one child per household to give equal weight to all sample households included in the estimations and hence to minimize a potential selection bias, considering that the HIECS is not designed to be representative for young children but households.

The mother sample datasets include the likely biological mothers or (female) caretakers of children ages 6–59 months who were selected for anthropometric measurement (including children with biologically implausible anthropometric measurements).[4] We dropped pregnant mothers because the BMIs yield incorrect indications of women's nutritional status during pregnancy. We identified mothers with biologically implausible BMIs using a common statistical definition of extreme outliers. We dropped any mother with a BMI that was above the third-quartile value in the core sample dataset (including mothers in both urban and rural areas) by a difference of three times the interquartile range (BMI = 44.79).[5] Like the child samples, the mother samples include only one individual per household.

The household sample datasets include all households with children 6–59 months old who were selected for anthropometric measurement (including children with biologically implausible anthropometric measurements).

Thus, all estimations are based on the same sets of individuals in the same households so that the estimates allow for drawing consistent conclusions across the different nutrition and diet quality indicators. The child datasets include 1,006 observations for the urban sample and 1,765 observations for the rural sample; the mother datasets include 1,140 observations for the urban sample and 1,823 observations for the rural sample; the child-mother pair datasets include 961 observations for the urban sample and 1,659 observations for the rural sample; and the household datasets include 1,130 observations for the urban sample and 1,911 observations for the rural sample.

OUTCOME VARIABLES

We estimated the effects of the Egyptian food subsidy system on four child nutrition indicators, two maternal nutrition indicators, two child-mother nutrition indicators, one household diet diversity indicator, and four household food frequency indicators (Table 4.1). In detail, the child nutrition indicators are child HAZ and child stunting (the respective binary indicator

4 In the following, we omit "caretaker" for ease of readability.

5 The lower bound value, calculated as below the first-quartile value in the core sample dataset by a difference of three times the interquartile range, is below zero, so no observations are dropped due to that.

TABLE 4.1 Overview of estimation model specifications with type of outcome and treatment variables

	Ration card program		Baladi bread & flour program
	PSM for program participation	Dose-response model: Subsidy level	Dose-response model: Subsidy level
Chronic child undernutrition			
Height-for-age z-score (HAZ)	continuous—binary	continuous—fractional	continuous—fractional
Stunting (HAZ < −2)	binary—binary	binary—fractional	binary—fractional
Overnutrition of . . .			
children			
Body-mass-index-for-age z-score (BMIZ)	continuous—binary	continuous—fractional	continuous—fractional
Overweight (BMIZ ≥ 2)	binary—binary	binary—fractional	binary—fractional
mothers			
Body mass index (BMI)	continuous—binary	continuous—fractional	continuous—fractional
Overweight (BMI ≥ 25)	binary—binary	binary—fractional	binary—fractional
Double burden of malnutrition at . . .			
individual level			
Child stunting & overweight (HAZ < −2 & BMIZ ≥ 2)	binary—binary	binary—fractional	binary—fractional
family level			
Child stunting (HAZ < −2) & maternal overweight (BMI ≥ 25)	binary—binary	binary—fractional	binary—fractional
Overnutrition of children and their mothers			
Child overweight (BMIZ ≥ 2) & maternal overweight (BMI ≥ 25)	binary—binary	binary—fractional	binary—fractional
Household diet quality			
Household dietary diversity score (HDDS)	categorical—binary	categorical—fractional	categorical—fractional
Consumption frequency of . . .			
vegetables	categorical—binary	categorical—fractional	categorical—fractional
legumes	categorical—binary	categorical—fractional	categorical—fractional
meat & fish	categorical—binary	categorical—fractional	categorical—fractional
milk & dairy products	categorical—binary	categorical—fractional	categorical—fractional

Source: Authors' representation.

Note: PSM = propensity score matching.

identifying chronic undernutrition) as well as child BMIZ and child overweight (the respective binary indicator identifying child overnutrition). Maternal nutrition indicators are mother's BMI and maternal overweight (the respective binary indicator identifying maternal overnutrition). The binary indicator of the double burden of malnutrition at the individual level is child stunting and overweight in combination. The binary indicator of the double burden of malnutrition at the family level is child stunting in combination with maternal overweight. For complementarity, we also include a binary indicator of child overweight in combination with maternal overweight.

The chosen household dietary diversity indicator is the household dietary diversity score (HDDS), which was developed by the Food and Nutrition Technical Assistance project of the United States Agency for International Development (Swindale and Bilinsky 2006a, 2006b). The HDDS counts the number of food groups that the household consumed over the seven-day recall period of the food security section. It has a maximum score of 12 food groups (cereals, starchy roots, legumes, vegetables, fruits, meat and fish, eggs, milk and dairy products, sugars, edible fats and oils, condiments, and other meal additions). The household food frequency indicators count the number of days that the household consumed a particular food group over the seven-day recall period. We chose four food groups that are of particular importance for physical and mental child development and micronutrient adequacy in the Egyptian context, namely (1) vegetables, (2) legumes, (3) meat and fish (including beef, mutton, poultry, offal, fish, and seafood), and (4) milk and dairy products.

TREATMENT VARIABLES

We estimated the nutritional and dietary effects for the Baladi bread and flour program and the food ration card program separately but sought some sort of comparability of the estimation results for the two programs. To consistently sum up the acquired benefits from the different subsidized food items under each program, we needed to identify a common, nutrition-sensible denominator for constructing the treatment variables in the datasets for the dose-response model estimations. To meet this methodological need and to closely correspond to our main hypothesis, we expressed the treatment variables on a calorie consumption basis.

In the datasets for estimating the Baladi bread and flour program's effects, the treatment variable—before it is converted into a fractional variable—is the average calorie consumption amount per capita and day that the household obtained from the consumption of subsidized Baladi bread and Baladi bread flour over the 15-day recall period of the food expenditure and consumption section in the basic HIECS (CAPMAS and WFP 2011). As for all processed foods, the HIECS data do not report the consumption quantity of Baladi bread but only the consumption expenditure, from which we derived the consumption quantity, using the fixed price of Baladi bread (EGP 0.05). The consumption quantities of Baladi bread flour and all foods subsidized under the ration card program are reported in the HIECS data. In the datasets for estimating the ration-card-program effects, the treatment variable—before converting it into a fractional variable—is the average calorie consumption amount per capita and day that the household obtained from the consumption of subsidized rice, sugar, and cooking oil over the 15-day recall period.[6]

In each estimation dataset, we first dropped households with outlier calorie consumption amounts that we defined as the observations above the 99-percentile value. Then, we converted the treatment variable into a fractional variable by dividing a household's calorie consumption amounts by the maximum calorie consumption amount in the dataset. Hence, the maximum value of the treatment variables is 1, and the minimum value is 0, indicating that—in the case of the ration card program—the particular household did not consume subsidized rice, sugar, or cooking oil, despite having a valid ration card. The binary treatment variable in the PSM estimations of the nutritional and dietary effects of participation in the ration card program takes values of 1 if the household has a valid ration card, and 0 otherwise. The household characteristics section of the HIECS consumption module questionnaire asked for this information explicitly.

INDEPENDENT VARIABLES

Our choice of the household characteristics variables to be included as covariates in the (binary and generalized) propensity score estimation models was guided by evidence from the food and health economics literature and our deep understanding of the Egyptian food subsidy system. We included only variables that simultaneously influence households' participation in the food subsidy programs or the acquired food subsidies and the nutrition outcome indicators. We also experimented extensively with alternative covariates, additional covariates, and the exact specification of the included covariates in preliminary work (not reported here). In all estimations, we used the same set

6 Black tea (without sugar) contains zero calories and is therefore excluded. Only 16.5 percent of all households with a valid ration card reported that they consumed subsidized black tea during the 15-day recall period (CAPMAS and WFP 2011).

of covariates—although the rationales for including some covariates differed across the estimations. This set includes categorical variables of household per capita income, household size, age of household head, and education level of household head as well as binary variables specifying whether the household is headed by a single woman; whether a household member receives a pension or social insurance or social assistance benefits; and whether a household member works in public administration, subsidy and social welfare services, education, health and civil service, or defense.[7] For executing the estimations, we transformed the categorical variables into binary variables, identifying income quintiles, five household size categories, and five age groups and four education levels for household heads.[8] The propensity score estimation equations also include binary variables identifying the location of the household by governorate (aggregate) and—for rural areas—a binary variable specifying whether the household farms agricultural land.[9]

As noted in the subsections describing the history of the Egyptian food subsidy system and its characteristics at the time of our survey data in the previous chapter, low household income status, single-female household head with dependents, pensioners, and beneficiaries of social insurance and social assistance programs were explicit criteria for household selection into the ration card program. Since the introduction of the ration card system, as well as throughout all past rounds of its expansion, households with low-income jobs and with economically and socially disadvantaged background were given highest priority. To the best of our knowledge, eligibility for the ration card program was usually defined through affiliation with a specific occupation or societal group. For example, households with members who were enrolled in public benefit programs or with the main income earner employed

---

7 Household income is the total net income of all household members as provided by CAPMAS. It includes wages and salaries, income from agricultural and nonagricultural activities—including value of own-consumption, income from financial and nonfinancial assets, value of cash and in-kind transfers, and imputed rent for owned housing.

8 Table A.11 in the Appendix presents the descriptive statistics of the estimation variables.

9 The urban sample includes 12 governorates or governorate aggregates. The rural sample includes 13 governorates or governorate aggregates. We aggregated some governorates because of insufficient observations by governorate. We aggregated governorates that were one governorate before 2010 (and meanwhile were partly consolidated again)—such as Giza and 6th of October Governorates, Luxor and Qena Governorates, and Cairo and (urban) Helwan Governorates—and that have similar demographic, ecological, and economic conditions, are located in the same region and bordering each other, and have similar food subsidy system coverage, such as the two Metropolitan governorates Port-Said and Suez; the urban areas of Kafr-Elsheikh and Gharbiya Governorates; the urban areas of Bni-Souef, Fayoum, and Menia Governorates; the rural areas of Domiyat and Dakahliya Governorates; the rural areas of Sharkiya and Ismailia Governorates; and the rural areas of Bni-Souef and Fayoum Governorates.

in the low-income public sector were among the primary beneficiaries. Moreover, public-sector employees in general are likely to be better connected than the rest of the population, which helped them to successfully apply for ration cards and get additional household members registered on the cards. In response to the food, fuel, and financial crises in 2007–2009, the ration card program was opened to all single female–headed households with dependents and other household groups with limited income-earning potential such as those who have no or low formal education. Therefore, we also account for household heads' attained education, differentiating between no formal education level and completed primary, secondary, and higher education.

Given the history and characteristics of the ration card program, we can expect that the longer a household has existed, the more likely it is that the household has managed to get into the ration card program; and the longer the household has been participating in the program, the more likely it is that the household has registered all (past) household members during one of the past expansion rounds. Because we have no data on the year when a household was established or the year when a beneficiary household entered the ration card program (Box 4.3), we use the age of the household head as a proxy variable, assuming that older household heads established their households earlier than younger ones.

We defined the five age categories in line with the duration between major modifications of the ration card program in the past. We grouped households whose head was 38 years or younger at the time of the HIECS in 2011, households whose head was older than 38 years and 48 years or younger, households whose head was older than 48 years and 58 years or younger, and households whose head was older than 58 years. A person 38 years of age in 2011 turned 18 years of age—the age of consent in Egypt—in 1991; that is, after automatic inclusion of newborns on the household ration cards was abolished. Still, this person was old enough to have founded a family and registered himself and his family during one of the rounds of program expansion, starting after 2005. A person 58 years of age in 2011 turned 18 years of age in 1971, that is, shortly after the beginning of Anwar Sadat's presidency and the rapid expansion of the ration card program in the 1970s. A household head 48 years of age in 2011 turned 18 years of age in 1981—the year of Sadat's assassination and the beginning of Hosni Mubarak's reign, so this man (or woman) was probably less likely to have been enrolled in the ration card program in his early adulthood as an independent household, given the tightening of the ration card program in the 1980s and 1990s.

Our rationale for the inclusion of household size as an independent variable and for the choice of household size categories follows a similar logic to that underlying the rationale for the household head age variable. Large households tend to incorporate more persons in different age groups than do small households. Containing a variety of age groups is likely to be associated with a higher probability of acquiring household ration cards and registering household members based on duration of household existence, whereas small households are more likely to have been recently established with a lower respective probability of acquiring cards and registering members. All else being equal, large households also have a higher probability of having at least one household member who fulfills the eligibility criteria for the ration card program. In combination with other variables included, the chosen household size categories allow for identification of certain household demographics that are likely to matter for selection into the ration card program and quota allotment. For example, a three-person household consisting of parents with one child is differentiated from a single-mother household with two children because of the variable identifying households headed by single women with dependents. Note that because of our estimation sample selection, all considered households have at least one young child (ages 6–59 months), so including a variable identifying two-person households leads to over-identification. As another example, a five-person household may consist of parents with their three children or grandparents with their daughter-in-law (or daughter) and her two children. Given patriarchal practices, the variables identifying the age category of household heads largely differentiate these two common cases.

Most Egyptian farm households are smallholder, semicommercialized farmers and thus may have been considered to be particularly vulnerable to food price and environmental shocks. These circumstances, in combination with the government's strong involvement in the agricultural sector in the past and the more recent (partial) agricultural liberalization, may have attracted particular attention to farmers as beneficiaries of public assistance (Ahmed et al. 2001). Until the mid-1980s, the production (and trade) of strategic food crops—mainly wheat, rice, and sugarcane, partly for supplying the food subsidy system—was centrally managed and fully under government control. Many Egyptian farmers are still organized in centrally established cooperatives, while membership in these cooperatives has possibly served as an eligibility criterion in rural areas.

All these variables are also likely to be associated with household participation in the Baladi bread and flour program. For example, poor households rely more on cheap Baladi bread than do rich households (Figure 3.4); single mothers tend to have time constraints for getting to the bread outlets and queuing up because of alternative time needs for income earning and childcare, whereas pensioners and beneficiaries of social insurance and social assistance programs may have more spare time; and Baladi bread outlets may be located near public-sector institutions so that their employees have easy access to Baladi bread. Household size and age and education of the household head—who is the main decisionmaker in the household—are likely determinants of household resource allocation, including decisions on household food consumption, as numerous studies in the food economics literature have shown (e.g., Behrman and Deolalikar 1987; Cortez and Senauer 1996; Pitt and Rosenzweig 1985; Thomas 1990). In addition, long-established households—proxied by the households' age—tend to reside in old neighborhoods, which are more likely to have a high density of Baladi bread outlets than newly constructed neighborhoods are. And farm households may be located farther away from Baladi bread outlets (and Baladi flour warehouses), may be less mobile, and may face more time constraints for acquiring Baladi bread and flour than other occupational groups do.

The coverage of, and hence households' physical access to, the ration card program and the Baladi bread and flour program varies by governorate because of different demographics and infrastructure. It may also vary because of differently influential representation in policy and administration, among other reasons. And Baladi bread flour was handed out in only some governorates at the time of the 2010–2011 HIECS.

All independent variables included in the propensity score estimation equations are also likely to affect household diet quality and individual nutritional outcomes, as evidence from the food and health economics literature suggests. Rich households can afford pricier, more nutritious food and better healthcare than poor households. More nutritious food and better healthcare are associated with better diet quality and lower risks of micronutrient deficiencies and chronic undernutrition (e.g., Brooks-Gunn and Duncan 1997; Ecker and Qaim 2011; Pinstrup-Andersen and Caicedo 1978; Ravallion 1990; Wolfe and Behrman 1983). Yet as discussed before in great detail, higher income does not necessarily lead to better nutrition.

The sex of the household head—as the main decisionmaker in the household—matters for the nutritional status of household members and for young children in particular, because it accounts for common gender differences in nutrition-relevant decisionmaking (e.g., Handa 1994; Kennedy and Peters 1992; Onyango, Tucker, and T. Eisemon 1994; Rashid, Smith, and Rahman 2011; Thiele, Mensink, and Beitz 2004). However, including just the sex of the household head as a covariate yields misleading results given the Egyptian context. According to our HIECS data (CAPMAS and WFP 2011), most female-headed households in Egypt (79.2 percent) are households where no adult male is present, so decision-making power is with her by necessity, whereas most households with adult males are headed by men (95.8 percent). Therefore, we included instead a variable that identifies households headed by single mothers because single mothers usually face major time constraints due to their often dual responsibility as main income earners and main child caretakers (and often even main meal preparers), which may adversely affect child nutrition.

Evidence from the health literature suggests that formal education is a strong predictor of nutrition—especially parental education for the nutritional status of young children (e.g., Semba et al. 2008; Strauss 1990; Thomas 1990). Given the Egyptian context, we included the education level of the—usually male—household head.[10] Similarly and as mentioned above, the age of the household head may influence decisionmaking on the allocation of household resources, and the household size matters for nutritional effects associated with (reverse) household economies of scale (Deaton and Paxson 1998; Lanjouw and Ravallion 1995; Nelson 1988) and sharing of childcare responsibilities (Doan and Bisharat 1990; Popkin 1980).

Households who receive social benefits or engage in public-sector activities may also have better access to nutrition-relevant public services, including primary healthcare. Farm households often have access to nutritious own-produce, such as vegetables, legumes, and animal-source foods but are also frequently exposed to parasites in (polluted) irrigation water, giving rise to secondary malnutrition (e.g., Berti, Krasevec, and FitzGerald 2004; Carletto et al. 2015; Sibhatu, Krishna, and Qaim 2015; Stephenson, Latham, and Ottesen 2000). Moreover, farming is a physical labor–intensive activity, so farmers have a lower risk of overweight due to high calorie expenditure. A household's location is likely to affect food consumption and individual nutrition due to the local infrastructure endowment and quality, such as consumer marketplaces, water and sanitation systems, and healthcare facilities, among others.

10 Alternative estimation specifications having the attained education level of the mother yield similar—though less strong—results (not reported here).

POTENTIAL ESTIMATION BIASES

As mentioned above, our identification strategy rests on the assumption that there are no other covariates than the ones considered that simultaneously influence treatment and outcome variables. This is a strong assumption for any empirical analysis of our kind, given survey data limitations. To make this assumption most plausible, we chose the empirical specifications to be consistent with established evidence from the food and health economics literature and our deep understanding of the Egyptian food subsidy system.

While we are confident that the chosen specifications of the estimation models exploited the full data potential, it is still conceivable that there are unobserved covariates that influence the treatment variables and the outcome variables at the same time. This could lead to biased estimates because the propensity score cannot adjust for the unobserved (systematic) differences between the treatment and comparison groups. Such a potential bias due to unobservables would arise if, for example, malnourished households manipulate their ration-card-program eligibility regarding the number of registered persons, whereas well-nourished households abstain from the possibility of this fraud. We doubt that this case is a likely source of a potential bias, however, as it assumes that only/predominantly malnourished households have some sort of (unobserved) means to successfully manipulate the selection process.

It should be clear that a potential bias due to unobservables arises only if the unobserved covariates influence both the treatment variable and the outcome variable. We acknowledge that there are likely several unobserved covariates that explain the selection into the ration card program and the acquired subsidy level under the ration card program and the Baladi bread and flour program, but we also believe that the probability that these covariates systematically influence the nutritional outcomes is fairly small. There are also variables that determine nutritional outcomes but are unlikely to influence the treatment variable. An example is children's age. Child stunting mainly evolves over the first two to three life years. However, neither the age of the children nor their number per household should influence households' participation in the ration card program or the received subsidy quotas because all children in our analysis are younger than five years of age, and the last expansion of the ration card program was before all of their births. Thus, we believe that the possibility of a bias due to unobservables is fairly small, and even if there is such an unobserved covariate, we believe that the potential bias does not compromise our main findings.

TABLE 4.2 Overview of PSM estimation results: Direction of causal effects

	Ration card program				Baladi bread & flour program	
	PSM for program participation[a]		Dose-response model: Subsidy level[b]		Dose-response model: Subsidy level[b]	
	Urban	Rural	Urban	Rural	Urban	Rural
Chronic child undernutrition						
Height-for-age z-score (HAZ)	+	+	–	0	0	–
Stunting (HAZ < –2)	–	+	+	+/–	0	0
Overnutrition of . . .						
children						
Body-mass-index-for-age z-score (BMIZ)	+	+	+	0	–/+	+
Overweight (BMIZ ≥ 2)	0	+	+	+/–	–/+	+
mothers						
Body mass index (BMI)	+	0	–/+	0	+	0
Overweight (BMI ≥ 25)	+	+	+	0	+	0
Double burden of malnutrition at . . .						
individual level						
Child stunting & overweight (HAZ < –2 & BMIZ ≥ 2)	–	+	+	+/–	–/+	0
family level						
Child stunting (HAZ < –2) & maternal overweight (BMI ≥ 25)	–	+	+/–	–/+	+/–	0
Overnutrition of children and their mothers						
Child overweight (BMIZ ≥ 2) & maternal overweight (BMI ≥ 25)	+	+	+	+/–	–/+	0

Estimation Results

This section presents our estimation results of the likely effects of the ration card program and the Baladi bread and flour program on individual nutrition and household diet quality among households with children ages 6–59 months—referred to as "families." Table 4.2 provides an overview of all results, indicating the direction of the estimated causal effects. First, we discuss the estimation results of the PSM with binary treatment that we used to assess the nutritional and dietary effects of participation in the ration card program compared to nonparticipation. Then, we discuss the estimation results of the PSM with continuous treatment for the ration card program. The results provide evidence on the hypothesized dose-response relationships

	Ration card program				Baladi bread & flour program	
	PSM for program participation[a]		Dose-response model: Subsidy level[b]		Dose-response model: Subsidy level[b]	
	Urban	Rural	Urban	Rural	Urban	Rural
Household diet quality						
Household dietary diversity score (HDDS)	0	–	**–/+**	–/+	+	**+/–**
Consumption frequency of . . .						
vegetables	–	+	**+**	**–/+**	+	0
legumes	+	–	**–**	0	**+/–**	0
meat & fish	–	–	–	**–/+**	+	**–**
milk & dairy products	–	**–**	**–**	**–/+**	**–/+**	**–/+**

Source: Authors' representation.

Note: PSM = propensity score matching.

[a] The signs indicate that the nutrition or dietary outcome indicator is higher (+) or lower (–), at the means, in the treatment group than in the comparison group. The 0 indicates that the mean difference is less than 1 percentage point. Bold signs indicate that goodness of fit is sufficient and an estimated coefficient of at least one subsidy-level variable is statistically significant at 10%. Normal, non-bold signs indicate that goodness of fit is sufficient but no coefficient of the subsidy-level variables is statistically significant at 10%. Bold gray signs indicate goodness of fit is insufficient and an estimated coefficient of at least one subsidy-level variable is statistically significant at 10%. Non-bold gray signs indicate goodness of fit is insufficient.

[b] The signs indicate that the nutritional or diet quality indicator continuously increases (+) or decreases (–) with higher subsidy levels, as suggested by the slope of the estimated dose-response function curve. The +/– and –/+ indicate that the estimated dose-response function follows an inverted or upright bell-shaped curve. The 0 indicates that the estimated dose-response function has a flat curve with no apparent slope. For defining the shape of the dose-response function curve, its confidence intervals are taken into consideration. Bold signs indicate that goodness of fit is sufficient and an estimated coefficient of at least one subsidy-level variable is statistically significant at 10%. Normal, non-bold signs indicate that goodness of fit is sufficient but no coefficient of the subsidy-level variables is statistically significant at 10%. Gray signs indicate goodness of fit is insufficient.

between the acquired food subsidy level (expressed on a calorie consumption basis and in relative terms) and nutrition and diet quality indicators among beneficiaries of the ration card program (identified by the possession of ration cards). Finally, we discuss the estimation results of the PSM with continuous treatment for the Baladi bread and flour program. The results provide evidence on the hypothesized dose-response relationships between the Baladi bread and flour subsidies and nutrition and diet quality outcomes among all families (considering that participation in the Baladi bread and flour program is unrestricted). Since the coefficients of the estimated dose-response functions have no direct interpretation, we present the estimated dose-response functions in graphical form.

Effects of Ration-Card-Program Participation

The goodness of fit of all the logistic regression models for the estimation of the binary propensity scores is decent (with pseudo R-squared scores between 0.22 and 0.25), and it is slightly higher for the rural samples than for the urban samples.[11] For all PSM estimations, the area of common support between the treatment group (that is, ration cardholders) and the comparison group (that is, non–ration-card holders) is fairly large. Imposing the common support condition drops 11–14 percent of the total number of observations in the urban samples and 9–11 percent of the total number of observations in the rural samples (Tables 4.3–4.6). The test statistics for the balancing property of the treatment and comparison groups after matching suggest that there is no substantial overall covariate imbalance in all logistic regression models. The overall biases tend to be slightly higher for the rural samples than for the urban samples.[12] As required, the pseudo R-squared scores are low, and the likelihood-ratio test statistics do not reject the null hypothesis of joint insignificance of the regressors. The mean biases for each variable included in the models are usually quite small and never exceed 10.5 percentage points. The highest mean biases occur due to matching on household size in the urban samples and the household head's education level in the rural samples. The estimated overall mean biases and overall median biases never exceed 4 percentage points and 3 percentage points, respectively. Rubin's B-value never exceeds 25, and Rubin's R-value is always between 0.5 and 2. Accordingly, the groups of the treated and untreated individuals/families can be considered as sufficiently balanced in all estimation models.

Overall, our PSM estimations with binary treatment provide ambiguous evidence of the causal effects of ration-card-program participation on individual nutrition and household diet quality. This finding is in line with our expectations, considering that there are large differences in household subsidy levels (and low subsidy levels are unlikely to create a significant nutritional response), so averaging over all families with ration cards might not be meaningful. Nevertheless, the ATT estimates indicate a few significant effects and some notable tendencies.

In urban areas, children from families with ration cards have on average significantly higher HAZs than their peers from families without ration cards, and child stunting tends to be less prevalent among ration cardholders,

---

11 Tables A.12–A.15 in the Appendix present the logistic regression results of the binary propensity score estimations.

12 Tables A.16–A.19 in the Appendix present the balancing property test statistics.

TABLE 4.3 Estimated ATT of ration-card-program participation on child nutrition

	Urban					Rural				
	Treated	Untreated	Diff.	Std. err.	t-stat	Treated	Untreated	Diff.	Std. err.	t-stat
HAZ	−0.861	−1.186	0.325	0.164	1.98	−0.930	−0.957	0.027	0.147	0.18
Stunting	0.271	0.320	−0.049	0.038	−1.30	0.262	0.251	0.011	0.034	0.34
BMIZ	1.055	0.877	0.177	0.147	1.21	1.030	0.922	0.108	0.132	0.82
Overweight	0.268	0.270	−0.002	0.038	−0.05	0.285	0.243	0.042	0.035	1.20
Stunting & overweight	0.139	0.159	−0.021	0.030	−0.70	0.121	0.119	0.002	0.026	0.09
Common support (observations)										
Total	390	616				1,082	683			
On-support	339	616				977	683			

Source: Authors' estimation based on data from CAPMAS and WFP (2011).

Note: ATT = average treatment effect on the treated; BMIZ = body-mass-index-for-age z-score; HAZ = height-for-age z-score.

TABLE 4.4 Estimated ATT of ration-card-program participation on maternal nutrition

	Urban					Rural				
	Treated	Untreated	Diff.	Std. err.	t-stat	Treated	Untreated	Diff.	Std. err.	t-stat
BMI	29.68	29.02	0.66	0.42	1.59	28.45	28.23	0.22	0.37	0.60
Overweight	0.832	0.758	0.074	0.033	2.28	0.713	0.736	−0.024	0.034	−0.70
Common support (observations)										
Total	445	695				1,127	696			
On-support	394	695				999	696			

Source: Authors' estimation based on data from CAPMAS and WFP (2011).

Note: ATT = average treatment effect on the treated; BMI = body mass index.

while the mean difference is statistically insignificant (at common levels) (Table 4.3). These children tend to also have higher average BMIZs, but there is no indication for an increased probability of overweight. In rural areas, the average BMIZ and the probability of overweight tend to be higher among children from beneficiary families than among those from nonbeneficiary families. The average BMI of mothers of young children tends to be higher among urban beneficiaries than urban nonbeneficiaries, and, consistent with this pattern, overweight among these mothers is significantly more likely (Table 4.4). There is no clear evidence for average effects of ration-card-program participation on maternal overnutrition in rural areas. Thus, on average, household participation in the ration card program seems to contribute to better nutrition among young children but also leads to overnutrition among

TABLE 4.5 Estimated ATT of ration-card-program participation on the double burden of malnutrition and the coexistence of child and maternal overnutrition at the family level

	Urban					Rural				
	Treated	Untreated	Diff.	Std. err.	t-stat	Treated	Untreated	Diff.	Std. err.	t-stat
Child stunting & maternal overweight	0.237	0.278	−0.041	0.036	−1.14	0.176	0.174	0.002	0.031	0.07
Child overweight & maternal overweight	0.246	0.217	0.029	0.037	0.78	0.206	0.169	0.037	0.033	1.13
Common support (observations)										
Total	367	594				1,028	631			
On-support	317	594				914	631			

Source: Authors' estimation based on data from CAPMAS and WFP (2011).

Note: ATT = average treatment effect on the treated.

TABLE 4.6 Estimated ATT of ration-card-program participation on household diet quality

	Urban					Rural				
	Treated	Untreated	Diff.	Std. err.	t-stat	Treated	Untreated	Diff.	Std. err.	t-stat
HDDS	10.58	10.68	−0.09	0.09	−1.05	10.35	10.45	−0.11	0.08	−1.34
Consumption frequency of										
vegetables	3.148	3.337	−0.188	0.163	−1.15	3.577	3.504	0.072	0.150	0.48
legumes	4.460	4.401	0.059	0.192	0.31	4.222	4.437	−0.215	0.166	−1.30
meat & fish	2.761	2.971	−0.210	0.138	−1.52	2.548	2.582	−0.035	0.110	−0.32
milk & dairy products	4.701	4.771	−0.070	0.179	−0.39	4.311	4.723	−0.411	0.166	−2.48
Common support (observations)										
Total	453	677				1,171	740			
On-support	398	677				1,063	740			

Source: Authors' estimation based on data from CAPMAS and WFP (2011).

Note: ATT = average treatment effect on the treated; HDDS = household dietary diversity score.

mothers of young children in urban areas, while it seems to contribute to child overnutrition without increasing maternal overnutrition notably in rural areas. Nevertheless, finding a family where the child and her mother are overweight is more likely among beneficiaries than nonbeneficiaries in both urban and rural areas (Table 4.5). However, the mean differences are statistically insignificant. The double burden of malnutrition at the family level tends to be less common among beneficiaries than among nonbeneficiaries in urban areas, while there is only a tiny (insignificant) difference in rural areas. The probabilities of the double burden of malnutrition and the coexistence of child and maternal overnutrition at the family level are considerably higher among both beneficiary and nonbeneficiary families in urban areas than families in rural areas.

Household diet quality tends to be somewhat lower overall among families with ration cards than families without ration cards in urban and rural areas. In particular, nutritious food groups tend to be consumed less frequently among beneficiary families; this is especially true of vegetables and meat and fish in urban areas, and of legumes and milk and dairy products in rural areas (Table 4.6). Yet the mean difference between beneficiaries and nonbeneficiaries is statistically significant only for the consumption frequency of milk and dairy products in rural areas. There is virtually no difference in household dietary diversity between beneficiaries and nonbeneficiaries in urban and rural areas. The mean differences vary around just 1 percent.

Effects of Ration-Card-Program Subsidies

The goodness of fit of all GLM estimates of the GPSs—in the first step of the dose-response models for assessing the effects of the subsidy levels of the ration card program among beneficiary families—is satisfactory (with Pearson scores between 0.11 and 0.15).[13] In the second step, the goodness of fit of the estimated dose-response functions is generally low (with R-squared and pseudo R-squared scores of less than 0.09).[14] However, low goodness-of-fit measures are not uncommon in cross-sectional regression models that explore variations in anthropometric measurements of individuals—especially for height-based indicators of child nutrition (e.g., Breisinger and Ecker 2014; Christiaensen and Alderman 2004), mainly due to large genetic variations and common measurement problems. Large heterogeneity in observed variables in combination with relatively small sample sizes possibly also contributes to low goodness-of-fit measures and statistically insignificant coefficient estimates in the second step of our dose-response models, especially in the case of the estimations of subsidy-level effects of the ration card program in urban areas. Nevertheless, our estimation results indicate consistent tendencies for several nutrition and diet quality indicators.

---

13 Tables A.20–A.23 in the Appendix show the GLM results of the GPS estimations for the ration-card-program subsidies.

14 Tables A.24–A.37 in the Appendix show the dose-response function estimates for the effects of ration-card-program subsidies.

FIGURE 4.1 Dose-response functions for child HAZ

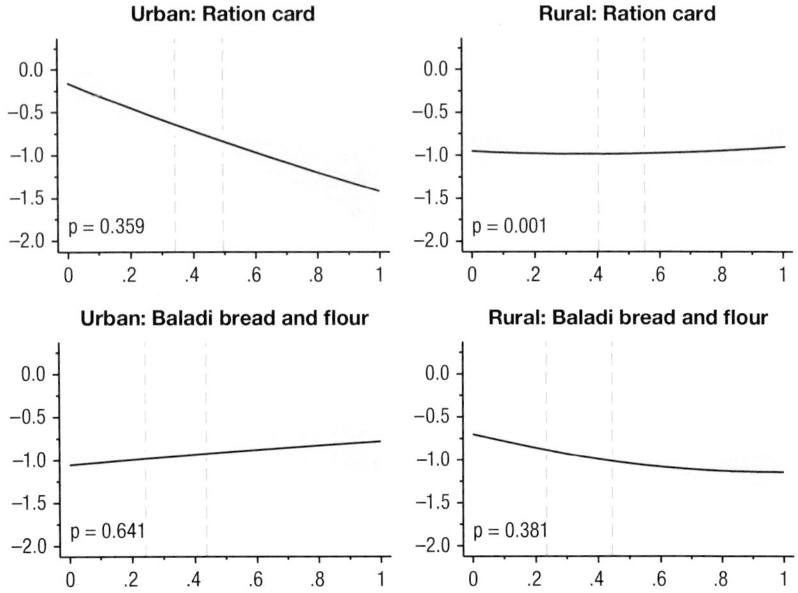

Source: Authors' estimation based on data from CAPMAS and WFP (2011).

Note: The y-axes indicate child height-for-age z-scores (HAZs), and the x-axes indicate household subsidy levels of the respective food subsidy programs in the respective residential areas.

p is the p-value of joint significance of the estimated dose-response function (Prob. > F). The gray-shaded area marks the 95 percent confidence interval. The vertical dashed lines mark the tertiles of the child samples, separating children from families with low, medium, and high subsidy levels.

In urban areas, the HAZs of children from families with ration cards tend to sharply decrease with increasing ration card subsidy levels in a linear manner, and the probability of child stunting tends to continuously increase across children from families with subsidy levels—other than very high subsidy levels (Figure 4.1 and Figure 4.2). Hence, the risk of chronic child undernutrition tends to increase with the consumed calories from subsidized rice, sugar, and cooking oil among urban beneficiary families. However, the average risk of chronic child undernutrition tends to be lower among urban beneficiaries compared to urban nonbeneficiaries, as the ATT estimates above suggest. Thus, it is the received subsidy amounts (above average) that tend to negatively affect children's nutritional status—but not household participation in the ration card program per se. Although the continuous and binary indicators of chronic undernutrition suggest a consistent tendency among ration cardholders in urban areas, it should be noted that the coefficient estimates in both

FIGURE 4.2 Dose-response functions for child stunting

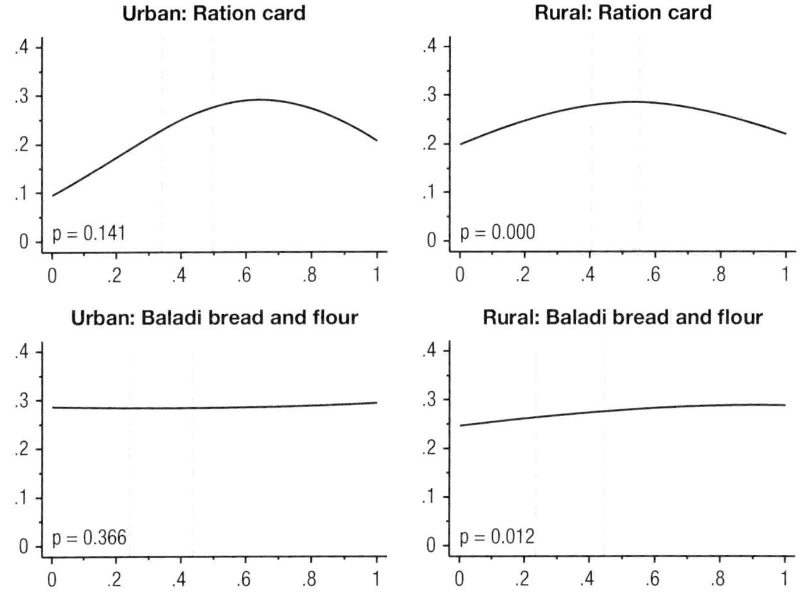

Source: Authors' estimation based on data from CAPMAS and WFP (2011).

Note: The y-axes indicate the probabilities of children being stunted, and the x-axes indicate household subsidy levels of the respective food subsidy programs in the respective residential areas.

p is the p-value of joint significance of the estimated dose-response function (Prob. > chi-sq.). The gray-shaded area marks the 95 percent confidence interval. The vertical dashed lines mark the tertiles of the child samples, separating children from families with low, medium, and high subsidy levels.

dose-response functions are statistically insignificant at common levels, and their goodness-of-fit measures are insufficient.

For rural areas, the dose-response functions indicate that the HAZs of children from beneficiary families and their probability of being stunted are quite unresponsive to different ration-card-program subsidy levels, with a slight—though statistically significant—tendency toward a higher child stunting probability at medium subsidy levels (Figure 4.1 and Figure 4.2). Differences in the responsiveness of nutrition indicators between urban and rural beneficiaries may be explained by various factors. A possible explanation for the differential effects on child HAZ and stunting is that children's physical growth in rural areas seems to be predominantly influenced by factors other than the acquired ration card subsidies and particularly by those factors that are accounted for by the GPS, such as infrastructural conditions at household locations. The coefficient estimates of the GPS (linear and quadratic)

FIGURE 4.3 Dose-response functions for child BMIZ

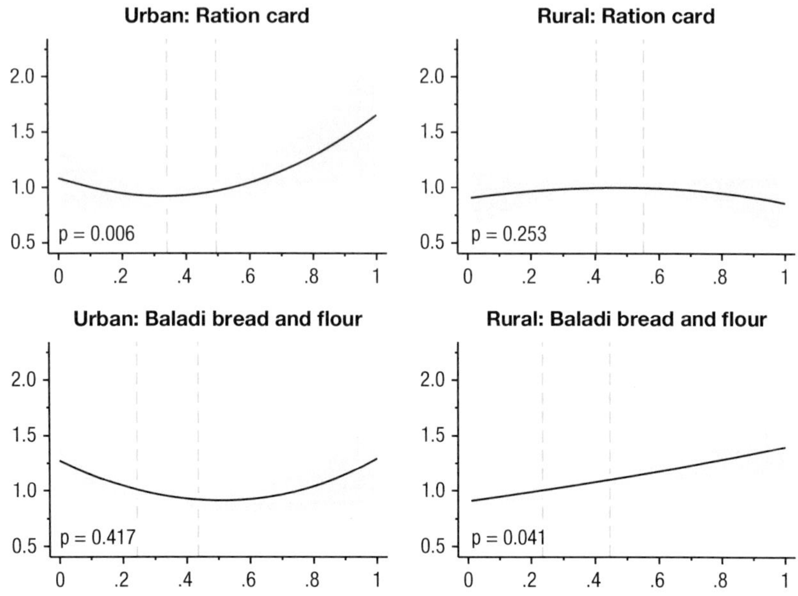

Source: Authors' estimation based on data from CAPMAS and WFP (2011).

Note: BMIZ = body-mass-index-for-age z-score.

The y-axes indicate child BMIZs, and the x-axes indicate household subsidy levels of the respective food subsidy programs in the respective residential areas.

p is the p-value of joint significance of the estimated dose-response function (Prob. > F). The gray-shaded area marks the 95 percent confidence interval. The vertical dashed lines mark the tertiles of the child samples, separating children from families with low, medium, and high subsidy levels.

variables in the dose-response functions for child HAZ and child stunting in rural areas are large and highly statistically significant (at the 1 percent level)—unlike those in the dose-response functions for child HAZ and child stunting in urban areas. And the GPS estimations for child nutrition in urban and rural areas show the largest differences in the coefficient estimates for several binary variables identifying the governorate where the beneficiary families reside.[15]

The BMIZs of children from urban beneficiary families increases with increasing ration-card-program subsidy levels, at least for children from families with medium and high subsidy levels (Figure 4.3). This estimation result is consistent with the ATT estimate above, according to which children from urban beneficiary families tend to have higher average BMIZ than children

15 See Tables A.20, A.24, and A.25 in the Appendix.

FIGURE 4.4 Dose-response functions for child overweight

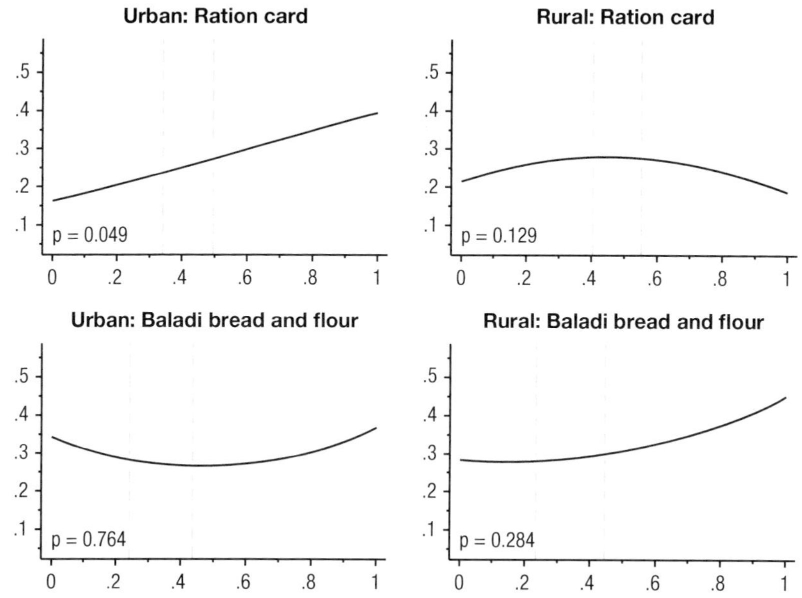

Source: Authors' estimation based on data from CAPMAS and WFP (2011).

Note: The y-axes indicate the probabilities of children being overweight, and the x-axes indicate household subsidy levels of the respective food subsidy programs in the respective residential areas.

p is the p-value of joint significance of the estimated dose-response function (Prob. > chi-sq.). The gray-shaded area marks the 95 percent confidence interval. The vertical dashed lines mark the tertiles of the child samples, separating children from families with low, medium, and high subsidy levels.

from urban nonbeneficiary families. Among urban beneficiaries, the probability of child overweight increases with increasing subsidy levels in a linear manner and at high margins (Figure 4.4). The goodness of fit of the dose-response functions for child BMIZ and child overweight is sufficient, and the coefficient estimates of the subsidy-level variables—which define the shape of the curves—are statistically significant, providing strong evidence for the effects of ration-card-program subsidies on child overnutrition in urban areas.[16]

This is different for the dose-response functions of the subsidy-level effects on child BMIZ and child overweight in rural areas. They have insufficient goodness-of-fit measures and—in the case of the estimation for the effect on child BMIZ—statistically insignificant coefficient estimates.[17] The

16 See Tables A.26 and A.27 in the Appendix.

17 See Tables A.26 and A.27 in the Appendix.

dose-response model estimation for the effect on child overweight indicates a slightly higher probability of child overweight at medium subsidy levels. Like chronic child undernutrition, child overnutrition seems to be more responsive to ration-card-program subsidies in urban areas than in rural areas. Possible explanations here are related to differences in household availability of subsidized calories and individual calorie expenditures. Rural families have, on average, lower calorie consumption from subsidized rice, sugar, and cooking oil than urban households do, and there are fewer families with very high subsidy levels in rural areas than in urban areas, given that the per capita quotas of rural beneficiary households exceed the number of actual household members less often than among urban households (Table 3.4).[18] In addition, children in rural areas may be more physically active than their peers in urban areas and burn off relatively more surplus calories, including those ingested with the subsidized foods.

The dose-response function of the subsidy-level effect of the ration card program on the BMIs of mothers from urban beneficiary families follows an inverted, flattened bell-shaped curve, implying that mothers' BMIs tend to be lowest at medium subsidy levels (Figure 4.5). However, it should be noted that the confidence interval expands considerably toward both ends of the curve and that the shape of the curve is essentially determined by the interaction between the subsidy level and the GPS variable, indicating that there is large heterogeneity at low and high subsidy levels and that the effect at a particular subsidy level distinctly varies subject to the covariates.[19] Moreover, the average BMI at the lowest point of the curve equals 29.8, while a BMI of 30 or more identifies obesity—the extreme form of overweight. Hence, a possible interpretation of this result is that, above a certain level of overnutrition, additional cheap calories from subsidized foods may not lead to markedly more weight gains. Investigating the effect on nutritional status relative to a cutoff level may be more revealing in such a case.

Accordingly, the dose-response model estimation for maternal overweight among urban families shows that the probability of maternal overweight in urban areas increases with higher subsidy levels at large—but declining—margins (Figure 4.6). The dose-response function has sufficient goodness of fit, and the respective coefficient estimates of the subsidy-level variables are highly statistically significant.[20] Mothers from urban families with medium

18 See Table A.11 in the Appendix.

19 See Table A.28 in the Appendix.

20 See Table A.29 in the Appendix.

FIGURE 4.5 Dose-response functions for mother's BMI

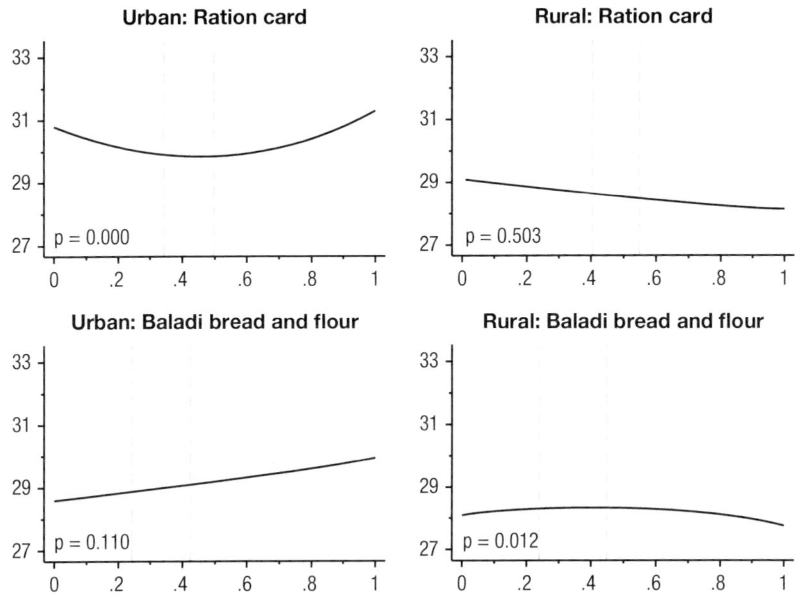

Source: Authors' estimation based on data from CAPMAS and WFP (2011).

Note: The y-axes indicate mothers' body mass indexes (BMIs), and the x-axes indicate household subsidy levels of the respective food subsidy programs in the respective residential areas.

p is the p-value of joint significance of the estimated dose-response function (Prob. > F). The gray-shaded area marks the 95 percent confidence interval. The vertical dashed lines mark the tertiles of the child samples, separating children from families with low, medium, and high subsidy levels.

or high subsidy levels have a risk of overweight that is on average more than 10 percentage points higher than the risk of mothers from urban families with low subsidy levels. Consistent with that, the respective ATT estimates above indicate that the average risk of maternal overweight is also significantly higher among urban beneficiaries than among urban nonbeneficiaries. Thus, we found strong evidence that the ration card program contributes to maternal overweight, in addition to child overweight, in urban areas.

The dose-response model estimations of the subsidy-level effects on mother's BMI and maternal overweight among rural beneficiary families yield coefficient estimates of the subsidy-level variables that are highly statistically insignificant, and the goodness of fit of the dose-response function for mother's BMI is far from being sufficient (Figure 4.5 and Figure 4.6). The seeming unresponsiveness of the maternal overnutrition indicators to ration-card-program subsidies in rural areas—as opposed to the responsiveness of the same indicators in urban areas—may be explained by overall lower consumption of

FIGURE 4.6 Dose-response functions for maternal overweight

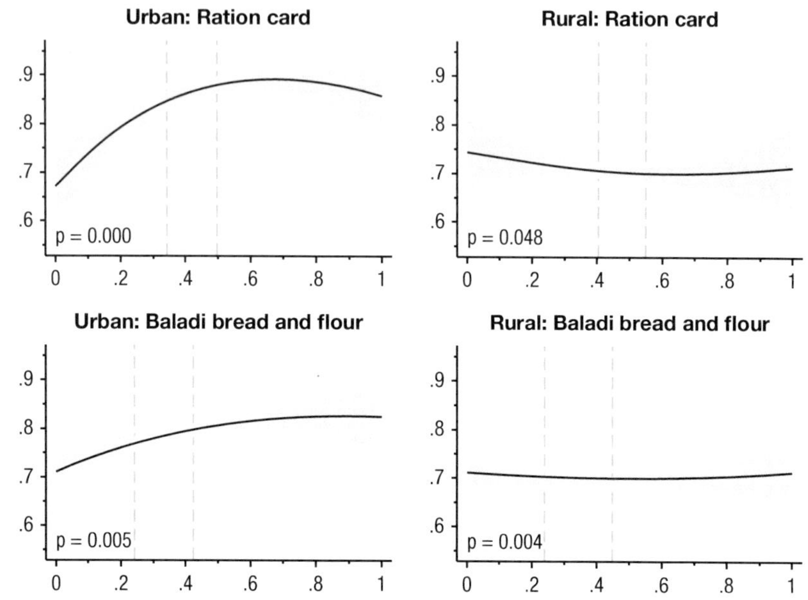

Source: Authors' estimation based on data from CAPMAS and WFP (2011).

Note: The y-axes indicate the probabilities of mothers being overweight, and the x-axes indicate household subsidy levels of the respective food subsidy programs in the respective residential areas.

p is the p-value of joint significance of the estimated dose-response function (Prob. > chi-sq.). The gray-shaded area marks the 95 percent confidence interval. The vertical dashed lines mark the tertiles of the child samples, separating children from families with low, medium, and high subsidy levels.

subsidized calories because of lower household per capita quotas as well as by higher individual calorie expenditures from physical activity, similar to the case of child overnutrition.

Consistent with the estimation result on child stunting and the estimation result on child overweight, the probability of stunting and overweight coexisting among children increases almost linearly with increasing subsidy levels of the ration card program among urban beneficiary families (at least across most of the subsidy range); among rural beneficiary families, it peaks at lower medium subsidy levels (Figure 4.7). Both dose-response functions have sufficient goodness of fit, and the coefficient estimates that define the shape of most of the curves are statistically significant.[21] Thus, the result for urban beneficiaries provides supportive evidence for our hypothesis that high

21 See Table A.30 in the Appendix.

FIGURE 4.7 Dose-response functions for child stunting and overweight

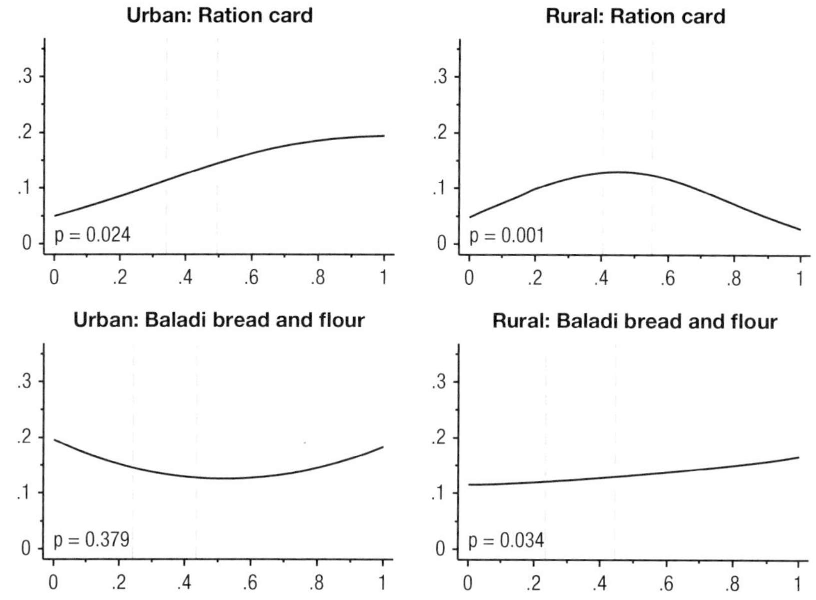

Source: Authors' estimation based on data from CAPMAS and WFP (2011).

Note: The y-axes indicate the probabilities of children being stunted and overweight at the same time, and the x-axes indicate household subsidy levels of the respective food subsidy programs in the respective residential areas.

p is the p-value of joint significance of the estimated dose-response function (Prob. > chi-sq.). The gray-shaded area marks the 95 percent confidence interval. The vertical dashed lines mark the tertiles of the child samples, separating children from families with low, medium, and high subsidy levels.

ration-card-program subsidies increase the risk of the double burden of malnutrition at the individual level—precisely among young children living in urban areas. Yet the average risk of the double burden of child malnutrition tends to be insignificantly lower among beneficiaries compared to nonbeneficiaries, as the respective ATT estimates above show. Hence, again, it is the received subsidy amounts that matter rather than the ration-card-program participation per se. Although statistically significant, the result for the effect on the double burden of child malnutrition among rural beneficiary families offers little insight, considering that the estimations for the effects on child under- and overnutrition separately produced no clear results.

The dose-response function estimation of the subsidy-level effect of the ration card program on the double burden of malnutrition at the family level among urban beneficiaries yields insufficient goodness of fit that disallows strong interpretation of the estimation result (Figure 4.8). Still, the coefficient

FIGURE 4.8 Dose-response functions for child stunting and maternal overweight

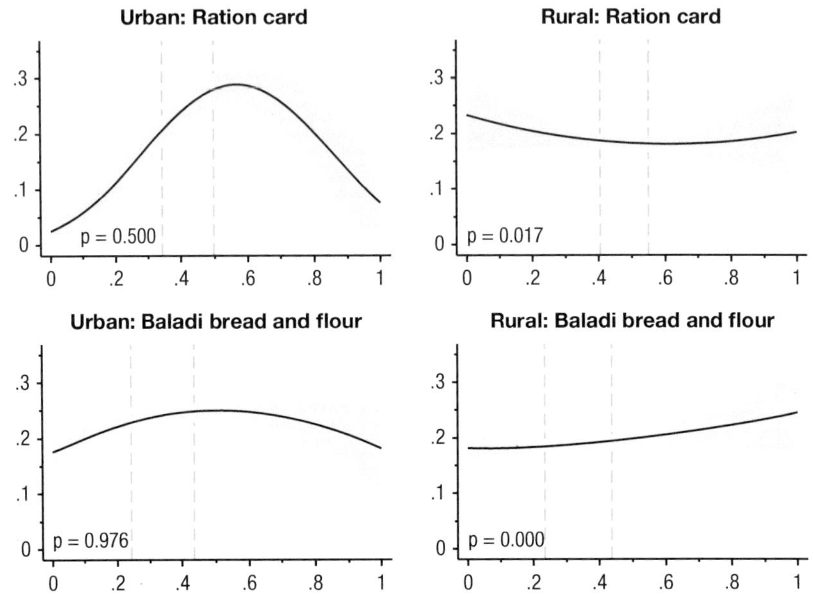

Source: Authors' estimation based on data from CAPMAS and WFP (2011).

Note: The y-axes indicate the probabilities of children being stunted and their mothers being overweight, and the x-axes indicate household subsidy levels of the respective food subsidy programs in the respective residential areas.

p is the p-value of joint significance of the estimated dose-response function (Prob. > chi-sq.). The gray-shaded area marks the 95 percent confidence interval. The vertical dashed lines mark the tertiles of the child samples, separating children from families with low, medium, and high subsidy levels.

estimate of the subsidy-level variable in quadratic form—defining the bell-shaped curve—is statistically significant.[22] The shape of the curve implies that the probability of child stunting and maternal overweight tends to be highest among urban families with medium-high subsidy levels and lower among urban families with low and very high subsidy levels.

The dose-response function for the ration-card-program subsidy-level effect on the double burden of malnutrition at the family level indicates no clear tendency among rural beneficiaries. There is only a slight tendency toward child stunting and maternal overweight being least probable at upper-medium subsidy levels. Although statistically significant, the result is not supported by clear results from the estimations of the subsidy-level effects on child stunting and on maternal overweight as separate indicators, so it should not be over-interpreted. Thus, neither the dose-response model

22 See Table A.31 in the Appendix.

FIGURE 4.9 Dose-response functions for child overweight and maternal overweight

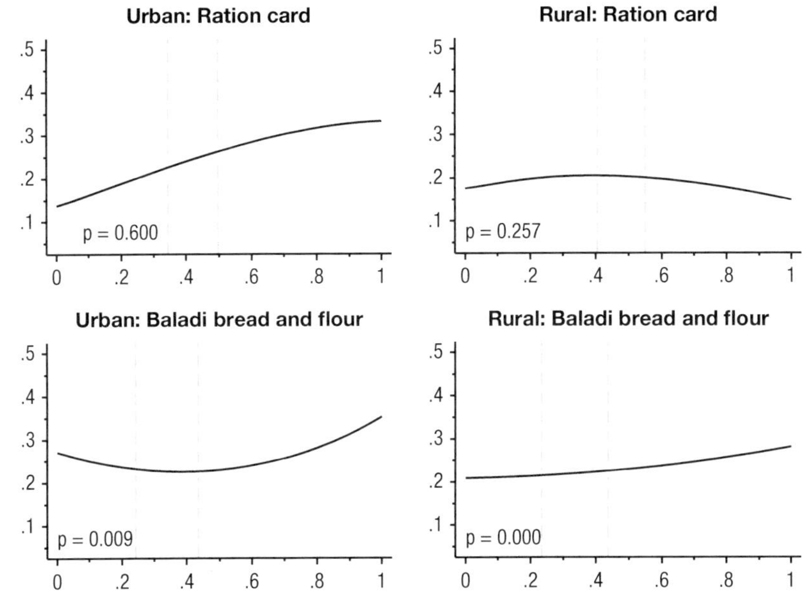

Source: Authors' estimation based on data from CAPMAS and WFP (2011).

Note: The y-axes indicate the probabilities of children being overweight and their mothers being overweight, and the x-axes indicate household subsidy levels of the respective food subsidy programs in the respective residential areas.

p is the p-value of joint significance of the estimated dose-response function (Prob. > chi-sq.). The gray-shaded area marks the 95 percent confidence interval. The vertical dashed lines mark the tertiles of the child samples, separating children from families with low, medium, and high subsidy levels.

estimations for the subsidy-level effects of the ration card program nor the PSM estimations for program participation provide supportive evidence for our hypothesis that the ration card program directly contributes to chronic undernutrition among children and overnutrition among their mothers at the same time.

For the subsidy-level effects on the coexistence of child and maternal overnutrition among urban and rural beneficiary families, the dose-response model estimations yield functions with insufficient goodness-of-fit measures and statistically insignificant coefficient estimates of the subsidy-level variables (Figure 4.9).[23] Nevertheless, the tendency of markedly increasing probability of child and maternal overweight with increasing subsidy levels among urban beneficiary families is consistent with the tendencies found for estimations of the effects on child overweight and maternal overweight as

23 See Table A.32 in the Appendix.

separate indicators. It is also consistent with the result from the corresponding PSM estimation, according to which the average risk of coexisting child and maternal overweight tends to be higher among urban beneficiaries than urban nonbeneficiaries.

Poor household diet quality—both insufficient diversity across all main food groups and infrequent consumption of nutritious food groups—is a likely pathway by which food subsidies can adversely affect child nutrition and hence drive the double burden of malnutrition, as hypothesized. Therefore, the dose-response model estimations for the subsidy-level effects of the ration card program on household diet quality indicators can provide complementary evidence for our hypothesis. The estimation results should be understood in conjunction with the findings from the analysis of Engel curves (presented in the previous chapter), according to which beneficiary and nonbeneficiary families with similar per capita household incomes have similar consumption expenditures for nutritious food groups across the income distribution. However, as noted above, this comparative analysis did not account for different subsidy levels and fell short of demonstrating causality. The dose-response model estimations address these limitations and hence can provide evidence for the hypothesized substitution effects that may occur between subsidized foods and more nutritious, nonsubsidized foods and that increase with rising subsidy levels. This would provide an explanation for the increased incidence of both chronic child undernutrition and child and maternal overnutrition found at high subsidy levels among urban beneficiaries of the ration card program.

The dose-response model estimations for the subsidy-level effects on household dietary diversity among urban and rural beneficiary families do not provide conclusive insights, although the relevant coefficient estimates of the subsidy-level variables are statistically significant (Figure 4.10).[24] Both dose-response functions follow an inverted, flattened bell-shaped curve with the lowest diversity at medium subsidy levels. For urban ration cardholders, the confidence levels of the curve considerably increase toward low and high subsidy levels, so that the curve shape is insufficiently robust for identifying a clear tendency. For the effect on dietary diversity among rural beneficiaries, the estimation yielded insufficient goodness of fit of the dose-response function, restricting its interpretation. It is important to note that the average HDDS at any subsidy level among urban and rural beneficiaries is consistently high, varying only between 10 and 11—out of a maximum of 12. And, the average HDDS among nonbeneficiaries is even slightly higher than

24 See Table A.33 in the Appendix.

FIGURE 4.10 Dose-response functions for HDDS

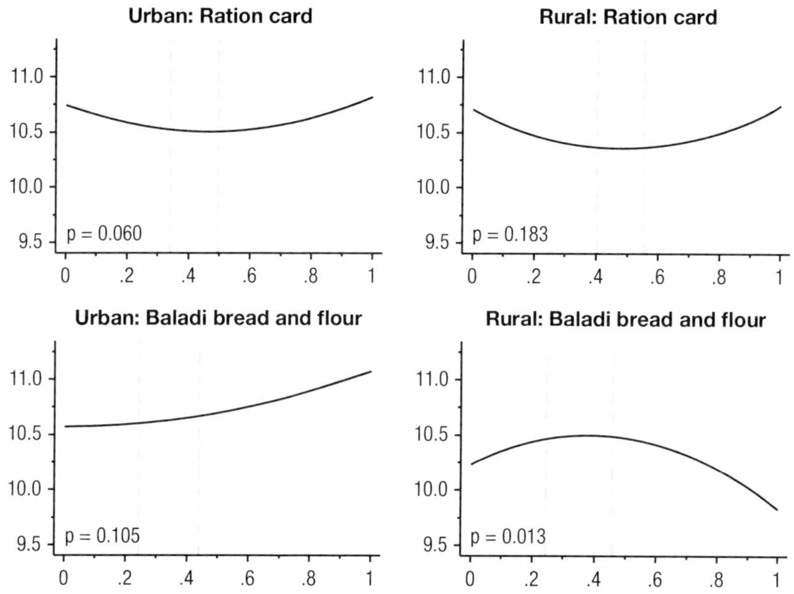

Source: Authors' estimation based on data from CAPMAS and WFP (2011).

Note: The y-axes indicate household dietary diversity scores (HDDSs), and the x-axes indicate household subsidy levels of the respective food subsidy programs in the respective residential areas.

p is the p-value of joint significance of the estimated dose-response function (Prob. > F). The gray-shaded area marks the 95 percent confidence interval. The vertical dashed lines mark the tertiles of the child samples, separating children from families with low, medium, and high subsidy levels.

among all beneficiaries, while its variance is quite low overall. Therefore, the HDDS alone appears to be a suboptimal indicator for assessing the effects of the ration card program on household diet quality, given the limitations of our data (Box 4.2).

The dose-response function estimations for the ration-card-program subsidy-level effects on the frequency of household consumption of nutritious food groups yield more revealing and statistically significant results—particularly for urban beneficiary families (Figure 4.11, Figure 4.12, Figure 4.13, and Figure 4.14). The goodness-of-fit measures of all dose-response functions are sufficient, except for legume consumption frequency among rural beneficiary families.[25] The estimation results indicate no clear tendency for the consumption frequency of other nutritious food groups among rural beneficiaries—similar to the results for most nutrition indicators.

25 See Tables A.34–A.37 in the Appendix.

FIGURE 4.11 Dose-response functions for frequency of household vegetable consumption

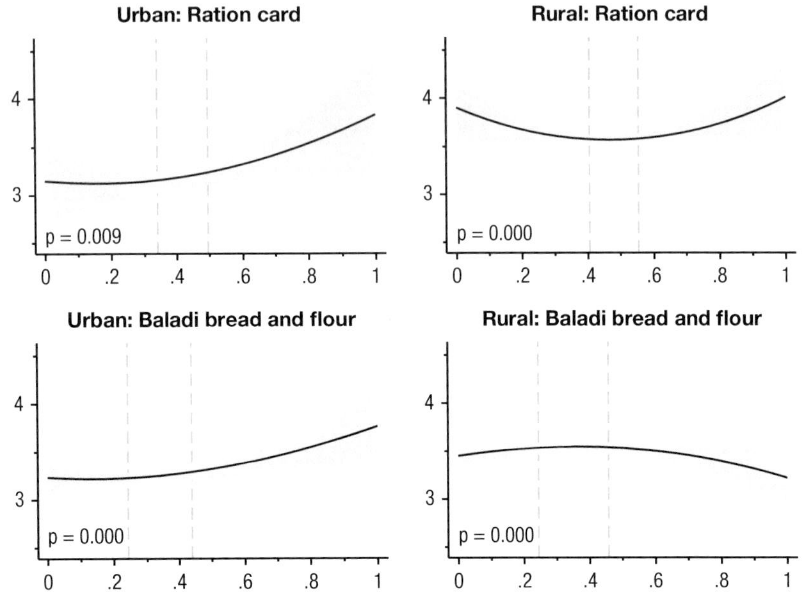

Source: Authors' estimation based on data from CAPMAS and WFP (2011).

Note: The y-axes indicate frequencies of household vegetable consumption, and the x-axes indicate household subsidy levels of the respective food subsidy programs in the respective residential areas.

p is the p-value of joint significance of the estimated dose-response function (Prob. > F). The gray-shaded area marks the 95 percent confidence interval. The vertical dashed lines mark the tertiles of the child samples, separating children from families with low, medium, and high subsidy levels.

In contrast, the estimation results for urban beneficiaries suggest that, with increasing subsidy levels, they consume vegetables slightly more frequently, but all other micronutrient-rich food groups—including legumes, meat and fish, and milk and dairy products—less frequently (which holds for legume consumption across most of the subsidy range but not for very high subsidy levels). Thus, these findings indeed confirm that urban beneficiaries of the ration card program substitute subsidized calorie-rich and micronutrient-poor foods for more nutritious foods and that this substitution effect increases with increasing subsidy levels, confirming our hypothesis. Animal-source products and legumes are rich in those absorbable micronutrients—especially zinc—and proteins that are important for children's physical and mental development and for preventing child stunting. Therewith, the findings provide an explanation for a likely pathway through which the Egyptian ration card program contributes not only to child and maternal overnutrition but also to chronic child undernutrition in urban areas.

FIGURE 4.12 Dose-response functions for frequency of household legume consumption

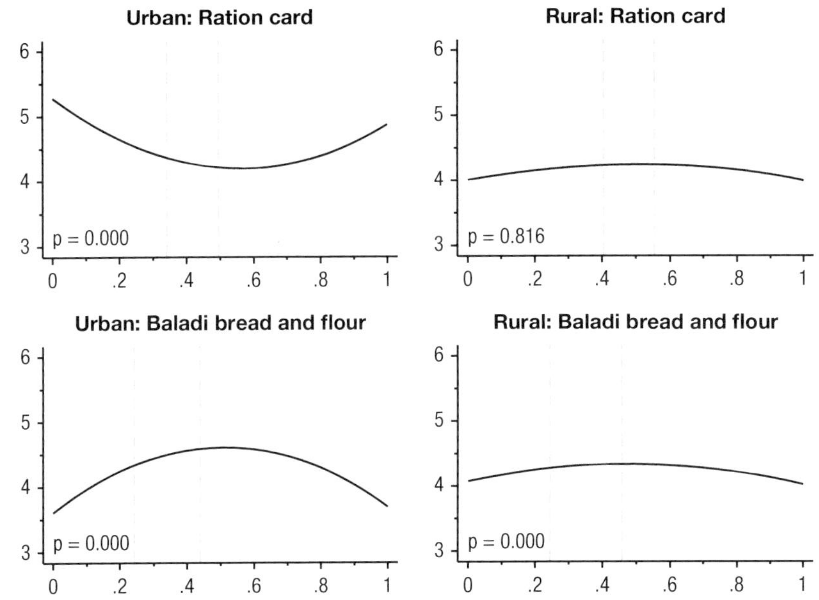

Source: Authors' estimation based on data from CAPMAS and WFP (2011).

Note: The y-axes indicate frequencies of household legume consumption, and the x-axes indicate household subsidy levels of the respective food subsidy programs in the respective residential areas.

p is the p-value of joint significance of the estimated dose-response function (Prob. > F). The gray-shaded area marks the 95 percent confidence interval. The vertical dashed lines mark the tertiles of the child samples, separating children from families with low, medium, and high subsidy levels.

Although the frequency of vegetable consumption among urban beneficiaries slightly increases with increasing subsidy levels, it is on average lower among urban beneficiaries than nonbeneficiaries, as the respective ATT estimates above show. The vegetable consumption frequency is generally low—among both beneficiaries and nonbeneficiaries as well as in urban and rural areas. On average, families consume vegetables on less than half of all days during one week, which is less frequently than they consume legumes and milk and dairy products. Such an infrequent vegetable consumption clearly falls short of healthy diet recommendations. Comparing the mean values and variations of the indicators of household dietary diversity and food group consumption frequency suggests that Egyptian diets tend to be inadequate in terms of the daily consumption of micronutrient-rich food groups, especially vegetables (although foods from almost all food groups are consumed over a period of one week, as the HDDS implies). Hence, the dietary shortfall seems to be a matter of low diversity of the regular meals, whereas weekend

FIGURE 4.13 Dose-response functions for frequency of household meat and fish consumption

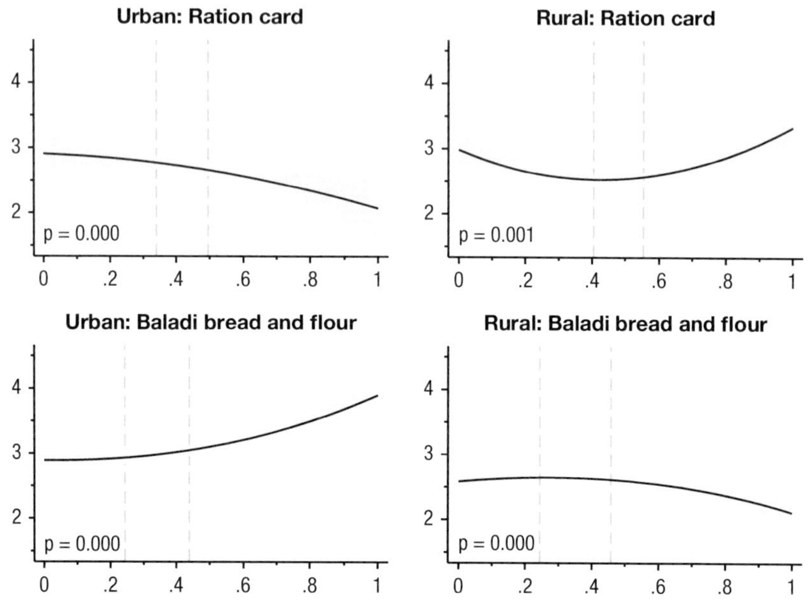

Source: Authors' estimation based on data from CAPMAS and WFP (2011).

Note: The y-axes indicate frequencies of household meat and fish consumption, and the x-axes indicate household subsidy levels of the respective food subsidy programs in the respective residential areas.

p is the p-value of joint significance of the estimated dose-response function (Prob. > F). The gray-shaded area marks the 95 percent confidence interval. The vertical dashed lines mark the tertiles of the child samples, separating children from families with low, medium, and high subsidy levels.

meals may be diverse in different foods, so the HDDS shows high overall dietary diversity.

Effects of Baladi Bread and Flour Subsidies

The goodness of fit of all GLM estimations of the GPS in the dose-response models for assessing the effects of Baladi bread and flour subsidies is decent (with Pearson scores between 0.20 and 0.26). These measures are higher than those in the dose-response models for assessing the effects of ration-card-program subsidies (possibly because of larger sample sizes).[26] The goodness-of-fit measures of the estimated dose-response functions are similarly low (with R-squared and pseudo R-squared scores of less than 0.13), but

26 Tables A.38–A.41 in the Appendix present the GLM results of the GPS estimates for Baladi bread and flour subsidies.

FIGURE 4.14 **Dose-response functions for frequency of household milk and dairy products consumption**

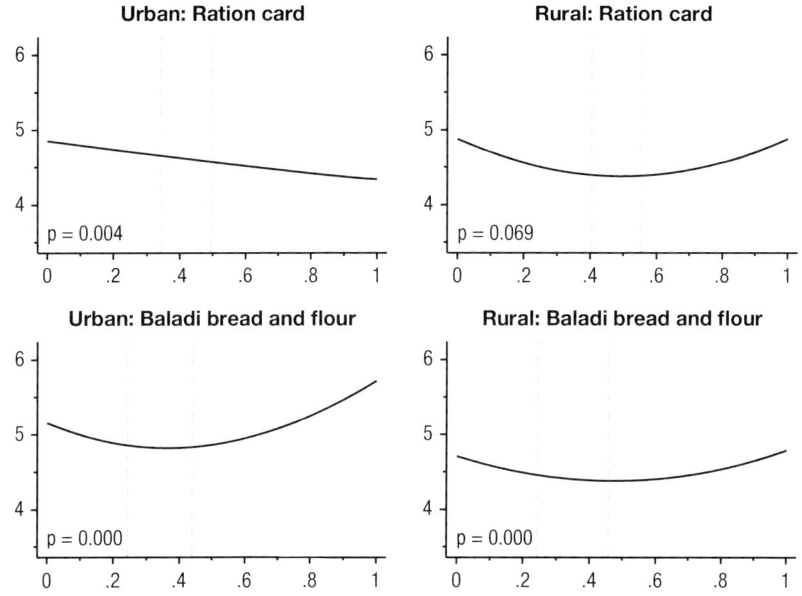

Source: Authors' estimation based on data from CAPMAS and WFP (2011).

Note: The y-axes indicate frequencies of household milk and dairy products consumption, and the x-axes indicate household subsidy levels of the respective food subsidy programs in the respective residential areas.

p is the p-value of joint significance of the estimated dose-response function (Prob. > F). The gray-shaded area marks the 95 percent confidence interval. The vertical dashed lines mark the tertiles of the child samples, separating children from families with low, medium, and high subsidy levels.

they are slightly higher for the dose-response functions of the effects on food group consumption frequency among rural families.[27]

Unlike the ration card program, the Baladi bread and flour program affects child nutrition primarily in rural areas, if at all. The goodness-of-fit measures of all dose-response functions of the effects on child over- or under-nutrition in urban areas are insufficient, and all coefficient estimates of the subsidy-level variables are statistically insignificant, disallowing strong interpretation of the results. In addition, they do not indicate any clear tendency for child nutrition in urban areas.

The dose-response function of the subsidy-level effect on child HAZ in rural areas indicates that a child's body height (relative to age) tends to

27 Tables A.42–A.55 in the Appendix present the dose-response function estimates for the effects of Baladi bread and flour subsidies.

decrease with increasing Baladi bread and flour subsidy levels at slightly declining margins (Figure 4.1). However, the probability of child stunting in rural areas is quite unresponsive to different subsidy levels, as the respective dose-response functions show (Figure 4.2). Both dose-response functions have statistically significant coefficient estimates of the subsidy-level variables, but the goodness of fit of the function for the effect on child HAZ is insufficient.[28]

The Baladi bread and flour program also seems to contribute to child overnutrition in rural areas. Child BMIZ tends to linearly increase with increasing subsidy levels (Figure 4.3), and the probability of child overnutrition tends to rise especially among families with high subsidy levels (Figure 4.4). However, it should be noted that the coefficient estimates of the subsidy-level variables in both dose-response functions are statistically insignificant (at common levels), and the goodness of fit of the function for the effect on child overweight is insufficient, too.[29]

Like the ration card program, the Baladi bread and flour program affects maternal overnutrition among urban families, whereas mothers' BMIs and the probability of maternal overweight among rural families are unresponsive to different levels of the Baladi bread and flour subsidy (Figure 4.5 and Figure 4.6).[30] The dose-response functions indicate that both mothers' BMIs and the probability of maternal overweight in urban areas tend to (almost) linearly increase with increasing subsidy levels. Thus, our estimation results consistently show that maternal overnutrition among urban families in Egypt is partly caused by food subsidies from both subsidy programs, while the effect of the ration card program on maternal overweight appears to be larger than that of the Baladi bread and flour program.

The double burden of malnutrition at the individual and the family levels in rural areas is largely unresponsive to different subsidy levels of the Baladi bread and flour program (Figure 4.7 and Figure 4.8). This also holds true for the incidence of child and maternal overweight in the same family in rural areas (Figure 4.9). These results are robust and consistent with the estimation results for child stunting and child and maternal overweight among rural families. In contrast, low goodness-of-fit measures and statistically insignificant coefficient estimates of the subsidy-level variables do not permit any interpretation of the dose-response functions of the subsidy-level effects on the double

28 See Tables A.42 and A.43 in the Appendix.

29 See Tables A.44 and A.45 in the Appendix.

30 See Tables A.46 and A.47 in the Appendix.

burden of malnutrition at the individual and the family levels in urban areas.[31] Thus, we do not find evidence to support our hypothesis that Baladi bread and flour subsidies contribute directly to the double burden of malnutrition. The dose-response function of the subsidy-level effect of the Baladi bread and flour program on the probability of coexisting child and maternal overweight in urban areas indicates a slightly decreasing probability up to a medium subsidy level and then a slightly increasing probability at higher subsidy levels.[32] However, this result is at best only weakly supported by the estimation results for child overweight and maternal overweight among urban families.

Keeping the aforementioned limitations of the HDDS in the context of this analysis in mind, we see that the dose-response function of the subsidy-level effect of the Baladi bread and flour program on household dietary diversity indicates a notable and statistically significant tendency for rural families.[33] It indicates that dietary diversity among rural families first slightly increases up to a medium subsidy level and decreases with higher subsidy levels at higher margins (Figure 4.10). According to that, there is an optimal, medium level for Baladi bread and flour subsidies in terms of their beneficial effect on household dietary diversity, while low subsidies have a less adverse dietary effect than high subsidies. Hence, above a certain subsidy level, higher amounts of cheap bread and flour tend to crowd out other—perhaps more nutritious—food groups and thereby likely contribute to overall unbalanced diets among rural families. The dose-response function of the subsidy-level effect on household dietary diversity among urban families indicates a tendency toward increasing dietary diversity with increasing subsidy levels. This tendency is not robust, however, given insignificant coefficient estimates of the subsidy-level variables. It should be noted that rural families have a significantly lower HDDS than that of urban families, and the indicator's variance is larger among rural families, which may help finding statistically significant results.

The dose-response model estimations for the subsidy-level effects of the Baladi bread and flour program on household consumption frequency of nutritious food groups yields ambiguous results. The frequencies of vegetable consumption and meat and fish consumption tend to slightly increase among urban families and slightly decrease among rural families at high (or medium-high) subsidy levels (Figure 4.11 and Figure 4.13). Yet the coefficient

31 See Tables A.48 and A.49 in the Appendix.

32 See Table A.50 in the Appendix.

33 See Table A.51 in the Appendix.

estimates of the subsidy-level variables are statistically insignificant in the dose-response functions for the effects among urban families.[34] At low and medium subsidy levels, the Baladi bread and flour program contributes to more frequent legume consumption among urban families; at high subsidy levels, however, the program contributes to less frequent legume consumption among urban families (Figure 4.12). The frequency of legume consumption among rural families seems to be unresponsive to different subsidy levels. Among both urban and rural families, the frequency of milk and dairy products consumption slightly decreases with increasing Baladi bread and flour subsidy levels across most of the subsidy range and increases only at very high subsidy levels again (Figure 4.14).

Overall, we found few consistent responses in the nutrition and diet quality indicators to different subsidy levels of the Baladi bread and flour program—with the important exceptions of child overnutrition among rural families and maternal overnutrition among urban families. Given that we did not find clear evidence for the effects of Baladi bread and flour subsidies on chronic child undernutrition, the dose-response estimations for the effects on household diet quality indicators have limited explanatory potential for the possible pathway through which these food subsidies could affect that nutrition outcome. In this sense, the ambiguous results of the dose-response model estimations for the effects on household diet quality are consistent with those for the effects on child stunting and the double burden of malnutrition at the individual and the family levels. A possible explanation for the disparity in the responsiveness of nutrition and diet quality indicators to the subsidies from the ration card program (among urban families) and the Baladi bread and flour program may relate to the fundamental differences in the design of the two programs (discussed in the previous chapter). Probably most crucially, Baladi bread is indeed an inferior good—unlike subsidized rice, sugar, and cooking oil. Further, the lack of (self-)targeting of the ration-card-program subsidies to the people in need and the selection of subsidized foods misaligned with people's real nutritional needs are what drive adverse nutritional outcomes.

34 See Tables A.51–A.55 in the Appendix.

Chapter 5

CONCLUSIONS

This study shows that Egypt faces two major nutritional challenges that are public health concerns and have critical, long-term implications for development and economic prosperity. Global comparisons indicate that both the double burden of malnutrition and the nutrition-growth disconnect are extremely pronounced in Egypt and were on the rise at least during the first decade of the 2000s. Considering the associated losses in development potential and economic costs for malnourished people and the general public, firm political commitment and comprehensive policy actions are needed to address these nutritional challenges effectively.

Egypt's exceptionalism in these nutritional challenges has likely been driven by a combination of four important interacting factors. The first factor is relatively rapid shifts in people's dietary patterns and lifestyles associated with the nutrition transition—a phenomenon present in many middle-income countries. The second factor is rising poverty due to the succession of economic crises in the 2000s and resulting adjustments in poor people's consumption patterns. The third factor is persistent underinvestment in nutrition-sensitive communal infrastructure and effective public services, in particular, healthcare, including specific interventions for child and maternal nutrition. The fourth factor is Egypt's large food subsidy system—the focus of our main empirical analysis. Egypt's own history of food subsidies, as well as evidence from the food economics literature, suggests that food price policies influence people's food consumption behavior and hence their nutritional status. Setting the right economic incentives at appropriate scale can do a great deal to reduce malnutrition, but unfavorable policies can further aggravate the nutritional challenges.

Although the purpose of the Egyptian food subsidy system has never been to influence nutrition, the market interventions and associated consumption incentives, in combination with the nutrition transition phenomenon, may have led to shifts in household diets toward more calorie-rich foods and less micronutrient-rich foods. The distortion of consumer preferences toward higher calorie intakes and less balanced diets may have been further aggravated in the course of the succession of economic crises in the 2000s, due to high food price inflation and volatility. Unlike open-market foods, the subsidized foods (Baladi bread and flour, rice, sugar, and cooking oil) were unaffected because their prices remained fixed at constant levels throughout. Hence, these calorie-rich foods became cheaper in real terms over time, and the household quotas of rice, sugar, and cooking oil—subsidized under the ration card program—were raised in response to the economic crises.

Ubiquitous household food insecurity, scarcity of basic foods in local markets, and volatile food prices during and after World War II prompted the government to introduce (temporary) food subsidies. Nowadays, this rationale is obsolete. The high prevalence of overweight and obesity along with still widespread chronic child undernutrition calls for a reorientation of Egypt's social safety net. Such a reorientation would include reforming the food subsidy system. In the past, nutritional concerns seem to have hardly played a relevant role in discussions on food subsidy reforms in Egypt. The reform debate has been mainly focused on the fiscal sustainability of the system, the presumed impact on household poverty, and potential implications for social stability. Discussions of the system's possible nutritional implications may have been neglected to some extent because of a lack of empirical evidence, which this study aimed to address.

In addition to documenting Egypt's current nutritional challenges and studying their likely key drivers, our empirical analysis investigated the hypothesized direct effects of the food subsidy system on child and maternal malnutrition in detail. The impact evaluation served to identify potential causal effects of the ration-card-program subsidies and the Baladi bread and flour program subsidies on various indicators of under- and overnutrition and their coexistence at individual and family levels. Identifying these causal relationships can provide fundamental evidence supporting (or disproving) our main hypothesis that Egypt's food subsidy system has been ineffective in reducing chronic child undernutrition and may rather have contributed to sustaining and even aggravating the double burden of malnutrition and the nutrition-growth disconnect. Fundamental to this hypothesis is that individuals' nutritional status responds negatively—or, at least, not positively—to the subsidies that their households receive.

Instead of analyzing only whether program participation affects nutritional outcomes or not, we were particularly interested in exploring the dose-response relationships that indicate the change in average nutritional outcomes due to changes in food subsidy levels. Such findings might be of greater value for policymakers concerned with reforming the food subsidy programs than findings that only allow inferences about situations with and without the programs. Because food subsidies are likely to directly affect child nutrition through the effects on their diets, we complemented our nutrition-focused analysis with two types of household diet quality indicators. They include indicators of household dietary diversity and the consumption frequency of food groups that are critical in child nutrition and for micronutrient adequacy in particular. Also, beyond its direct nutritional effect through food consumption, the food subsidy system may have contributed to Egypt's nutritional challenges through its heavy burden on the public budget. The funds that have been allocated to the food subsidy system have been unavailable for possibly more nutrition-beneficial investments. Our study refrained from estimating the potential effects through this pathway, due to a lack of appropriate data.

Summary of Main Findings

Overall, our estimation results suggest that the ration card program considerably affects under- and overnutrition, mainly in urban areas. The Baladi bread and flour program has notable effects on overnutrition in both urban and rural areas. The nutritional effects of the ration card program are generally larger than those of the Baladi bread and flour program. Our estimations provide no statistically significant indication that higher food subsidies lead to improved nutritional outcomes. On the contrary, we found that higher food subsidies increase the risk of malnutrition among both children and their mothers, especially the risk of overnutrition. In urban areas, the probability of child overweight and the probability of maternal overweight increase with the subsidy levels that the families acquire from the ration card program. Children and mothers from urban families with ration cards tend to also have higher average BMIZ and BMI than their peers from urban families without ration cards. In addition, mothers' BMIs and their risk of overweight tend to increase with increasing Baladi bread and flour subsidies among urban families. In rural areas, Baladi bread and flour subsidies seem to contribute to increasing BMIZs of children and their risk of overweight, especially at high subsidy levels.

Related to chronic child undernutrition, our dose-response model estimations yielded statistically insignificant results for urban areas and functions that indicate no clear tendency for rural areas. The results from the dose-response model estimations for the subsidy-level effects of the ration card program in urban areas are noteworthy, however, because they provide a consistent picture in combination with other, statistically significant estimation results. They indicate that the HAZs of children from urban families with higher ration card subsidy levels is much lower, and their probability of being stunted much higher, than among their peers from urban families with lower subsidy levels. Consistent with this and the finding on the risk of child overweight, the estimated dose-response function of the effects on the double burden of child malnutrition suggests that the probability of children being stunted and overweight at the same time significantly increases with increasing ration-card-program subsidy levels among urban beneficiaries. Nevertheless, on average, children from urban beneficiary families tend to have higher HAZs and a lower probability of stunting, as well as higher BMIZs without an increased probability of overweight, compared to children from urban nonbeneficiary families.

Taken together, these results suggest that participation in the ration card program per se has no uniformly adverse effect on urban children's nutrition; it is the acquired subsidy level in high-beneficiary families that leads to increased risks of chronic undernutrition, overnutrition, and the double burden at the child level. At the same time, the ration card program contributes to maternal overnutrition among urban families, with an increasing risk of overweight at increasing subsidy levels. However, none of our estimations provide sufficiently robust results for an increased risk of the double burden of malnutrition at the family level caused by the food subsidies.

The findings on child malnutrition in urban areas are supported by our results from the estimations on household diet quality. The PSM estimations for ration-card-program participation suggest that household dietary diversity and the frequencies of vegetable consumption and meat and fish consumption tend to be lower, on average, among urban beneficiaries than urban nonbeneficiaries. Further, the results from the dose-response model estimations show that the frequencies of meat and fish consumption, milk and dairy product consumption, and legume consumption (for the most part) decrease with increasing subsidy levels among urban beneficiaries of the ration card program.

Thus, the ration card program seems to indeed adversely affect child nutrition in urban areas by incentivizing a diet that is too laden in calorie-rich foods; unbalanced across food groups; and lacks micronutrient-rich foods, which impair normal physical growth. With increasing subsidy levels of the ration card program, urban beneficiaries seem to increasingly substitute expensive, nonstaple foods that are important for child nutrition with calorie-rich and micronutrient-poor foods mainly made from cheap, subsidized sugar and rice. Lower child HAZ and higher probability of child stunting among families with high subsidy levels may therefore be explained by reduced consumption of animal-source foods, legumes, and (some) vegetables—foods that are all rich sources of critical micronutrients, especially zinc, and high-quality protein. These substitution effects were likely fueled by rising prices of these foods in the course of the economic crises in the 2000s and the government's decision to hold the prices of the subsidized foods constant and to even increase ration card quotas to help beneficiary households to cope with real income losses from price increases of open-market goods. Such substitution effects were also found by previous studies based on other household survey data from Egypt (Kavle et al. 2015a; Ramadan and Thomas 2011).

Our estimation results also suggest that child and maternal nutrition indicators in rural areas are largely unresponsive to food subsidies from both programs, except for child overnutrition in response to Baladi bread and flour subsidies. Regarding household diet quality in rural areas, we found the strongest effect for household dietary diversity in response to Baladi bread and flour subsidies. The dose-response function indicates that the diversity of rural families' diets first slightly increases with increasing subsidy levels up to a medium level and decreases with higher levels at higher margins. According to that, there is an optimal, medium level for Baladi bread and flour subsidies in terms of their beneficial effects on household dietary diversity, while low subsidies have less adverse dietary effects than high subsidies. However, we do not find robust evidence that this or other, less strong dietary effects are reflected in child undernutrition indicators in rural areas, so the explanatory potential of inadequate household diet quality as a possible pathway of the hypothesized nutritional effects is limited here.

In conclusion, the results of our empirical analysis provide supportive evidence for our hypothesis that the food subsidy system has been ineffective in reducing chronic undernutrition and has contributed to aggravating the double burden of malnutrition and probably the growth-nutrition disconnect in Egypt. In combination with other developments in recent decades, Egypt's large food subsidies can help to explain the country's exceptionalism in the global comparison in terms of these nutritional challenges to some extent (although data limitations prevent quantifying the precise contribution). Indeed, Egypt is not the only country with a long and continuing history of large food subsidies; another one is India. India's PDS dates from the beginning of World War II and is quite similar to Egypt's ration card program (Measham and Chatterjee 1999; Mooij 1998). Since 1997, the Targeted PDS (TPDS) provides rations of staple food grains (rice and wheat), sugar, and cooking oil to ration cardholders through a network of public distribution shops (Grosh et al. 2008; Jha et al. 2013; Tarozzi 2005). The TPDS has been found to fail in targeting the majority of the (officially) poor and to be ineffective in improving household food insecurity and reducing child undernutrition (Jha et al. 2013; Kochar 2005; Svedberg 2012; Tarozzi 2005). Yet the coverage of India's TPDS has been much smaller than Egypt's food ration card program (24.4 percent household coverage in India compared to 58.5 percent of Egyptian households with ration cards in 2004–2005, and 68.4 percent of Egyptian households in early 2011)—as well as the share of food subsidies in national GDP (0.7 percent in India compared to 1.8 percent in Egypt in 2008 and 2.4 percent in Egypt in 2010–2011) (Al-Shawarby and El-Laithy 2010; Svedberg 2012; see above). However, India resembles Egypt in that progress in reducing chronic undernutrition has been slow, despite high rates of economic growth (Deaton and Drèze 2009; Stevens et al. 2012; Subramanyam et al. 2010).

Our empirical findings consistently suggest that—from a nutritional perspective—primarily Egypt's ration card program, especially in urban areas, needed major changes to reduce the incentives to overconsume calorie-rich and unbalanced diets. The ration card program had stronger adverse effects on child and maternal nutrition than the Baladi bread and flour program, which may be explained by four crucial differences in the designs of the two programs:

> First, unlike Baladi bread, rice, sugar, and cooking oil do not seem to be inferior goods (at least among households with young children), so their consumption tends to increase with growing household incomes. Therefore, it cannot be assumed that non-poor households with ration cards forego utilizing their quotas for consuming these subsidized foods. In other words, hoping for self-targeting of the subsidies among ration-card-program beneficiaries is unrealistic. Restricting access to these subsidized foods (as has been done through allocation of ration cards) is necessary.

> Second, the ration card program (as in place until May 2014) was poorly targeted and provided food subsidies to most non-poor households, and the allotted per capita quotas were even higher among high-income beneficiary households than low-income beneficiary households—especially in urban areas. Hence, particularly households with no actual financial need were incentivized to overconsume subsidized rice, sugar, and cooking oil. Many of them also managed to acquire large per capita quotas.

Third, the selection of the foods to subsidize was contrary to the real nutritional needs of the vast majority of the Egyptian population—and probably even more contrary to the needs of the beneficiary population of the ration card program, which excluded one-third and one-fourth of the lowest income quintiles in urban and rural areas, respectively (Table 3.2). Child and maternal undernutrition from calorie deficiency has not been a prevalent nutritional problem in Egypt in recent years, as our descriptive analysis of the patterns of malnutrition shows.

Fourth, household per capita quotas of the subsidized foods—and therefore the availability of cheap calories—were larger, on average, among urban beneficiary households than rural beneficiary households. In contrast, individual calorie expenditures tend to be higher in rural areas because of higher physical activity levels from manual labor–intensive economic activities (in agriculture and related sectors) among adults, outdoor playtime activities for children, and less use of motorized means of transportation, among other reasons. Thus, in urban areas, higher availability of cheap calories coincide with lower physiological calorie requirements—leading to more excess calories.

Policy Implications

In addition to providing a strong nutritional rationale for reforming the Egyptian food subsidy system, our empirical analysis has six reform recommendations that emerge directly from it:

First, food subsidies for all (non-inferior) calorie-rich foods (subsidized under the ration card program) should be cut to reduce the incentives for their overconsumption. Instead, consumption of a variety of micronutrient-rich foods—and especially foods important for child nutrition—could be subsidized to increase the incentives for consuming nutritious and diverse diets.

Second, the fixed-quota scheme of the ration card program should be abolished to allow beneficiaries more flexibility in choosing foods according to their individual needs.

Third, the consumption of Baladi bread (and flour) should be restricted to reduce the incentive for its overconsumption if the Baladi bread and flour program as such is maintained.

Fourth, the fixed-price regime of the Egyptian food subsidy system should be phased out, and prices of subsidized foods should eventually be allowed to fully vary with open-market prices in order to avoid price distortions and related consumption incentives. This could be realized through switching to a voucher-based system like the Supplemental Nutrition Assistance Program (SNAP) of the United States. This system change would make subsidization of individual food items and differentiation to open-market products—as well as operation of a separate procurement and marketing system for subsidized products—redundant.

Fifth, household eligibility for food subsidies under the ration card program should be reviewed, and food subsidies—or, more generally, food assistance—should be better targeted to the needy population. Means tests could be used for targeting food assistance, and under- and overnutrition indicators should be considered, in addition to household wealth indicators.

Sixth, benefit differentiation corresponding to beneficiaries' neediness should be reintroduced. For example, Egypt could adopt a two-level system consisting of a high-assistance level, which includes a broad basket of subsidized products for the neediest beneficiaries, and a reduced-assistance level with a narrower basket limited to key nutritious foods, for the less needy beneficiaries.

Following the presidential election in May 2014, the new Egyptian government did begin to fundamentally reform the food subsidy system. The rapidly growing fiscal burden as well as the system's ineffectiveness as a social protection instrument and factor for social stability—rather than nutritional concerns—have likely motived the initiation of reform. Nevertheless, the revised food subsidy system shows notable modifications that can be expected to have nutrition-beneficial implications. The modifications already implemented are consistent with the reform recommendations emerging from our empirical analysis but still fall short of most of them.

The changes made to the food ration program with expected positive dietary effects are the transition from food quantity–based quotas to cash assistance for selected food and nonfood products and the expansion of the subsidized food basket. Removing the fixed quotas for rice, sugar, and cooking oil reduced—but did not eliminate—the incentives to overconsume these calorie-rich foods, especially considering that the quotas under the old program were well above recommendations for healthy diets. Rice, sugar, and cooking oil remain in the subsidized consumption basket, and other foods rich in carbohydrates and dietary fat were added, including rice of higher quality, pasta, other cooking oils, and shortening.[1] The issuance of cash allotments and the expansion of the basket of subsidized foods allow beneficiaries to choose the commodities with greater concern for their dietary needs and to select somewhat more micronutrient-rich foods such as lentils, fava beans, meat, chicken, fish, milk, and cheese.

The new subsidy system restricts purchases of Baladi bread to holders of subsidy cards and is entirely based on electronic smart cards. This system provides a basis for implementing improved targeting to the households in (food) need; it also offers the technical flexibility to easily align the amount of cash assistance with the level of beneficiaries' neediness. Limiting the number of handed-out Baladi bread loaves and allowing for substitution of the unused bread rations with other subsidized commodities reduce the incentives of Baladi bread overconsumption (and waste) and enable beneficiaries to acquire larger quantities of more micronutrient-rich and calorie-lean foods at subsidized prices. Recently, the Egyptian government also began to take first steps to reduce the number of holders of subsidy cards by appealing to people's social responsibility and asking them to hand in unneeded subsidy cards voluntarily. Yet the regime of fixed prices and the government-controlled procurement and marketing system for subsidized products remain in place.

Potential next reform steps to make the current system more nutrition sensitive include eliminating the remaining adverse dietary incentives and creating more nutrition-beneficial ones, introducing under- and overnutrition indicators as eligibility criteria, utilizing the system for food fortification programs, and complementing it with nutrition awareness campaigns and nutrition education programs. Perhaps most critically, the new system still incentivizes consumption of calorie-rich diets, and the revised basket of subsidized foods now includes even relatively superior sources of carbohydrates and dietary fat, such as rice of higher quality, pasta, and varieties of cooking oil and shortening. It also includes non-nutritious nonessentials such as chicken bouillon, instant coffee, and black tea. In contrast, the consumption of micronutrient-rich fresh vegetables and fruits—critical for child nutrition in particular—is not subsidized. Similarly, infant formula—an expensive but vital product for nonbreastfed infants and young toddlers—is excluded from the subsidized food basket. Poor households are not able to regularly afford

1 See Table A.9 in the Appendix.

high-quality formula, which may also contribute to poor child nutrition to some extent.

Targeting food assistance based on under- and overnutrition indicators—in addition to household wealth indicators—as well as monitoring the system's effectiveness in terms of nutritional outcomes would certainly set a milestone. It would require that the Egyptian government commit, as an explicit goal of the food assistance system, to reducing malnutrition. For implementing a need-based allocation of food assistance at the subnational level, the required anthropometric data are available at least at the governorate level and in regular, multiyear intervals from the DHS. Anthropometric data for individual household members could be collected through the (reforming) public health system and possibly even be stored on the smart card, in addition to other eligibility criteria.

The subsidized foods provide excellent vehicles for fortification programs. The fortification of Baladi bread with iron and of oil with vitamin A should be resumed, and the coverage of the fortification program should be expanded to the entire country, while the stability of the added nutrients needs to be ensured. Expanding the fortification program to some of the newly subsidized foods, as well as fortification with additional micronutrients such as zinc, could be explored.

In addition to economic factors, key determinants of consumer food preferences include food habits and consumers' nutritional knowledge. As our Engel curve analysis shows, per capita consumption of sugars and edible oils and fats continuously increases with increasing household incomes among beneficiary and nonbeneficiary families of the ration card program—irrespective of widespread overweight and obesity. It implies that there is little consciousness of nutritional health—even among the rich, who are usually more educated. Nutrition awareness campaigns and nutrition education programs, particularly ones related to overnutrition, unhealthy diets, and "modern" food habits are needed. The high consumption of junk foods and sugary soft drinks—especially among young children—is of particular concern (Kavle et al. 2015b; Musaiger 2011). For example, sponge cakes and sugary biscuits are not perceived as unhealthy and are often considered as "ideal" common complementary foods for toddlers (Kavle et al. 2015b). Moreover, the implications of sedentary lifestyles for nutrition and health need to be debated publically, and physical activity should be promoted (Han et al. 2010; Musaiger and Al-Hazzaa 2012; Rahim et al. 2014; Mehio Sibai et al. 2010).

To develop effective complementary nutrition education programs, Egypt can draw from experiences in other countries with similar food assistance programs. For example, impact evaluation studies of various nutrition education interventions among SNAP beneficiary households in the United States show that professional nutrition education for both children and their parents in controlled environments (such as health centers) can be effective in improving children's diets at home (Williams et al. 2014, 2015). As with SNAP in the United States, several nutrition interventions should be tested and rigorously analyzed in order to identify the most effective and feasible ones to be implemented. Further down the road, making food assistance conditional on participation in nutrition education programs should be taken into consideration, and its feasibility explored.

The reform steps undertaken by the Egyptian government since June 2014 mark the beginning of the end of one of the world's oldest food subsidy systems. Nevertheless, the current voucher-based system may be only an intermediate solution toward a (conditional) cash transfer system, which has been shown to be most cost-effective in reducing poverty and food insecurity in developing countries (e.g., Grosh et al. 2008; Hidrobo et al. 2014; Rawlings and Rubio 2005). With this, Egypt would follow several other countries, including Algeria, Jordan, and Mexico, which shifted their social safety net from a food subsidy–based to a cash transfer–based system. The experiences in these countries may provide important lessons for a successful transition process in Egypt (Grosh et al. 2008). However, to the best of our knowledge, the nutritional effects of neither the reforms in these countries nor those in other developing countries that have had large food subsidy systems (in the past), such as Bangladesh, India, Iran, and Iraq, have been analyzed rigorously and comprehensively. The current literature also contains very little evidence of program impact evaluations that can help to assess the potential nutritional effects of different reform alternatives—especially in terms of their effects on overnutrition. This lack of evidence calls for more rigorous research in that direction, and Egypt has the opportunity to let research-based evidence guide the decisionmaking in future reform steps.

Although the transition from a food subsidy–based to a (conditional) cash transfer–based system may have helped to substantially reduce child and maternal undernutrition and to slow the double burden of malnutrition in other countries, having a conditional cash transfer program in place is no panacea. Using data from rural areas in southern Mexico, Leroy et al. (2014) show that increasing household wealth—possibly thanks to the national cash transfer program—is associated with an increased probability of coexisting child stunting and maternal overweight. However, the authors also show that maternal education effectively mitigates the negative nutritional effects of increasing household wealth. Hence, where maternal schooling is low, income support needs to be accompanied by formal female education and behavior change communication to effectively reduce child stunting and to protect women from unhealthy weight gain (Leroy et al. 2014). Consequently, independent of the present system of public assistance, education—and nutrition education in particular—is indispensable to effectively reduce the double burden of malnutrition and the growth-nutrition disconnect in Egypt.

Limitations and Research Implications

Finally, our main empirical analysis has several limitations emerging from the household survey data used and the methodology (which is conditioned by the available data) applied. Our findings should be understood under consideration of the study's limitations, which may also be motivation for follow-up research:

> First, no time-series household survey data are available for evaluating the effects of the Egyptian food subsidy system and its past reforms over time. Given that our estimation relies on cross-sectional data, for example, our results are likely to underestimate the long-term effects that may arise from the intergenerational transmission of malnutrition. For the same reason, we are unable to analyze the drivers of the observed growth-nutrition disconnect at the household level in greater detail.
>
> Second, because of a lack of respective survey questions, the HIECS data (CAPMAS and WFP 2011) do not allow (or insufficiently allow) for analyzing the nutritional effects of inadequate child and infant feeding practices, eating and lifestyle habits, diseases, and poor infrastructure and public service provision. Therefore, our analysis permits drawing precise conclusions on the nutritional effects of underinvestment in infrastructure; public services; and direct nutrition, health, and education interventions, as well as on the possible indirect nutritional effects of food subsidies through the allocation of the public budget.
>
> Third, the HIECS data fall short of the ideal set of variables for our impact evaluation analysis (which can probably only be obtained from a specialized survey). We made great efforts to minimize a potential bias due to unobservables in our PSM estimations. We acknowledge that the possibility of such a potential bias exists, but we also believe that even if there is such a possible bias, it is unlikely to compromise our main findings.

Fourth, although PSM methods are suited for assessing the changes in an outcome variable in response to a treatment or a treatment level, they fall short in explaining the mechanism through which the changes occur. Hence, we are unable to econometrically identify the precise impact pathways and to quantify the relative importance of the nutritional effects of the food subsidy system compared to (all) other potential effects. However, the results from the complementary estimations for the effects on household diet quality provide supportive evidence that food subsidies affect people's nutrition through incentivizing calorie-overladen and unbalanced diets. Our estimation results are also supported by the results from our Engel curve analysis and are consistent with evidence from the food and health economics literature—including studies from Egypt.

Fifth, the data that have been used and are currently available are unsuited for evaluating the nutritional and dietary effects of the ongoing reform. At least with respect to the evaluation of the reform's food consumption effects, the forthcoming data from the 2014–2015 HIECS, in combination with the 2010–2011 and 2012–2013 HIECSs, may overcome some of the data limitations. Part of the 2012–2013 and 2014–2015 HIECS sample is a panel of the households interviewed in the 2010–2011 HIECS, which would allow tracking their food consumption over time and identifying changes in consumption patterns. Yet neither the 2012–2013 HIECS nor the 2014–2015 HIECS include anthropometric measurements—essential for assessing the effects on nutritional outcomes—or diet-related questions. Thanks to the support from WFP, the existence of the food security and nutrition module complementing the basic 2010–2011 HIECS made our analysis possible and, at least for that reason, so unique and valuable.

Follow-up research that evaluates the impact of future reform steps on food consumption and nutritional outcomes may be of great value, particularly for policy makers who are in charge of the reform implementation. Properly designed research can inform the political decision-making process regarding, for example, the likely income, dietary, and nutritional implications of different reform alternatives and thereby help to create a more effective and possibly more nutrition-sensitive social safety net in Egypt. Experimental impact evaluation studies could be designed to examine the transition from voucher-based food assistance to cash transfers or the introduction of complementary nutrition education programs with and without conditionality.

Before implementing such substantial—and perhaps costly—reform steps on a large scale or even nationwide, they could be tested on a smaller scale and rigorously analyzed in order to assess their practicability, effectiveness, and social acceptance. Indeed, such research requires political intent and firm commitment by relevant governmental institutions to close collaboration in research implementation.

References

Abdelmegeid, A., A. Brasington, E. Sarriot, R. Taylor, N. Hassenien, O. Yehia, and A. Assran. 2015. *Maternal and Child Survival Program: Raedat Rafiat Assessment Report.* Cairo, Egypt: USAID.

Abegunde, D., C. Mathers, T. Adam, M. Ortegon, and K. Strong. 2007. "The Burden and Costs of Chronic Diseases in Low-Income and Middle-Income Countries." *Lancet* 370 (9603): 1929–1938.

Adams, R. 2000. "Self-Targeted Subsidies: The Political and Distributional Impact of the Egyptian Food Subsidy System." *Economic Development and Cultural Change* 49 (1): 115–136.

Adams, R., and J. Page. 2003. "Poverty, Inequality and Growth in Selected Middle East and North Africa Countries, 1980–2000." *World Development* 31 (12): 2027–2048.

Aguëro, J., M. Carter, and I. Woolard. 2006. *The Impact of Unconditional Cash Transfers on Nutrition: The South African Child Support Grant.* Working Paper 06/08. Cape Town: Southern Africa Labour and Development Research Unit.

Ahmed, A., and H. Bouis. 2002. "Weighing What's Practical: Proxy Means Tests for Targeting Food Subsidies in Egypt." *Food Policy* 27 (5): 519–540.

Ahmed, A., H. Bouis, T. Gutner, and H. Löfgren. 2001. *The Egyptian Food Subsidy System: Structure, Performance, and Options for Reform.* Research Report 119. Washington, DC: International Food Policy Research Institute.

Ahmed, S. 2014. "The Impact of Food and Global Economic Crises (2008) on Food Security in Egypt." *African and Asian Studies* 13 (1–2): 205–236.

Alderman, H. 1986. *The Effect of Food Price and Income Changes on the Acquisition of Food by Low-Income Households.* Washington, DC: International Food Policy Research Institute.

Alderman, H., and J. von Braun. 1984. *The Effects of the Egyptian Food Ration and Subsidy System on Income Distribution and Consumption.* Research Report 45. Washington, DC: International Food Policy Research Institute.

Alderman, H., J. von Braun, and S. Sakr. 1982. *Egypt's Food Subsidy and Rationing System: A Description*. Research Report 34. Washington, DC: International Food Policy Research Institute.

Ali, S., and R. Adams. 1996. "The Egyptian Food Subsidy System: Operation and Effects on Income Distribution." *World Development* 24 (11): 1777–1791.

Al-Shawarby, S., and H. El-Laithy. 2010. *Egypt's Food Subsidies: Benefit Incidence and Leakages*. Cairo, Egypt: World Bank.

Alwan, A., D. MacLean, L. Riley, E. d'Espaignet, C. Mathers, G. Stevens, and D. Bettcher. 2010. "Monitoring and Surveillance of Chronic Non-communicable Diseases: Progress and Capacity in High-Burden Countries." *Lancet* 376 (9755): 1861–1868.

Andrews, D., and M. Buchinsky. 2000. "A Three-Step Method for Choosing the Number of Bootstrap Repetitions." *Econometrica* 68 (1): 23–51.

Asfaw, A. 2006. "The Role of Food Price Policy in Determining the Prevalence of Obesity: Evidence from Egypt." *Review of Agricultural Economics* 28 (3): 305–312.

———. 2007a. "Do Government Food Price Policies Affect the Prevalence of Obesity? Empirical Evidence from Egypt." *World Development* 35 (4): 687–701.

———. 2007b. "Micronutrient Deficiency and the Prevalence of Mothers' Overweight/Obesity in Egypt." *Economics and Human Biology* 5 (3): 471–483.

Austin, A., A. Hill, and W. Fawzi. 2013. "Maternal Obesity Trends in Egypt 1995–2005." *Maternal and Child Nutrition* 9 (2): 167–179.

Austin, P. 2009. "Balance Diagnostics for Comparing the Distribution of Baseline Covariates between Treatment Groups in Propensity-Score Matched Samples." *Statistics in Medicine* 28 (25): 3083–3107.

Barker, D. 1988. "Childhood Causes of Adult Diseases." *Archives of Disease in Childhood* 63 (7): 867–869.

———. 2004. "The Developmental Origins of Adult Disease." *Journal of the American College of Nutrition* 23 (S6): 588S–595S.

———. 2012. "Developmental Origins of Chronic Disease." *Public Health* 126 (3): 185–189.

Beaton, G., R. Martorell, K. Aronson, B. Edmonston, G. McCabe, A. Ross, and B. Harvey. 1994. "Vitamin A Supplementation and Child Morbidity and Mortality in Developing Countries." *Food and Nutrition Bulletin* 15: 282–289.

Behrman, J., and A. Deolalikar. 1987. "Will Developing Country Nutrition Improve with Income? A Case Study for Rural South India." *Journal of Political Economy* 95 (3): 492–507.

Berhane, G., D. Gilligan, J. Hoddinott, N. Kumar, and A. Seyoum Taffesse. 2014. "Can Social Protection Work in Africa? The Impact of Ethiopia's Productive Safety Net Programme." *Economic Development and Cultural Change* 63 (1): 1–26.

Berti, P., J. Krasevec, and S. FitzGerald. 2004. "A Review of the Effectiveness of Agriculture Interventions in Improving Nutrition Outcomes." *Public Health Nutrition* 7 (5): 599–609.

Bhutta, Z., T. Ahmed, R. Black, S. Cousens, K. Dewey, E. Giugliani, B. Haider, et al. 2008. "What Works? Interventions for Maternal and Child Undernutrition and Survival." *Lancet* 371 (9610): 417–440.

Bhutta, Z., J. Das, A. Rizvi, M. Gaffey, N. Walker, S. Horton, P. Webb, A. Lartey, and R. Black. 2013. "Evidence-Based Interventions for Improvement of Maternal and Child Nutrition: What Can Be Done and at What Cost?" *Lancet* 382 (9890): 452–477.

Bia, M., and A. Mattei. 2008. "A Stata Package for the Estimation of the Dose-Response Function through Adjustment for the Generalized Propensity Score." *Stata Journal* 8 (3): 354–373.

Black, R., L. Allen, Z. Bhutta, L. Caulfield, M. de Onis, M. Ezzati, C. Mathers, and J. Rivera. 2008. "Maternal and Child Undernutrition: Global and Regional Exposures and Health Consequences." *Lancet* 371 (9608): 243–260.

Bleich, S., D. Cutler, C. Murray, and A. Adams. 2008. "Why Is the Developed World Obese?" *Annual Review of Public Health* 29: 273–295.

Bolbol, A., A. Fatheldin, and M. Omran. 2005. "Financial Development, Structure, and Economic Growth: The Case of Egypt, 1974–2002." *Research in International Business and Finance* 19 (1): 171–194.

Bove, I., T. Miranda, C. Campoy, R. Uauy, and M. Napol. 2012. "Stunting, Overweight and Child Development Impairment Go Hand in Hand as Key Problems of Early Infancy: Uruguayan Case." *Early Human Development* 88 (9): 747–751.

Branca, F., and M. Ferrari. 2002. "Impact of Micronutrient Deficiencies on Growth: The Stunting Syndrome." *Annals of Nutrition and Metabolism* 46 (S1): 8–17.

Breisinger, C., P. Al-Riffai, O. Ecker, R. Abuismail, J. Waite, N. Abdelwahab, A. Zohery, et al. 2013. *Tackling Egypt's Rising Food Insecurity in a Time of Transition*. Joint IFPRI-WFP Country Policy Note. Washington, DC: International Food Policy Research Institute; Cairo, Egypt: World Food Programme.

Breisinger, C., and O. Ecker. 2014. "Simulating Economic Growth Effects on Food and Nutrition Security in Yemen: A New Macro-Micro Modeling Approach." *Economic Modelling* 43: 100–113.

Breisinger, C., O. Ecker, and P. Al-Riffai. 2011. *Economics of the Arab Awakening: From Revolution to Transformation and Food Security*. Policy Brief 18. Washington, DC: International Food Policy Research Institute.

Breisinger, C., O. Ecker, P. Al-Riffai, and B. Yu. 2012. *Beyond the Arab Awakening: Policies and Investments for Poverty Reduction and Food Security.* Washington, DC: International Food Policy Research Institute.

Breisinger, C., O. Ecker, J.-F. Maystadt, J.-F. Trinh Tan, P. Al-Riffai, K. Bouzar, A. Sma, and M. Abdelgadir. 2014. *How To Build Resilience to Conflict: The Role of Food Security.* Washington, DC: International Food Policy Research Institute.

Brooks-Gunn, J., and G. Duncan. 1997. "The Effects of Poverty on Children." *Future of Children* 7 (2): 55–71.

Brown, K., S. Wuehler, and J. Peerson. 2001. "The Importance of Zinc in Human Nutrition and Estimation of the Global Prevalence of Zinc Deficiency." *Food and Nutrition Bulletin* 22 (2): 113–125.

Bryce, J., D. Coitinho, I. Darnton-Hill, D. Pelletier, and P. Pinstrup-Andersen. 2008. "Maternal and Child Undernutrition: Effective Action at National Level." *Lancet* 371 (9611): 510–526.

Bryson, A., R. Dorsett, and S. Purdon. 2002. *The Use of Propensity Score Matching in the Evaluation of Active Labour Market Policies.* Working Paper 4. London: Policy Studies Institute and National Centre for Social Research.

Bush, R. 2010. "Food Riots: Poverty, Power and Protest." *Journal of Agrarian Change* 10 (1): 119–129.

Caliendo, M., and S. Kopeinig. 2008. "Some Practical Guidance for the Implementation of Propensity Score Matching." *Journal of Economic Surveys* 22 (1): 31–72.

CAPMAS (Egypt, Central Agency for Public Mobilization and Statistics). 2013. *The Egyptian Subsidies.* Cairo, Egypt: Central Agency for Public Mobilization and Statistics.

———. 2014. *Statistical Yearbook 2014.* Cairo, Egypt. http://www.capmas.gov.eg/pdf/Electronic%20Static%20Book2014//PDF/population/Untitled.pdf.

CAPMAS and WFP (Egypt, Central Agency for Public Mobilization and Statistics and World Food Programme). 2011. 2010–2011 Egypt Household Income, Expenditure, and Consumption Survey. Unpublished applied datasets.

Carletto, G., M. Ruel, P. Winters, and A. Zezza. 2015. "Farm-Level Pathways to Improved Nutritional Status: Introduction to the Special Issue." *Journal of Development Studies* 51 (8): 945–957.

Carneiro, P., and M. Rodrigues. 2009. *Evaluating the Effect of Maternal Time on Child Development Using the Generalized Propensity Score.* Working Paper. London: University College London.

Caulfield, L., S. Richard, J. Rivera, P. Musgrove, and R. Black. 2006. "Stunting, Wasting and Micronutrient Deficiency Disorders." In *Disease Control Priorities in Developing Countries*, edited by D. Jamison, J. Breman, A. Measham, G. Alleyne, M. Claeson, D. Evans, P. Jha, A. Mills, and P. Musgrove, 551–567. 2nd ed. Washington, DC: World Bank.

Central Bank of Egypt. 2014. "The State Budget—Expenditures." Accessed March 10, 2014. http://www.cbe.org.eg/English/Economic+Research/Time+Series/.

Chambers, E., and D. Cox. 1967. "Discrimination between Alternative Binary Response Models." *Biometrika* 54 (3–4): 573–578.

Chang, G. 2002. "The Cause and Cure of China's Widening Income Disparity." *China Economic Review* 13 (4): 335–340.

Chen, Z., S. Yen, D. Eastwood. 2005. "Effects of Food Stamp Participation on Body Weight and Obesity." *American Journal of Agricultural Economics* 87 (5): 1167–1173.

Chou, S.-Y., M. Grossman, and H. Saffer. 2004. "An Economic Analysis of Adult Obesity: Results from the Behavioral Risk Factor Surveillance System." *Journal of Health Economics* 23 (3): 565–587.

Christiaensen, L., and H. Alderman. 2004. "Child Malnutrition in Ethiopia: Can Maternal Knowledge Augment the Role of Income?" *Economic Development and Cultural Change* 52 (2): 287–312.

Coelli, T. 2010. *The Cost Efficiency in the Production and Distribution of Subsidised Bread in Egypt*. Cairo, Egypt: World Bank.

Corsi, D., H. Kyu, and S. Subramanian. 2011. "Socioeconomic and Geographic Patterning of Under- and Overnutrition among Women in Bangladesh." *Journal of Nutrition* 141 (4): 631–638.

Cortez, R., and B. Senauer. 1996. "Taste Changes in the Demand for Food by Demographic Groups in the United States: A Nonparametric Empirical Analysis." *American Journal of Agricultural Economics* 78 (2): 280–289.

CSO (Yemen, Central Statistical Organization). 2006. Yemen Household Budget Survey 2005–2006. Unpublished applied datasets.

Dabelea, D. 2007. "The Predisposition to Obesity and Diabetes in Offspring of Diabetic Mothers." *Diabetes Care* 30 (S2): S169-S174.

Dabelea, D., and T. Crume. 2011. "Maternal Environment and the Transgenerational Cycle of Obesity and Diabetes." *Diabetes* 60 (7): 1849–1855.

Dabelea, D., R. Hanson, R. Lindsay, D. Pettitt, G. Imperatore, M. Gabir, J. Roumain, P. Bennett, and W. Knowler. 2000. "Intrauterine Exposure to Diabetes Conveys Risks for Type 2 Diabetes and Obesity: A Study of Discordant Sibships." *Diabetes* 49 (12): 2208–2211.

Dahi, O. 2012. "The Political Economy of the Egyptian and Arab Revolt." *IDS Bulletin* 43 (1): 47–53.

Dai, X., and L. Cheng. 2015. "The Effect of Public Subsidies on Corporate R&D Investment: An Application of the Generalized Propensity Score." *Technological Forecasting and Social Change* 90 (B): 410–419.

Deaton, A., and J. Drèze. 2009. "Food and Nutrition in India: Facts and Interpretations." *Economic and Political Weekly* 44 (7): 42–65.

Deaton, A., and C. Paxson. 1998. "Economies of Scale, Household Size, and the Demand for Food." *Journal of Political Economy* 106 (5): 897–930.

Dehejia, R., and S. Wahba. 2002. "Propensity Score-Matching Methods for Nonexperimental Causal Studies." *Review of Economics and Statistics* 84 (1): 151–161.

Dinour, L., D. Bergen, and M.-C. Yeh. 2007. "The Food Insecurity–Obesity Paradox: A Review of the Literature and the Role Food Stamps May Play." *Journal of the American Dietetic Association* 107 (11): 1952–1961.

Doan, R., and L. Bisharat. 1990. "Female Autonomy and Child Nutritional Status: The Extended-Family Residential Unit in Amman, Jordan." *Social Science and Medicine* 31 (7): 783–789.

Drewnowski, A., and B. Popkin. 1997. "The Nutrition Transition: New Trends in the Global Diet." *Nutrition Reviews* 55 (2): 31–43.

Duffey, K., P. Gordon-Larsen, J. Shikany, D. Guilkey, D. Jacobs, and B. Popkin. 2010. "Food Price and Diet and Health Outcomes: 20 Years of the CARDIA Study." *Archives of Internal Medicine* 170 (5): 420–426.

ECES (Egyptian Center for Economic Studies). 2010. *The Subsidy System in Egypt: Alternatives for Reform*. Policy Viewpoint 25. Cairo, Egypt: Egyptian Center for Economic Studies.

Ecker, O., and M. Qaim. 2011. "Analyzing Nutritional Impacts of Policies: An Empirical Study for Malawi." *World Development* 39 (3): 412–428.

Elhakim, N., A. Laillou, A. El Nakeeb, R. Yacoub, and M. Shehata. 2012. "Fortifying Baladi Bread in Egypt: Reaching More Than 50 Million People through the Subsidy Program." *Food and Nutrition Bulletin* 33 (S3): 260S–271S.

El Taguri, A., F. Besmar, A. Monem, I. Betilmal, C. Ricour, and M. Rolland-Cachera. 2009. "Stunting Is a Major Risk Factor for Overweight: Results from National Surveys in 5 Arab Countries." *Eastern Mediterranean Health Journal* 15 (3): 549–562.

El-Zanaty, F., and A. Way. 2006. *Egypt Demographic and Health Survey 2005*. Cairo, Egypt: Ministry of Health and Population; National Population Council; El-Zanaty and Associates; ORC Macro.

———. 2009. *Egypt Demographic and Health Survey 2008*. Cairo, Egypt: Ministry of Health; El-Zanaty and Associates; Macro International.

Engle, P., M. Black, J. Behrman, M. Cabral de Mello, P. Gertler, L. Kapiriri, R. Martorell, and M. Young. 2007. "Strategies to Avoid the Loss of Developmental Potential in More Than 200 Million Children in the Developing World." *Lancet* 369 (9557): 229–242.

Eriksson, J., T. Forsen, J. Tuomilehto, P. Winter, C. Osmond, and D. Barker. 1999. "Catchup Growth in Childhood and Death from Coronary Heart Disease: Longitudinal Study." *British Medical Journal* 318 (7181): 427–431.

Ezzati, M., S. Vander Hoorn, C. Lawes, R. Leach, W. James, A. Lopez, A. Rodgers, and C. Murray. 2005. "Rethinking the 'Diseases of Affluence' Paradigm: Global Patterns of Nutritional Risks in Relation to Economic Development." *PLoS Medicine* 2 (5): e133.

Fan, J., and I. Gijbels. 1996. *Local Polynomial Modelling and Its Applications*. New York: Chapman and Hall/CRC.

FAO (Food and Agriculture Organization of the United Nations). 1996. "Rome Declaration on World Food Security and World Food Summit Plan of Action." Accessed January 3, 2012. http://www.fao.org/DOCREP/003/W3613E/W3613E00.HTM.

———. 2009. *Declaration of the World Summit on Food Security*. WSFS 2009/2. Rome: Food and Agriculture Organization of the United Nations.

FAOSTAT (Food and Agriculture Organization of the United Nations, Statistics Division). 2014. Food Balance Sheets. Accessed November 3, 2014. http://faostat3.fao.org/home/E.

Filmer, D., J. Hammer, and L. Pritchett. 2000. "Weak Links in the Chain: A Diagnosis of Health Policy in Poor Countries." *World Bank Research Observer* 15 (2): 199–224.

Filmer, D., and L. Pritchett. 1999. "The Impact of Public Spending on Health: Does Money Matter?" *Social Science and Medicine* 49 (10): 1309–1323.

Finkelstein, E., I. Fiebelkorn, and G. Wang. 2003. "National Medical Spending Attributable to Overweight and Obesity: How Much, and Who's Paying?" *Health Affairs (Web Exclusive)*: W3–219.

Finkelstein, E., C. Ruhm, and K. Kosa. 2005. "Economic Causes and Consequences of Obesity." *Annual Review of Public Health* 26: 239–257.

Finucane, M., G. Stevens, M. Cowan, G. Danaei, J. Lin, C. Paciorek, G. Singh, et al. 2011. "National, Regional, and Global Trends in Body-Mass Index since 1980: Systematic Analysis of Health Examination Surveys and Epidemiological Studies with 960 Country-Years and 9.1 Million Participants." *Lancet* 377 (9765): 557–567.

Fotso, J.-C. 2007. "Urban-Rural Differentials in Child Malnutrition: Trends and Socioeconomic Correlates in Sub-Saharan Africa." *Health and Place* 13 (1): 205–223.

Freinkel, N. 1980. "Banting Lecture 1980: Of Pregnancy and Progeny." *Diabetes* 29 (12): 1023–1035.

Fryges, H. 2009. "The Export-Growth Relationship: Estimating a Dose-Response Function." *Applied Economics Letters* 16 (18): 1855–1859.

Gabbert, S., and H.-P. Weikard. 2001. "How Widespread Is Undernourishment? A Critique of Measurement Methods and New Empirical Results." *Food Policy* 26 (3): 209–228.

Galal, O. 2002. "The Nutrition Transition in Egypt: Obesity, Undernutrition and the Food Consumption Context." *Public Health Nutrition* 5 (1A): 141–148.

Garrett, J., and M. Ruel. 2005. "Stunted Child–Overweight Mother Pairs: Prevalence and Association with Economic Development and Urbanization." *Food and Nutrition Bulletin* 26 (2): 209–221.

Gertler, P., S. Martinez, P. Premand, L. Rawlings, and C. Vermmersch. 2011. *Impact Evaluation in Practice.* Washington, DC: World Bank.

Ghoneim, H. 2013. *Ration Cards in Egypt: Targeting, Leakage, and Costs.* Working Paper 36. Cairo, Egypt: German University in Cairo.

Gillespie, S., L. Haddad, V. Mannar, P. Menon, N. Nisbett, and Maternal and Child Nutrition Study Group. 2013. "The Politics of Reducing Malnutrition: Building Commitment and Accelerating Progress." *Lancet* 382 (9891): 552–569.

Gluckman, P., and M. Hanson. 2008. "Developmental and Epigenetic Pathways to Obesity: An Evolutionary-Developmental Perspective." *International Journal of Obesity* 32: S62–S71.

Grantham-McGregor, S., Y. Cheung, S. Cueto, P. Glewwe, L. Richter, B. Strupp, and International Child Development Steering Group. 2007. "Developmental Potential in the First 5 Years for Children in Developing Countries." *Lancet* 369 (9555): 60–70.

Grosh, M., C. del Ninno, E. Tesliuc, and A. Ouerghi. 2008. *For Protection and Promotion: The Design and Implementation of Effective Safety Nets.* Washington, DC: World Bank.

Guardabascio, B., and M. Ventura. 2014. "Estimating the Dose-Response Function through a Generalized Linear Model Approach." *Stata Journal* 14 (1): 141–158.

Gutner, T. 2002. "The Political Economy of Food Subsidy Reform: The Case of Egypt." *Food Policy* 27 (5): 455–476.

Haddad, L., H. Alderman, S. Appleton, L. Song, and Y. Yohannes. 2003. "Reducing Child Malnutrition: How Far Does Income Growth Take Us?" *World Bank Economic Review* 17 (1): 107–131.

Haider, B., and Z. Bhutta. 2012. "Multiple-Micronutrient Supplementation for Women during Pregnancy." *Cochrane Database of Systematic Reviews* 11.

Hales, C., and D. Barker. 1992. "Type 2 (Non-Insulin-Dependent) Diabetes Mellitus: The Thrifty Phenotype Hypothesis." *Diabetologia* 35 (7): 595–601.

———. 2001. "The Thrifty Phenotype Hypothesis." *British Medical Bulletin* 60 (1): 5–20.

Han, J., D. Lawlor, and S. Kimm. 2010. "Childhood Obesity." *Lancet* 375 (9727): 1737–1748.

Han, Z., S. Mulla, J. Beyene, G. Liao, and S. McDonald. 2011. "Maternal Underweight and the Risk of Preterm Birth and Low Birth Weight: A Systematic Review and Meta-Analyses." *International Journal of Epidemiology* 40 (1): 65–101.

Handa, S. 1994. "Gender, Headship and Intrahousehold Resource Allocation." *World Development* 22 (10): 1535–1547.

Hannusch, D. 2008. *Marketing of Food in Egypt: Food Subsidies, Social and Economic Considerations.* Cairo, Egypt: World Food Programme, Regional Bureau for Middle East, Central Asia, and Eastern Europe.

Hassine, N. 2012. "Inequality of Opportunity in Egypt." *World Bank Economic Review* 26 (2): 265–295.

Haughton, J., and S. Khandker. 2009. *Handbook on Poverty and Inequality.* Washington, DC: World Bank.

Headey, D., O. Ecker, and J.-F. Trinh Tan. 2014. "Shocks to the System: Monitoring Food Security in a Volatile World." In *Handbook on Food: Demand, Supply, Sustainability and Security*, edited by R. Jha, R. Gaiha, and A. Deolalikar, 41–71. Gloucestershire, UK: Edward Elgar Publishing.

Heckman, J., H. Ichimura, and P. Todd. 1997. "Matching as an Econometric Evaluation Estimator: Evidence from Evaluating a Job Training Programme." *Review of Economic Studies* 64 (4): 605–654.

———. 1998. "Matching as an Econometric Evaluation Estimator." *Review of Economic Studies* 65 (2): 261–294.

Heckman, J., and R. Robb. 1985. "Alternative Methods for Evaluating the Impact of Interventions: An Overview." *Journal of Econometrics* 30 (1–2): 239–267.

Hediger, M., M. Overpeck, A. McGlynn, R. Kuczmarski, K. Maurer, and W. Davis. 1999. "Growth and Fatness at Three to Six Years of Age of Children Born Small- or Large-for-Gestational Age." *Pediatrics* 104 (3): e33.

Hefni, M., and C. Witthöft. 2011. "Increasing the Folate Content in Egyptian Baladi Bread Using Germinated Wheat Flour." LWT-Food *Science and Technology* 44 (3): 706–712.

Herman, W., M. Ali, R. Aubert, M. Engelgau, S. Kenny, E. Gunter, A. Malarcher, et al. 1995. "Diabetes Mellitus in Egypt: Risk Factors and Prevalence." *Diabetic Medicine* 12 (12): 1126–1131.

Hidrobo, M., J. Hoddinott, A. Peterman, A. Margolies, and V. Moreira. 2014. "Cash, Food, or Vouchers? Evidence from a Randomized Experiment in Northern Ecuador." *Journal of Development Economics* 107: 144–156.

Hirano, K., and G. Imbens. 2004. "The Propensity Score with Continuous Treatments." In *Applied Bayesian Modeling and Causal Inference from Incomplete-Data Perspectives*, edited by A. Gelman and X.-L. Meng, 73–84. West Sussex, UK: J. Wiley and Sons.

Hoddinott, J., G. Berhane, D. Gilligan, N. Kumar, and A. Seyoum Taffesse. 2012. "The Impact of Ethiopia's Productive Safety Net Programme and Related Transfers on Agricultural Productivity." *Journal of African Economies* 21 (5): 761–786.

Hoddinott, J., J. Maluccio, J. Behrman, J. Flores, and R. Martorell. 2008. "Effect of a Nutrition Intervention during Early Childhood on Economic Productivity in Guatemalan Adults." *Lancet* 371 (9610): 411–416.

Hoffman, D., A. Sawaya, W. Coward, A. Wright, P. Martins, C. de Nascimento, K. Tucker, and S. Roberts. 2000a. "Energy Expenditure of Stunted and Nonstunted Boys and Girls Living in the Shantytowns of Sao Paulo, Brazil." *American Journal of Clinical Nutrition* 72 (4): 1025–1031.

Hoffman, D., A. Sawaya, I. Verreschi, K. Tucker, and S. Roberts. 2000b. "Why Are Nutritionally Stunted Children at Increased Risk of Obesity? Studies of Metabolic Rate and Fat Oxidation in Shantytown Children from Sao Paulo, Brazil." *American Journal of Clinical Nutrition* 72 (3): 702–707.

Horton, S. 1999. "Opportunities for Investments in Nutrition in Low-Income Asia." *Asia Development Review* 17 (1–2): 246–273.

Horton, S., and J. Ross. 2003. "The Economics of Iron Deficiency." *Food Policy* 28 (1): 51–75.

Horton, S., M. Shekar, C. McDonald, A. Mahal, and J. Brooks. 2010. *Scaling Up Nutrition: What Will It Cost?* Washington, DC: World Bank.

Ianchovichina, E., J. Loening, and C. Wood. 2014. "How Vulnerable Are Arab Countries to Global Food Price Shocks?" *Journal of Development Studies* 50 (9): 1302–1319.

ICF International. 2014. STATcompiler. Accessed July 5, 2014. http://www.statcompiler.com/.

IFPRI (International Food Policy Research Institute). 2014. *Global Nutrition Report 2014: Actions and Accountability to Accelerate the World's Progress on Nutrition*. Washington, DC: International Food Policy Research Institute.

Imbens, G. 2004. "Nonparametric Estimation of Average Treatment Effects under Exogeneity: A Review." *Review of Economics and Statistics* 86 (1): 4–29.

IMF (International Monetary Fund). 2014. World Economic Outlook Database, April 2014. Accessed July 26, 2014. https://www.imf.org/external/pubs/ft/weo/2014/01/weodata/index.aspx.

IZiNCG (International Zinc Nutrition Consultative Group). 2004. "Assessment of the Risk of Zinc Deficiency in Populations and Options for Its Control." *Food and Nutrition Bulletin* 25 (1, suppl. 2): S94–S203.

Jensen, R., and N. Miller. 2011. "Do Consumer Price Subsidies Really Improve Nutrition?" *Review of Economics and Statistics* 93 (4): 1205–1223.

Jha, R., R. Gaiha, M. Pandey, and N. Kaicker. 2013. "Food Subsidy, Income Transfer and the Poor: A Comparative Analysis of the Public Distribution System in India's States." *Journal of Policy Modeling* 35 (6): 887–908.

Jiang, M., and E. Foster. 2013. "Duration of Breastfeeding and Childhood Obesity: A Generalized Propensity Score Approach." *Health Services Research* 48 (2pt1): 628–651.

Karlberg, J., and K. Albertsson-Wikland. 1995. "Growth in Full-Term Small-for-Gestational-Age Infants: From Birth to Final Height." *Pediatric Research* 38 (5): 733–739.

Katona, P., and J. Katona-Apte. 2008. "The Interaction between Nutrition and Infection." *Clinical Infectious Diseases* 46 (10): 1582–1588.

Kavle, J., F. El-Zanaty, M. Landry, and R. Galloway. 2015a. "The Rise in Stunting in Relation to Avian Influenza and Food Consumption Patterns in Lower Egypt in Comparison to Upper Egypt: Results from 2005 and 2008 Demographic and Health Surveys." *BMC Public Health* 15 (1): 285.

Kavle, J., V. Flax, A. Abdelmegeid, F. Salah, S. Hafez, M. Ramzy, D. Hamed, G. Saleh, and R. Galloway. 2016. "Factors Associated with Early Growth in Egyptian Infants: Implications for Addressing the Dual Burden of Malnutrition." *Maternal and Child Nutrition* 12 (1): 139–151.

Kavle, J., S. Mehanna, G. Saleh, M. Fouad, M. Ramzy, D. Hamed, M. Hassan, G. Khan, and R. Galloway. 2015b. "Exploring Why Junk Foods Are 'Essential' Foods and How Culturally Tailored Recommendations Improved Feeding in Egyptian Children." *Maternal and Child Nutrition* 11 (3): 346–370.

Kennedy, E., and H. Alderman. 1987. *Comparative Analyses of Nutritional Effectiveness of Food Subsidies and Other* Food-Related *Interventions*. Washington, DC: International Food Policy Research Institute.

Kennedy, E., and P. Peters. 1992. "Household Food Security and Child Nutrition: The Interaction of Income and Gender of Household Head." *World Development* 20 (8): 1077–1085.

Khandker, S., G. Koowal, and H. Samad. 2010. *Handbook on Impact Evaluation: Quantitative Methods and Practices*. Washington, DC: World Bank.

Kilpi, F., L. Webber, A. Musaigner, A. Aitsi-Selmi, T. Marsh, K. Rtveladze, K. McPherson, and M. Brown. 2013. "Alarming Predictions for Obesity and Non-communicable Diseases in the Middle East." *Public Health Nutrition* 17 (5): 1078–1086.

Kochar, A. 2005. "Can Targeted Food Programs Improve Nutrition? An Empirical Analysis of India's Public Distribution System." *Economic Development and Cultural Change* 54 (1): 203–235.

Koletzko, B., B. Brands, L. Poston, K. Godfrey, and H. Demmelmair. 2012. "Early Nutrition Programming of Long-Term Health." *Proceedings of the Nutrition Society* 71 (3): 371–378.

Kuku, O., S. Garasky, and C. Gundersen. 2012. "The Relationship between Childhood Obesity and Food Insecurity: A Nonparametric Analysis." *Applied Economics* 44 (21): 2667–2677.

Laillou, A., S. Hafez, A. Mahmoud, M. Mansour, F. Rohner, S. Fortin, J. Berger, N. Ibrahim, and R. Moench-Pfanner. 2012. "Vegetable Oil of Poor Quality Is Limiting the Success of Fortification with Vitamin A in Egypt." *Food and Nutrition Bulletin* 33 (3): 186–193.

Lanjouw, P., and M. Ravallion. 1995. "Poverty and Household Size." *Economic Journal* 105 (433): 1415–1434.

Lechner, M. 2002. "Program Heterogeneity and Propensity Score Matching: An Application to the Evaluation of Active Labor Market Policies." *Review of Economics and Statistics* 84 (2): 205–220.

Leger, J., C. Levy-Marchal, J. Bloch, A. Pinet, D. Chevenne, D. Porquet, D. Collin, and P. Czernichow. 1997. "Reduced Final Height and Indications for Insulin Resistance in 20 Year Olds Born Small for Gestational Age: Regional Cohort Study." *BMJ* 315 (7104): 341–347.

Leroy, J. 2011. "*zscore06*: Stata Command for the Calculation of Anthropometric Z-Scores Using the 2006 WHO Child Growth Standards." Accessed July 13, 2016. http://fmwww.bc.edu/repec/bocode/z/zscore06.html.

Leroy, J., P. Gadsden, T. de Cossío, and P. Gertler. 2013. "Cash and In-Kind Transfers Lead to Excess Weight Gain in a Population of Women with a High Prevalence of Overweight in Rural Mexico." *Journal of Nutrition* 143 (3): 378–383.

Leroy, J., J.-P. Habicht, T. González de Cossío, and M. Ruel. 2014. "Maternal Education Mitigates the Negative Effects of Higher Income on the Double Burden of Child Stunting and Maternal Overweight in Rural Mexico." *Journal of Nutrition* 144 (5): 765–770.

Leuven, E., and B. Sianesi. 2003. "PSMATCH2: Stata Module to Perform Full Mahalanobis and Propensity Score Matching, Common Support Graphing, and Covariate Imbalance Testing." Accessed July 14, 2016. http://ideas.repec.org/c/boc/bocode/s432001.html.

———. 2012. PSTEST Stata Module. User-Created Stata Command.

Löfgren, H., and M. El-Said. 2001. "Food Subsidies in Egypt: Reform Options, Distribution and Welfare." *Food Policy* 26 (1): 65–83.

Mansour, S. 2012. *Egypt: Grain and Feed Annual—Wheat and Corn Production on the Rise.* Global Agricultural Information Network (GAIN) Report. Cairo, Egypt: United States Department of Agriculture Foreign Agricultural Service.

Matte, T., M. Bresnahan, M. Begg, and E. Susser. 2001. "Influence of Variation in Birth Weight within Normal Range and Within Sibships on IQ at Age 7 Years: Cohort Study." *BMJ* 323 (7308): 310–314.

Mayer, J. 1976. "The Dimensions of Human Hunger." *Scientific American* 235 (3): 40–49.

Mayo-Wilson, E., A. Imdad, K. Herzer, M. Yawar Yakoob, and Z. Bhutta. 2011. "Vitamin A Supplements for Preventing Mortality, Illness, and Blindness in Children Aged under 5: Systematic Review and Meta-Analysis." *BMJ* 343: d5094.

McDonald, S. 2010. "Overweight and Obesity in Mothers and Risk of Preterm Birth and Low Birth Weight Infants: Systematic Review and Meta-Analyses." *BMJ* 341: c3428.

Measham, A., and M. Chatterjee. 1999. *Wasting Away: The Crisis of Malnutrition in India.* Washington, DC: World Bank.

Mehio Sibai, A., L. Nasreddine, A., Mokdad, N. Adra, M. Tabet, and N. Hwalla. 2010. "Nutrition Transition and Cardiovascular Disease Risk Factors in Middle East and North Africa Countries: Reviewing the Evidence." *Annals of Nutrition and Metabolism* 57 (3–4): 193–203.

Mendez, M., C. Monteiro, and B. Popkin. 2005. "Overweight Exceeds Underweight among Women in Most Developing Countries" *American Journal of Clinical Nutrition* 81 (3): 714–721.

Meyerhoefer, C., and Y. Pylypchuk. 2008. "Does Participation in the Food Stamp Program Increase the Prevalence of Obesity and Health Care Spending?" *American Journal of Agricultural Economics* 90 (2): 287–305.

Mistry, S., and S. Puthussery. 2015. "Risk Factors of Overweight and Obesity in Childhood and Adolescence in South Asian Countries: A Systematic Review of the Evidence." *Public Health* 129 (3): 200–209.

MOF (Egypt, Ministry of Finance). 2014. "The Financial Monthly Bulletin." Accessed March 10, 2014. http://www.mof.gov.eg/English/publications/MOF_Publications/Pages/The_Financial_Monthly_Bulletin.aspx.

MOH (Egypt, Ministry of Health), El-Zanaty and Associates, and Macro International. 2008. Egypt 2008 Standard Demographic and Health Survey dataset. Accessed March 3, 2014. http://dhsprogram.com/data/available-datasets.cfm.

Mohd Shariff, Z., and G. Khor. 2005. "Obesity and Household Food Insecurity: Evidence from a Sample of Rural Households in Malaysia." *European Journal of Clinical Nutrition* 59 (9): 1049–1058.

MOHP (Egypt, Ministry of Health and Population), El-Zanaty and Associates, and ICF International. 2015. *Egypt Health Issue Survey 2015.* Cairo, Egypt: Ministry of Health and Population; Rockville, MD, US: ICF International.

MOHP (Egypt, Ministry of Health and Population), NPC (Egypt, National Population Council), and ORC Macro. 2000. Egypt 2005 Standard Demographic and Health Survey dataset. Accessed March 3, 2014. http://dhsprogram.com/data/available-datasets.cfm.

MOHP (Egypt, Ministry of Health and Population), NPC (Egypt, National Population Council), El-Zanaty and Associates, and ORC Macro. 2003. Egypt 2003 Interim Demographic and Health Survey dataset. Accessed March 3, 2014. http://dhsprogram.com/data/available-datasets.cfm.

———. 2005. Egypt 2005 Standard Demographic and Health Survey dataset. Accessed March 3, 2014. http://dhsprogram.com/data/available-datasets.cfm.

Mooij, J. 1998. "Food Policy and Politics: The Political Economy of the Public Distribution System in India." *Journal of Peasant Studies* 25 (2): 77–101.

MSIT (Egypt, Ministry of Supply and Internal Trade). 2014a. "Number of Ration Cards and Beneficiaries: 2010 Compared to 2004." Accessed December 4, 2014. http://bit.ly/2aah30D.

———. 2014b. "Number of Ration Cards and Beneficiaries: November 2011, after Adding Newborns." Accessed December 4, 2014. http://bit.ly/2aah30D.

———. 2014c. "A Clarifying Notification of the New System for Bread across Governorates." Accessed December 5, 2014. http://bit.ly/29S7Y9h.

———. 2015. "The New Ration Card System." Accessed April 24, 2015. http://bit.ly/29LND4S.

MSS (Egypt, Ministry of Social Solidarity). 2010. *Monthly Bulletin*. Issue 182. Cairo, Egypt: Ministry of Social Solidarity.

———. 2012. "A Declaration of the Quantity and Price of Subsidized Commodities Allotted to the Ration Card." Cairo, Egypt: Ministry of Social Solidarity.

Musaiger, A. 2011. "Overweight and Obesity in Eastern Mediterranean Region: Prevalence and Possible Causes." *Journal of Obesity* 2011: 1–17.

Musaiger, A., and H. Al-Hazzaa. 2012. "Prevalence and Risk Factors Associated with Nutrition-Related Noncommunicable Diseases in the Eastern Mediterranean Region." *International Journal of General Medicine* 5: 199–217.

Negro-Calduch, E., S. Elfadaly, M. Tibbo, P. Ankers, and E. Bailey. 2013. "Assessment of Biosecurity Practices of Small-Scale Broiler Producers in Central Egypt." *Preventive Veterinary Medicine* 110 (2): 253–262.

Nelson, J. 1988. "Household Economies of Scale in Consumption: Theory and Evidence." *Econometrica* 56 (6): 1301–1314.

Ng, M., T. Fleming, M. Robinson, B. Thomson, N. Graetz, C. Margono, E. Mullany, et al. 2014. "Global, Regional, and National Prevalence of Overweight and Obesity in Children and Adults during 1980–2013: A Systematic Analysis for the Global Burden of Disease Study 2013." *Lancet* 384 (9945): 766–781.

Ng, S., E. Norton, and B. Popkin. 2009. "Why Have Physical Activity Levels Declined among Chinese Adults? Findings from the 1991–2006 China Health and Nutrition Surveys." *Social Science and Medicine* 68 (7): 1305–1314.

Ng, S., and B. Popkin. 2012. "Time Use and Physical Activity: A Shift Away from Movement across the Globe." *Obesity Reviews* 13 (8): 659–680.

Nubé, M. 2001. "Confronting Dietary Energy Supply with Anthropometry in the Assessment of Undernutrition Prevalence at the Level of Countries." *World Development* 29 (7): 1275–1289.

Onyango, A., K. Tucker, and T. Eisemon. 1994. "Household Headship and Child Nutrition: A Case Study in Western Kenya." *Social Science and Medicine* 39 (12): 1633–1639.

Pinstrup-Andersen, P., and E. Caicedo. 1978. "The Potential Impact of Changes in Income Distribution on Food Demand and Human Nutrition." *American Journal of Agricultural Economics* 60 (3): 402–415.

Pitt, M., and M. Rosenzweig. 1985. "Health and Nutrient Consumption across and within Farm Households." *Review of Economics and Statistics* 67 (2): 212–223.

Plagemann, A. 2008. "A Matter of Insulin: Developmental Programming of Body Weight Regulation." *Journal of Maternal-Fetal and Neonatal Medicine* 21 (3): 143–148.

Poi, B. 2004. "From the Help Desk: Some Bootstrapping Techniques." *Stata Journal* 4 (3): 312–328.

Popkin, B. 1980. "Time Allocation of the Mother and Child Nutrition." *Ecology of Food and Nutrition* 9 (1): 1–14.

———. 1993. "Nutritional Patterns and Transitions." *Population and Development Review* 19 (1): 138–157.

———. 1994. "The Nutrition Transition in Low-Income Countries: An Emerging Crisis." *Nutrition Reviews* 52 (9): 285–298.

———. 1998. "The Nutrition Transition and Its Health Implications in Lower-Income Countries." *Public Health Nutrition* 1 (1): 5–21.

———. 1999. "Urbanization, Lifestyle Changes and the Nutrition Transition." *World Development* 27 (11): 1905–1916.

———. 2001. "The Nutrition Transition and Obesity in the Developing World." *Journal of Nutrition* 131 (3): 871S–873S.

———. 2002a. "The Shift in Stages of the Nutrition Transition in the Developing World Differs from Past Experiences!" *Public Health Nutrition* 5 (1A): 205–214.

———. 2002b. "The Dynamics of the Dietary Transition in the Developing World." In *The Nutrition Transition: Diet and Disease in the Developing World*, edited by B. Caballero and B. Popkin, 111–128. London: Academic Press.

Popkin, B., L. Adair, and S. Wen Ng. 2012. "Global Nutrition Transition and the Pandemic of Obesity in Developing Countries." *Nutrition Reviews* 70 (1): 3–21.

Popkin, B., S. Kim, E. Russev, S. Du, and C. Zizza. 2006. "Measuring the Full Economic Costs of Diet, Physical Activity and Obesity-Related Chronic Diseases." *Obesity Reviews* 7 (3): 271–293.

Popkin, B., M. Richards, and C. Montiero. 1996. "Stunting Is Associated with Overweight in Children of Four Nations That Are Undergoing the Nutrition Transition." *Journal of Nutrition* 126 (12): 3009–3016.

Prentice, A. 2006. "The Emerging Epidemic of Obesity in Developing Countries." *International Journal of Epidemiology* 35 (1): 93–99.

Rahim, H., A. Sibai, Y. Khader, N. Hwalla, I. Fadhil, H. Alsiyabi, A. Mataria, S. Mendis, A. Mokdad, and A. Husseini. 2014. "Non-communicable Diseases in the Arab World." *Lancet* 383 (9914): 356–367.

Ramadan, R., and A. Thomas. 2011. "Evaluating the Impact of Reforming the Food Subsidy Program in Egypt: A Mixed Demand Approach." *Food Policy* 36 (5): 638–646.

Rashid, D., L. Smith, and T. Rahman. 2011. "Determinants of Dietary Quality: Evidence from Bangladesh." *World Development* 39 (12): 2221–2231.

Ravallion, M. 1990. "Income Effects on Undernutrition." *Economic Development and Cultural Change* 38 (3): 489–515.

Rawlings, L., and G. Rubio. 2005. "Evaluating the Impact of Conditional Cash Transfer Programs." *World Bank Research Observer* 20 (1): 29–55.

Rivera, J., S. Barquera, F. Campirano, I. Campos, M. Safdie, and V. Tovar. 2002. "Epidemiological and Nutritional Transition in Mexico: Rapid Increase of Non-communicable Chronic Diseases and Obesity." *Public Health Nutrition* 5 (1A): 113–122.

Rivera, J., S. Barquera, T. González-Cossío, G. Olaiz, and J. Sepulveda. 2004. "Nutrition Transition in Mexico and in Other Latin American Countries." *Nutrition Reviews* 62 (S2): S149–S157.

Rivera, J., C. Hotz, T. González-Cossío, L. Neufeld, and A. García-Guerra. 2003. "The Effect of Micronutrient Deficiencies on Child Growth: A Review of Results from Community-Based Supplementation Trials." *Journal of Nutrition* 133 (11): 4010S–4020S.

Rosenbaum, P., and D. Rubin. 1983. "The Central Role of the Propensity Score in Observational Studies for Causal Effects." *Biometrika* 70 (1): 41–55.

———. 1985. "Constructing a Control Group Using Multivariate Matched Sampling Methods That Incorporate the Propensity Score." *American Statistician* 39 (1): 33–38.

Rubin, D. 2001. "Using Propensity Scores to Help Design Observational Studies: Application to the Tobacco Litigation." *Health Services and Outcomes Research Methodology* 2 (3–4): 169–188.

Ruel, M., J. Harris, and K. Cunningham. 2013. "Diet Quality in Developing Countries." In *Diet Quality: An Evidence-Based Approach*. Vol. 2, edited by V. Preedy, L.-H. Hunter, and V. Patel, 239–261. Heideberg, Germany: Humana Press.

Sachs, R. 2012. *On Bread and Circuses: Food Subsidy Reform and Popular Opposition in Egypt*. Working Paper. Stanford, CA, US: Stanford University, Center for International Security and Cooperation.

Sahn, D., and D. Stifel. 2003. "Urban-Rural Inequality in Living Standards in Africa." *Journal of African Economies* 12 (4): 564–597.

Sawaya, A., and S. Roberts. 2003. "Stunting and Future Risk of Obesity: Principal Physiological Mechanisms." *Cadernos de Saúde Pública* 19: S21–S28.

Schmidhuber, J., and P. Shetty. 2005. "The Nutrition Transition to 2030. Why Developing Countries Are Likely to Bear the Major Burden." *Acta Agriculturae Scandinavica, Section C* 2 (3–4): 150–166.

Scholl, T., and M. Hediger. 1994. "Anemia and Iron-Deficiency Anemia: Compilation of Data on Pregnancy Outcome." *American Journal of Clinical Nutrition* 59 (2): 492S–500S.

Schroeder, D., R. Martorell, and R. Flores. 1999. "Infant and Child Growth and Fatness and Fat Distribution in Guatemalan Adults." *American Journal of Epidemiology* 149 (2): 177–185.

Selowsky, M., and L. Taylor. 1973. "The Economics of Malnourished Children: An Example for Disinvestment in Human Capital." *Economic Development and Cultural Change* 22 (1): 17–30.

Semba, R., S. de Pee, K. Sun, M. Sari, N. Akhter, and M. Bloem. 2008. "Effect of Parental Formal Education on Risk of Child Stunting in Indonesia and Bangladesh: A Cross-Sectional Study." *Lancet* 371 (9609): 322–328.

Shetty, P. 2013. "Nutrition Transition and Its Health Outcomes." *Indian Journal of Pediatrics* 80 (1): 21–27.

Shrimpton, R., and C. Rokx. 2012. *The Double Burden of Malnutrition: A Review of Global Evidence*. HNP Discussion Paper 79525. Washington, DC: World Bank.

Sianesi, B. 2004. "An Evaluation of the Swedish System of Active Labour Market Programmes in the 1990s." *Review of Economics and Statistics* 86 (1): 133–155.

Sibhatu, K., V. Krishna, and M. Qaim. 2015. "Production Diversity and Dietary Diversity in Smallholder Farm Households." *Proceedings of the National Academy of Sciences* 112 (34): 10657–10662.

Smith, L. 1998. "Can FAO's Measure of Chronic Undernourishment Be Strengthened?" *Food Policy* 23 (5): 425–445.

Smith, L., and L. Haddad. 2000. *Explaining Child Malnutrition in Developing Countries: A Cross-Country Analysis*. Washington, DC: International Food Policy Research Institute.

———. 2002. "How Potent Is Economic Growth in Reducing Undernutrition? What Are the Pathways of Impact? New Cross-Country Evidence." *Economic Development and Cultural Change* 51 (1): 55–76.

Smith, L., M. Ruel, and A. Ndiaye. 2005. "Why Is Child Malnutrition Lower in Urban Than in Rural Areas? Evidence from 36 Developing Countries." *World Development* 33 (8): 1285–1305.

Smith, J., and P. Todd. 2005. "Does Matching Overcome LaLonde's Critique of Nonexperimental Estimators?" *Journal of Econometrics* 125 (1–2): 305–353.

Stephenson, L., M. Latham, and A. Ottesen. 2000. "Malnutrition and Parasitic Helminth Infections." *Parasitology* 121 (S1): S23–S38.

Stevens, G., G. Singh, Y. Lu, G. Danaei, J. Lin, M. Finucane, A. Bahalim, et al. 2012. "National, Regional, and Global Trends in Adult Overweight and Obesity Prevalences." *Population Health Metrics* 10 (1): 22.

Strauss, J. 1990. "Households, Communities, and Preschool Children's Nutrition Outcomes: Evidence from Rural Côte d'Ivoire." *Economic Development and Cultural Change* 38 (2): 231–261.

Strauss, R., and W. Dietz. 1998. "Growth and Development of Term Children Born with Low Birth Weight: Effects of Genetic and Environmental Factors." *Journal of Pediatrics* 133 (1): 67–72.

Subramanian, S., J. Perkins, and K. Khan. 2009. "Do Burdens of Underweight and Overweight Coexist among Lower Socioeconomic Groups in India?" *American Journal of Clinical Nutrition* 90 (2): 369–376.

Subramanyam, M., I. Kawachi, L. Berkman, and S. Subramanian. 2010. "Socioeconomic Inequalities in Childhood Undernutrition in India: Analyzing Trends between 1992 and 2005." *PLoS ONE* 5 (6): e1392.

Svedberg, P. 1999. "841 Million Undernourished?" *World Development* 27 (12): 2081–2098.

———. 2002. "Undernutrition Overestimated." *Economic Development and Cultural Change* 51 (1): 5–36.

———. 2012. "Reforming or Replacing the Public Distribution System with Cash Transfers?" *Economic and Political Weekly* 47 (7): 53–62.

Swindale, A., and P. Bilinsky. 2006a. "Development of a Universally Applicable Household Food Insecurity Measurement Tool: Process, Current Status, and Outstanding Issues." *Journal of Nutrition* 136 (5): 1449S–1452S.

———. 2006b. *Household Dietary Diversity Score (HDDS) for Measurement of Household Food Access: Indicator Guide*. Version 2. Washington, DC: Food and Nutrition Technical Assistance (FANTA) Project, Academy for Educational Development.

Tarozzi, A. 2005. "The Indian Public Distribution System as Provider of Food Security: Evidence from Child Nutrition in Andhra Pradesh." *European Economic Review* 49 (5): 1305–1330.

Thiele, S., G. Mensink, and R. Beitz. 2004. "Determinants of Diet Quality." *Public Health Nutrition* 7 (1): 29–37.

Thomas, D. 1990. "Intra-Household Resource Allocation: An Inferential Approach." *Journal of Human Resources* 25 (4): 635–664.

Thow, A., S. Jan, S. Leeder, and B. Swinburn. 2010. "The Effect of Fiscal Policy on Diet, Obesity and Chronic Disease: A Systematic Review." *Bulletin of the World Health Organization* 88 (8): 609–614.

Timmer, P., W. Falcon, and S. Pearson. 1983. *Food Policy Analysis*. Baltimore: Johns Hopkins University Press.

Trego, R. 2011. "The Functioning of the Egyptian Food-Subsidy System during Food-Price Shocks." *Development in Practice* 21 (4–5): 666–678.

Trogdon, J., E. Finkelstein, T. Hylands, P. Dellea, and S. Kamal-Bahl. 2008. "Indirect Costs of Obesity: A Review of the Current Literature." *Obesity Reviews* 9 (5): 489–500.

Turcksin, R., S. Bel, S. Galjaard, and R. Devlieger. 2014. "Maternal Obesity and Breastfeeding Intention, Initiation, Intensity and Duration: A Systematic Review." *Maternal and Child Nutrition* 10 (2): 166–183.

Uauy, R., J. Kain, V. Mericq, J. Rojas, and C. Corvalan. 2008. "Nutrition, Child Growth, and Chronic Disease Prevention." *Annals of Medicine* 40: 11–20.

UN-DESA (United Nations Department of Economic and Social Affairs). 2014. World Population Prospects Database. Accessed July 5, 2014. http://esa.un.org/unpd/wpp/.

UNICEF (United Nations Children's Fund). 1990. *Strategy for Improved Nutrition of Children and Women in Developing Countries*. UNICEF Policy Review. New York: United Nations Children's Fund.

UNSTAT (United Nations Statistics Division). 2014. National Accounts Main Aggregates Database. Accessed July 5, 2014. http://unstats.un.org/unsd/snaama/Introduction.asp.

Ver Ploeg, M., L. Mancino, B.-H. Lin, and C.-Y. Wang. 2007. "The Vanishing Weight Gap: Trends in Obesity among Adult Food Stamp Participants (US) (1976–2002)." *Economics and Human Biology* 5 (1): 20–36.

Verme, P., B. Milanovic, S. Al-Shawarby, S. El Tawila, M. Gadallah, and E. El-Majeed. 2014. *Inside Inequality in the Arab Republic of Egypt: Facts and Perceptions across People, Time, and Space.* Washington, DC: World Bank.

Victora, C., L. Adair, C. Fall, P. Hallal, R. Martorell, L. Richter, and H. Sachdev. 2008. "Maternal and Child Undernutrition: Consequences for Adult Health and Human Capital." *Lancet* 371 (9609): 340–357.

Victora, C., M. de Onis, P. Hallal, M. Blössner, and R. Shrimpton. 2010. "Worldwide Timing of Growth Faltering: Revisiting Implications for Interventions." *Pediatrics* 125(3): e474–480.

Villamor, E., and W. Fawzi. 2000. "Vitamin A Supplementation: Implications for Morbidity and Mortality in Children." *Journal of Infectious Diseases* 182 (S1): S122–S133.

Walker, S., T. Wachs, J. Meeks Gardner, B. Lozoff, G. Wasserman, E. Pollitt, and J. Carter. 2007. "Child Development: Risk Factors for Adverse Outcomes in Developing Countries." *Lancet* 369 (9556): 145–157.

Webb, P., and S. Block. 2012 "Support for Agriculture during Economic Transformation: Impacts on Poverty and Undernutrition." *Proceedings of the National Academy of Sciences* 109 (31): 12309–12314.

WFP (World Food Programme). 2008. *Vulnerability Analysis and Review of Food Subsidy in Egypt.* Cairo, Egypt: World Food Programme.

———. 2013. *The Status of Poverty and Food Security in Egypt: Analysis and Policy Recommendations—Preliminary Summary Report.* Cairo, Egypt: World Food Programme.

WHO (World Health Organization). 2011. *Global Status Report on Noncommunicable Diseases 2010.* Geneva: World Health Organization.

Williams, P., S. Cates, J. Blitstein, J. Hersey, V. Gabor, M. Ball, K. Kosa, H. Wilson, S. Olson, and A. Singh. 2014. "Nutrition-Education Program Improves Preschoolers' At-Home Diet: A Group Randomized Trial." *Journal of the Academy of Nutrition and Dietetics* 114 (7): 1001–1008.

Williams, P., S. Cates, J. Blitsein, J. Hersey, K. Kosa, V. Long, A. Singh, and D. Berman. 2015. "Evaluating the Impact of Six Supplemental Nutrition Assistance Program Education Interventions on Children's At-Home Diets." *Health Education and Behavior* 42 (3): 329–338.

Wolfe, B., and J. Behrman. 1983. "Is Income Overrated in Determining Adequate Nutrition?" *Economic Development and Cultural Change* 31 (3): 525–549.

World Bank. 2006. *Repositioning Nutrition as Central to Development: A Strategy for Large-Scale Action.* Washington, DC: World Bank.

———. 2007. *Arab Republic of Egypt: Poverty Assessment Update.* Report 39885-EG. Cairo, Egypt: Ministry of Economic Development, World Bank.

———. 2012. Poverty and Inequality Analysis Portal. Accessed January 3, 2012. http://go.worldbank.org/VFPEGF7FU0.

———. 2014. World Development Indicators Databank. Accessed July 5, 2014. http://data.worldbank.org/data-catalog/world-development-indicators.

Wu, G., F. Bazer, T. Cudd, C. Meininger, and T. Spencer. 2004. "Maternal Nutrition and Fetal Development." *Journal of Nutrition* 134 (9): 2169–2172.

Yang, D. 1999. "Urban-Biased Policies and Rising Income Inequality in China." *American Economic Review* 89 (2): 306–310.

Yi, S.-W., Y.-J. Han, and H. Ohrr. 2013. "Anemia before Pregnancy and Risk of Preterm Birth, Low Birth Weight and Small-for-Gestational-Age Birth in Korean Women." *European Journal of Clinical Nutrition* 67 (4): 337–342.

Youssef, M., M. Mohsen, N. Abou El-Soud, and Y. Kazem. 2010. "Energy Intake, Diet Composition among Low Social Class Overweight and Obese Egyptian Adolescents." *Journal of American Science* 6 (9): 160–168.

Zagorsky, J., and P. Smith. 2009. "Does the U.S. Food Stamp Program Contribute to Adult Weight Gain?" *Economics and Human Biology* 7 (2): 246–258.

Appendix

TABLE A.1 Prevalence of female overweight and annual average change in Egypt

	2000 (%)	2003[a] (%)	2005 (%)	2008[b] (%)	2011 (%)	2000–2011 (percentage points)	2005–2011 (percentage points)
Total	**77.9**	**78.0**	**80.5**	**78.6**	**72.6**	**−0.5**	**−1.3**
By region and residential area[c]							
Metropolitan	88.4	88.8	89.1	84.6	74.0	−1.3	−2.5
Lower Egypt	84.3	83.6	85.3	85.5	78.3	−0.5	−1.2
Urban	89.5	86.8	89.8	89.4	78.5	−1.0	−1.9
Rural	82.2	82.3	83.7	84.1	78.2	−0.4	−0.9
Upper Egypt	64.0	65.4	70.7	66.7	65.6	0.1	−0.8
Urban	78.9	77.7	82.3	76.6	71.5	−0.7	−1.8
Rural	56.4	59.6	65.0	62.0	62.8	0.6	−0.4
By wealth/income quintile and residential area							
Quintile 1 (poorest)	61.1	65.6	66.1	65.6	66.2	0.5	0.0
Quintile 2	72.8	72.2	76.0	74.7	71.2	−0.1	−0.8
Quintile 3	80.0	77.3	81.3	81.3	75.1	−0.4	−1.0
Quintile 4	85.8	83.6	86.0	84.6	75.3	−0.9	−1.8
Quintile 5 (richest)	90.2	86.8	89.9	84.3	75.0	−1.4	−2.5
Urban	86.0	85.2	87.3	83.4	74.3	−1.1	−2.2
Quintile 1 (poorest)	77.7	76.9	81.7	77.6	72.6	−0.5	−1.5
Quintile 2	83.4	85.9	85.8	84.0	77.0	−0.6	−1.5
Quintile 3	88.7	87.5	88.0	86.2	74.2	−1.3	−2.3
Quintile 4	89.5	87.5	89.2	85.2	76.1	−1.2	−2.2
Quintile 5 (richest)	90.5	87.2	91.1	83.1	71.6	−1.7	−3.3

	2000 (%)	2003[a] (%)	2005 (%)	2008[b] (%)	2011 (%)	2000–2011 (percentage points)	2005–2011 (percentage points)
Rural	71.2	72.4	75.5	75.1	71.3	0.0	−0.7
Quintile 1 (poorest)	56.8	60.4	62.7	62.5	62.3	0.5	−0.1
Quintile 2	66.6	70.7	70.0	70.4	69.6	0.3	−0.1
Quintile 3	72.1	72.4	76.8	75.4	71.0	−0.1	−1.0
Quintile 4	76.3	75.3	79.7	81.1	74.9	−0.1	−0.8
Quintile 5 (richest)	83.1	78.6	83.7	83.6	78.8	−0.4	−0.8

Source: Authors' estimation based on DHS data (2000–2008) (MOH, El-Zanaty and Associates, and Macro International 2008; MOHP, NPC, and ORC Macro 2000; MOHP et al. 2003; MOHP et al. 2005) and data from CAPMAS and WFP (2011).

Note: The samples include nonpregnant women 20–49 years of age with biologically plausible body mass indexes (BMIs) ($5.2 \leq$ BMI ≤ 52.1). The prevalence rate of female overweight is defined as the proportion of women with BMIs equal to 25 and above.

The Demographic and Health Surveys (DHSs) from 2000, 2005, and 2008 (MOH, El-Zanaty and Associates, and Macro International 2008; MOHP, NPC, and ORC Macro 2000; MOHP et al. 2003; MOHP et al. 2005) are standard DHSs, and the respective samples contain 13,608, 16,843, and 14,388 observations from all governorates in Egypt. The 2011 Household Income, Expenditure, and Consumption Survey (HIECS) sample (CAPMAS and WFP 2011) contains 9,778 observations from all governorates. The household disaggregation by wealth/income quintile in the DHS samples is based on the distribution of asset wealth (measured by a composite index), and the household disaggregation in the HIECS sample is based on the distribution of household income per capita.

[a] The 2003 DHS is an interim DHS and contains 7,923 observations. It excludes the Frontier Governorates and oversampled Menia Governorate (located in Upper Egypt) and the slum areas of Greater Cairo (belonging to the Metropolitan area).

[b] The 2008 DHS data yield implausible subnational prevalence rates.

[c] Estimates for Frontier Governorates are not reported because of insufficient observations.

TABLE A.2 Prevalence of female obesity and annual average change in Egypt

	2000 (%)	2003[a] (%)	2005 (%)	2008[b] (%)	2011 (%)	2000–2011 (percentage points)	2005–2011 (percentage points)
Total	**41.5**	**36.3**	**47.2**	**40.1**	**33.9**	**−0.7**	**−2.2**
By region and residential area[c]							
Metropolitan	47.8	48.9	59.8	42.8	33.9	−1.3	−4.3
Lower Egypt	48.8	38.3	52.6	46.7	40.9	−0.7	−2.0
Urban	56.3	42.3	56.3	50.6	39.7	−1.5	−2.8
Rural	45.7	36.7	51.3	45.4	41.4	−0.4	−1.7
Upper Egypt	28.9	27.1	34.7	30.1	25.8	−0.3	−1.5
Urban	42.5	34.9	47.9	38.2	29.4	−1.2	−3.1
Rural	22.0	23.4	28.2	26.2	24.1	0.2	−0.7
By wealth/income quintile and residential area							
Quintile 1 (poorest)	24.9	28.4	32.8	30.4	27.6	0.2	−0.9
Quintile 2	36.9	30.0	39.5	37.2	32.4	−0.4	−1.2
Quintile 3	44.5	35.1	47.3	42.6	36.6	−0.7	−1.8
Quintile 4	50.0	39.6	54.7	44.1	37.5	−1.1	−2.9
Quintile 5 (richest)	51.6	45.0	58.0	44.1	35.5	−1.5	−3.8
Urban	48.7	43.2	55.5	43.5	34.2	−1.3	−3.6
Quintile 1 (poorest)	38.7	37.3	48.2	39.3	31.4	−0.7	−2.8
Quintile 2	47.8	42.5	52.2	42.4	36.7	−1.0	−2.6
Quintile 3	54.0	42.3	57.7	46.8	35.8	−1.7	−3.7
Quintile 4	52.6	46.2	59.9	45.5	36.2	−1.5	−3.9
Quintile 5 (richest)	50.3	46.7	58.3	42.7	30.7	−1.8	−4.6

	2000 (%)	2003[a] (%)	2005 (%)	2008[b] (%)	2011 (%)	2000–2011 (percentage points)	2005–2011 (percentage points)
Rural	35.5	30.9	41.2	37.5	33.8	−0.2	−1.2
Quintile 1 (poorest)	21.9	25.4	29.9	28.0	25.5	0.3	−0.7
Quintile 2	29.5	29.1	34.3	35.4	31.0	0.1	−0.5
Quintile 3	37.0	29.8	40.0	36.0	33.4	−0.3	−1.1
Quintile 4	42.2	32.7	45.0	43.2	37.3	−0.5	−1.3
Quintile 5 (richest)	45.9	35.1	51.7	43.3	41.8	−0.4	−1.7

Source: Authors' estimation based on DHS data (2000–2008) (MOH, El-Zanaty and Associates, and Macro International 2008; MOHP, NPC, and ORC Macro 2000; MOHP et al. 2003; MOHP et al. 2005) and data from CAPMAS and WFP (2011).

Note: The samples include nonpregnant women 20–49 years of age with biologically plausible body mass indexes (BMIs) ($5.2 \leq BMI \leq 52.1$). The prevalence rate of female obesity is defined as the proportion of women with BMIs equal to 30 and above.

The Demographic and Health Surveys (DHSs) from 2000, 2005, and 2008 (MOH, El-Zanaty and Associates, and Macro International 2008; MOHP, NPC, and ORC Macro 2000; MOHP et al. 2003; MOHP et al. 2005) are standard DHSs, and the respective samples contain 13,608, 16,843, and 14,388 observations from all governorates in Egypt. The 2011 Household Income, Expenditure, and Consumption Survey (HIECS) sample (CAPMAS and WFP 2011) contains 9,778 observations from all governorates. The household disaggregation by wealth/income quintile in the DHS samples is based on the distribution of asset wealth (measured by a composite index), and the household disaggregation in the HIECS sample is based on the distribution of household income per capita.

[a] The 2003 DHS is an interim DHS and contains 7,923 observations. It excludes the Frontier Governorates and oversampled Menia Governorate (located in Upper Egypt) and the slum areas of Greater Cairo (belonging to the Metropolitan area).

[b] The 2008 DHS data yield implausible subnational prevalence rates.

[c] Estimates for Frontier Governorates are not reported because of insufficient observations.

TABLE A.3 Prevalence of child stunting and annual average change in Egypt

	2000 (%)	2003[a] (%)	2005 (%)	2008[b] (%)	2011 (%)	2000–2011 (percentage points)	2005–2011 (percentage points)
Total	**23.3**	**19.3**	**23.4**	**32.0**	**31.2**	**0.7**	**1.3**
By region and residential area[c]							
Metropolitan	11.6	18.4	21.5	24.3	30.8	1.7	1.6
Lower Egypt	21.2	13.1	17.1	38.1	27.1	0.5	1.7
Urban	18.9	12.9	18.5	42.8	24.7	0.5	1.0
Rural	22.1	13.2	16.7	36.7	27.8	0.5	1.8
Upper Egypt	31.1	25.8	30.2	28.0	34.7	0.3	0.8
Urban	25.8	20.2	24.8	24.2	39.2	1.2	2.4
Rural	33.2	27.9	32.3	29.5	33.4	0.0	0.2
By wealth/income quintile and residential area							
Quintile 1 (poorest)	31.7	26.7	33.6	31.5	34.0	0.2	0.1
Quintile 2	27.4	19.4	26.0	34.0	32.3	0.4	1.0
Quintile 3	23.2	19.4	23.2	31.2	29.2	0.5	1.0
Quintile 4	19.3	14.9	19.4	32.1	27.2	0.7	1.3
Quintile 5 (richest)	14.7	18.9	17.8	31.3	33.1	1.7	2.5
Urban	17.7	17.2	21.6	29.7	31.9	1.3	1.7
Quintile 1 (poorest)	22.5	22.0	29.9	30.6	33.0	0.9	0.5
Quintile 2	20.8	13.4	21.8	29.2	32.3	1.1	1.8
Quintile 3	16.4	13.6	22.9	29.0	31.9	1.4	1.5
Quintile 4	16.3	19.5	19.2	30.5	33.0	1.5	2.3
Quintile 5 (richest)	12.8	18.0	15.6	29.4	29.4	1.5	2.3

	2000 (%)	2003[a] (%)	2005 (%)	2008[b] (%)	2011 (%)	2000–2011 (percentage points)	2005–2011 (percentage points)
Rural	27.2	20.7	24.5	33.4	30.8	0.3	1.0
Quintile 1 (poorest)	33.0	25.9	36.0	32.7	32.3	−0.1	−0.6
Quintile 2	29.4	21.9	28.1	33.0	33.8	0.4	1.0
Quintile 3	27.8	18.7	23.9	33.0	30.7	0.3	1.1
Quintile 4	25.9	21.6	22.1	30.9	26.8	0.1	0.8
Quintile 5 (richest)	20.4	17.6	17.2	36.9	30.3	0.9	2.2

Source: Authors' estimation based on DHS data (2000–2008) (MOH, El-Zanaty and Associates, and Macro International 2008; MOHP, NPC, and ORC Macro 2000; MOHP et al. 2003; MOHP et al. 2005) and data from CAPMAS and WFP (2011).

Note: The samples include children ages 6–59 months with biologically plausible height-for-age z-scores (HAZs) ($-6 \leq HAZ \leq 6$). The prevalence rate of child stunting is defined as the proportion of children with HAZs below −2.

The Demographic and Health Surveys (DHSs) from 2000, 2005, and 2008 (MOH, El-Zanaty and Associates, and Macro International 2008; MOHP, NPC, and ORC Macro 2000; MOHP et al. 2003; MOHP et al. 2005) are standard DHSs, and the respective samples contain 8,350, 10,878, and 8,646 observations from all governorates in Egypt. The 2011 Household Income, Expenditure, and Consumption Survey (HIECS) sample (CAPMAS and WFP 2011) contains 3,852 observations from all governorates. The household disaggregation by wealth/income quintile in the DHS samples is based on the distribution of asset wealth (measured by a composite index), and the household disaggregation in the HIECS sample is based on the distribution of household income per capita.

[a] The 2003 DHS is an interim DHS and contains 5,200 observations. It excludes the Frontier Governorates and oversampled Menia Governorate (located in Upper Egypt) and the slum areas of Greater Cairo (belonging to the Metropolitan area). The 2008 DHS data yield implausible subnational prevalence estimates.

[b] The 2008 DHS data yield implausible subnational prevalence rates.

[c] Estimates for Frontier Governorates are not reported because of insufficient observations.

TABLE A.4 Prevalence of child wasting and annual average change in Egypt

	2000 (%)	2003[a] (%)	2005 (%)	2008[b] (%)	2011 (%)	2000–2011 (percentage points)	2005–2011 (percentage points)
Total	**2.4**	**4.6**	**4.3**	**7.2**	**4.7**	**0.2**	**0.1**
By region and residential area[c]							
Metropolitan	2.1	3.8	10.2	11.0	5.6	0.3	−0.8
Lower Egypt	2.6	3.4	2.7	6.2	4.1	0.1	0.2
Urban	3.1	2.9	2.0	5.8	4.0	0.1	0.3
Rural	2.4	3.7	3.0	6.3	4.1	0.2	0.2
Upper Egypt	2.4	6.0	3.7	6.9	5.2	0.3	0.3
Urban	2.4	7.1	3.9	8.4	5.1	0.2	0.2
Rural	2.4	5.6	3.6	6.3	5.3	0.3	0.3
By wealth/income quintile and residential area							
Quintile 1 (poorest)	2.9	5.9	4.9	7.0	5.8	0.3	0.2
Quintile 2	2.5	3.4	2.4	7.8	4.3	0.2	0.3
Quintile 3	2.4	5.1	2.9	7.6	3.3	0.1	0.1
Quintile 4	2.5	4.8	4.1	6.2	6.0	0.3	0.3
Quintile 5 (richest)	1.6	4.0	7.1	7.5	4.4	0.3	−0.5
Urban	2.4	4.5	6.0	8.7	5.0	0.2	−0.2
Quintile 1 (poorest)	4.1	5.5	4.1	11.4	5.8	0.2	0.3
Quintile 2	3.5	4.5	5.0	7.9	2.1	−0.1	−0.5
Quintile 3	1.2	5.3	4.1	6.6	4.2	0.3	0.0
Quintile 4	1.1	4.8	7.2	7.6	6.8	0.5	−0.1
Quintile 5 (richest)	2.4	2.7	9.2	10.5	5.9	0.3	−0.6

	2000 (%)	2003[a] (%)	2005 (%)	2008[b] (%)	2011 (%)	2000–2011 (percentage points)	2005–2011 (percentage points)
Rural	2.4	4.6	3.3	6.3	4.6	0.2	0.2
Quintile 1 (poorest)	2.3	6.5	5.3	7.3	5.6	0.3	0.1
Quintile 2	3.4	4.5	3.5	6.6	4.8	0.1	0.2
Quintile 3	1.8	3.4	2.0	7.4	3.9	0.2	0.3
Quintile 4	1.8	3.9	2.3	7.3	5.6	0.3	0.5
Quintile 5 (richest)	2.5	5.4	3.7	3.5	3.3	0.1	−0.1

Source: Authors' estimation based on DHS data (2000–2008) (MOH, El-Zanaty and Associates, and Macro International 2008; MOHP, NPC, and ORC Macro 2000; MOHP et al. 2003; MOHP et al. 2005) and data from CAPMAS and WFP (2011).

Note: The samples include children ages 6–59 months with biologically plausible weight-for-height z-score (WHZ) ($-5 \leq WHZ \leq 5$). The prevalence rate of child wasting is defined as the proportion of children with WHZ below −2.

The Demographic and Health Surveys (DHSs) from 2000, 2005, and 2008 (MOH, El-Zanaty and Associates, and Macro International 2008; MOHP, NPC, and ORC Macro 2000; MOHP et al. 2003; MOHP et al. 2005) are standard DHSs, and the respective samples contain 8,343, 10,866, and 8,532 observations from all governorates in Egypt. The 2011 Household Income, Expenditure, and Consumption Survey (HIECS) sample (CAPMAS and WFP 2011) contains 3,664 observations from all governorates. The household disaggregation by wealth/income quintile in the DHS samples is based on the distribution of asset wealth (measured by a composite index), and the household disaggregation in the HIECS sample is based on the distribution of household income per capita.

[a] The 2003 DHS is an interim DHS and contains 5,196 observations. It excludes the Frontier Governorates and oversampled Menia Governorate (located in Upper Egypt) and the slum areas of Greater Cairo (belonging to the Metropolitan area).

[b] The 2008 DHS data yield implausible subnational prevalence rates.

[c] Estimates for Frontier Governorates are not reported because of insufficient observations.

TABLE A.5 Prevalence of child underweight and annual average change in Egypt

	2000 (%)	2003[a] (%)	2005 (%)	2008[b] (%)	2011 (%)	2000–2011 (percentage points)	2005–2011 (percentage points)
Total	**3.3**	**7.2**	**4.4**	**6.6**	**6.9**	**0.3**	**0.4**
By region and residential area[c]							
Metropolitan	1.8	5.5	6.6	6.2	6.9	0.5	0.0
Lower Egypt	2.0	3.9	3.1	5.9	6.0	0.4	0.5
Urban	2.1	2.8	2.9	5.2	8.3	0.6	0.9
Rural	1.9	4.4	3.1	6.1	5.4	0.3	0.4
Upper Egypt	5.6	11.1	4.9	7.5	7.4	0.2	0.4
Urban	3.3	10.0	4.0	7.7	6.9	0.3	0.5
Rural	6.6	11.5	5.3	7.5	7.6	0.1	0.4
By wealth/income quintile and residential area							
Quintile 1 (poorest)	5.6	11.9	5.3	7.9	8.7	0.3	0.6
Quintile 2	3.7	7.0	4.5	8.0	7.0	0.3	0.4
Quintile 3	3.5	6.7	3.7	6.4	6.3	0.3	0.4
Quintile 4	2.1	5.6	3.7	5.8	5.5	0.3	0.3
Quintile 5 (richest)	1.6	6.6	4.9	5.2	6.8	0.5	0.3
Urban	2.3	5.9	4.7	6.4	7.5	0.5	0.5
Quintile 1 (poorest)	2.9	7.0	4.6	9.3	8.7	0.5	0.7
Quintile 2	3.6	5.2	6.3	7.6	7.5	0.4	0.2
Quintile 3	1.9	6.3	3.3	4.6	5.6	0.3	0.4
Quintile 4	1.6	7.2	5.2	5.4	7.6	0.5	0.4
Quintile 5 (richest)	1.7	4.3	4.1	5.7	7.9	0.6	0.6

	2000 (%)	2003[a] (%)	2005 (%)	2008[b] (%)	2011 (%)	2000–2011 (percentage points)	2005–2011 (percentage points)
Rural	4.0	8.1	4.2	6.7	6.5	0.2	0.4
Quintile 1 (poorest)	5.9	11.9	6.8	9.4	7.7	0.2	0.2
Quintile 2	5.6	9.5	3.8	7.3	7.1	0.1	0.6
Quintile 3	2.9	7.0	4.0	6.4	7.9	0.5	0.7
Quintile 4	4.0	6.3	3.4	6.3	4.9	0.1	0.2
Quintile 5 (richest)	1.8	7.3	3.7	4.7	4.9	0.3	0.2

Source: Authors' estimation based on DHS data (2000–2008) (MOH, El-Zanaty and Associates, and Macro International 2008; MOHP, NPC, and ORC Macro 2000; MOHP et al. 2003; MOHP et al. 2005) and data from CAPMAS and WFP (2011).

Note: The samples include children ages 6–59 months with biologically plausible weight-for-age z-score (WAZ) ($-6 \leq WAZ \leq 5$). The prevalence rate of child underweight is defined as the proportion of children with WAZ below −2.

The Demographic and Health Surveys (DHSs) from 2000, 2005, and 2008 (MOH, El-Zanaty and Associates, and Macro International 2008; MOHP, NPC, and ORC Macro 2000; MOHP et al. 2003; MOHP et al. 2005) are standard DHSs, and the respective samples contain 8,445, 11,150, and 8,959 observations from all governorates in Egypt. The 2011 Household Income, Expenditure, and Consumption Survey (HIECS) sample (CAPMAS and WFP 2011) contains 4,084 observations from all governorates. The household disaggregation by wealth/income quintile in the DHS samples is based on the distribution of asset wealth (measured by a composite index), and the household disaggregation in the HIECS sample is based on the distribution of household income per capita.

[a] The 2003 DHS is an interim DHS and contains 5,258 observations. It excludes the Frontier Governorates and oversampled Menia Governorate (located in Upper Egypt) and the slum areas of Greater Cairo (belonging to the Metropolitan area).

[b] The 2008 DHS data yield implausible subnational prevalence rates.

[c] Estimates for Frontier Governorates are not reported because of insufficient observations.

TABLE A.6 Prevalence of child overweight and annual average change in Egypt

	2000 (%)	2003[a] (%)	2005 (%)	2008[b] (%)	2011 (%)	2000–2011 (percentage points)	2005–2011 (percentage points)
Total	**21.6**	**10.1**	**14.9**	**22.8**	**29.2**	**0.7**	**2.4**
By region and residential area[c]							
Metropolitan	10.0	13.4	15.7	24.8	29.5	1.8	2.3
Lower Egypt	27.2	10.1	15.2	29.5	30.7	0.3	2.6
Urban	29.1	8.7	12.7	34.5	27.1	−0.2	2.4
Rural	26.4	10.7	16.0	28.0	31.7	0.5	2.6
Upper Egypt	20.0	8.8	14.5	14.4	27.0	0.6	2.1
Urban	18.4	8.8	13.1	13.8	28.1	0.9	2.5
Rural	20.6	8.8	15.1	14.6	26.7	0.5	1.9
By wealth/income quintile and residential area							
Quintile 1 (poorest)	21.3	7.5	18.0	14.8	27.9	0.6	1.7
Quintile 2	22.1	9.3	15.0	20.7	28.9	0.6	2.3
Quintile 3	23.3	9.4	14.8	23.5	28.7	0.5	2.3
Quintile 4	21.9	12.6	13.5	26.7	26.6	0.4	2.2
Quintile 5 (richest)	19.1	10.4	14.2	26.6	33.7	1.3	3.2
Urban	18.2	10.6	14.0	24.4	28.8	1.0	2.5
Quintile 1 (poorest)	18.1	9.5	14.6	20.1	26.4	0.8	2.0
Quintile 2	18.0	10.0	11.7	24.0	29.9	1.1	3.0
Quintile 3	19.5	12.0	13.9	26.0	27.4	0.7	2.3
Quintile 4	18.4	10.3	14.8	24.9	30.4	1.1	2.6
Quintile 5 (richest)	16.8	10.9	15.0	26.1	30.1	1.2	2.5

	2000 (%)	2003[a] (%)	2005 (%)	2008[b] (%)	2011 (%)	2000–2011 (percentage points)	2005–2011 (percentage points)
Rural	23.9	9.7	15.5	21.8	29.3	0.5	2.3
Quintile 1 (poorest)	21.2	7.3	17.7	13.9	27.1	0.5	1.6
Quintile 2	21.2	9.7	15.8	17.7	28.2	0.6	2.1
Quintile 3	23.8	8.2	17.0	21.6	31.6	0.7	2.4
Quintile 4	24.5	9.6	14.8	25.4	25.9	0.1	1.9
Quintile 5 (richest)	28.4	12.6	13.5	28.7	34.0	0.5	3.4

Source: Authors' estimation based on DHS data (2000–2008) (MOH, El-Zanaty and Associates, and Macro International 2008; MOHP, NPC, and ORC Macro 2000; MOHP et al. 2003; MOHP et al. 2005) and data from CAPMAS and WFP (2011).

Note: The samples include children ages 6–59 months with biologically plausible body-mass-index-for-age z-scores (BMIZs) ($-5 \leq$ BMIZ ≤ 5). The prevalence rate of child obesity is defined as the proportion of children with BMIZs equal to 2 and above.

The Demographic and Health Surveys (DHSs) from 2000, 2005, and 2008 (MOH, El-Zanaty and Associates, and Macro International 2008; MOHP, NPC, and ORC Macro 2000; MOHP et al. 2003; MOHP et al. 2005) are standard DHSs, and the respective samples contain 8,313, 10,790, and 8,401 observations from all governorates in Egypt. The 2011 Household Income, Expenditure, and Consumption Survey (HIECS) sample (CAPMAS and WFP 2011) contains 3,631 observations from all governorates. The household disaggregation by wealth/income quintile in the DHS samples is based on the distribution of asset wealth (measured by a composite index), and the household disaggregation in the HIECS sample is based on the distribution of household income per capita.

[a] The 2003 DHS is an interim DHS and contains 5,195 observations. It excludes the Frontier Governorates and oversampled Menia Governorate (located in Upper Egypt) and the slum areas of Greater Cairo (belonging to the Metropolitan area).

[b] The 2008 DHS data yield implausible subnational prevalence rates.

[c] Estimates for Frontier Governorates are not reported because of insufficient observations.

TABLE A.7 Prevalence of stunted children with overweight mothers and annual average change in Egypt

	2000 (%)	2003[a] (%)	2005 (%)	2008[b] (%)	2011 (%)	2000–2011 (percentage points)	2005–2011 (percentage points)
Total	**19.4**	**16.2**	**19.1**	**25.8**	**22.3**	**0.3**	**0.5**
By region and residential area[c]							
Metropolitan	13.8	15.8	19.1	22.1	26.9	1.2	1.3
Lower Egypt	20.2	14.5	16.4	33.4	20.6	0.0	0.7
Urban	20.0	14.0	20.6	40.0	20.4	0.0	0.0
Rural	20.2	14.7	14.9	31.3	20.7	0.0	1.0
Upper Egypt	21.4	18.3	22.0	18.3	21.5	0.0	–0.1
Urban	22.0	17.3	21.5	17.6	25.6	0.3	0.7
Rural	21.1	18.7	22.2	18.6	20.2	–0.1	–0.3
By wealth/income quintile and residential area							
Quintile 1 (poorest)	20.7	15.2	20.1	20.9	20.0	–0.1	0.0
Quintile 2	21.0	16.6	20.5	24.9	22.2	0.1	0.3
Quintile 3	19.8	17.3	19.8	25.0	22.8	0.3	0.5
Quintile 4	19.2	14.2	18.0	29.8	20.3	0.1	0.4
Quintile 5 (richest)	16.0	17.6	17.6	27.4	26.1	0.9	1.4
Urban	17.8	15.6	20.3	25.9	25.3	0.7	0.8
Quintile 1 (poorest)	21.3	17.1	24.1	24.8	21.8	0.0	–0.4
Quintile 2	18.0	12.4	21.7	25.5	25.5	0.7	0.6
Quintile 3	18.7	14.8	20.5	26.0	26.4	0.7	1.0
Quintile 4	15.6	17.7	18.9	28.2	29.9	1.3	1.8
Quintile 5 (richest)	15.5	16.3	16.5	24.9	22.9	0.7	1.1

	2000 (%)	2003[a] (%)	2005 (%)	2008[b] (%)	2011 (%)	2000–2011 (percentage points)	2005–2011 (percentage points)
Rural	20.6	16.7	18.4	25.8	20.6	0.0	0.4
Quintile 1 (poorest)	21.7	13.6	21.3	20.1	17.6	−0.4	−0.6
Quintile 2	19.9	15.2	18.6	25.7	22.4	0.2	0.6
Quintile 3	21.4	17.4	18.9	22.4	22.4	0.1	0.6
Quintile 4	19.4	18.6	19.3	26.9	18.8	−0.1	−0.1
Quintile 5 (richest)	20.7	17.1	15.0	32.2	21.9	0.1	1.2

Source: Authors' estimation based on DHS data (2000–2008) (MOH, El-Zanaty and Associates, and Macro International 2008; MOHP, NPC, and ORC Macro 2000; MOHP et al. 2003; MOHP et al. 2005) and data from CAPMAS and WFP (2011).

Note: The samples include children ages 6–59 months with biologically plausible height-for-age z-scores (HAZs) ($-6 \leq$ HAZ ≤ 6) and their nonpregnant mothers 20–49 years of age with biologically plausible body mass indexes (BMIs) ($5.2 \leq$ BMI $\leq$ 52.1). The prevalence rate of child stunting is defined as the proportion of children with HAZs below −2. The prevalence rate of female overweight is defined as the proportion of women with BMIs equal to 25 and above.

The Demographic and Health Surveys (DHSs) from 2000, 2005, and 2008 (MOH, El-Zanaty and Associates, and Macro International 2008; MOHP, NPC, and ORC Macro 2000; MOHP et al. 2003; MOHP et al. 2005) are standard DHSs, and the respective samples contain 6,237, 8,100, and 6,729 observations from all governorates in Egypt. The 2011 Household Income, Expenditure, and Consumption Survey (HIECS) sample (CAPMAS and WFP 2011) contains 3,661 observations from all governorates. The household disaggregation by wealth/income quintile in the DHS samples is based on the distribution of asset wealth (measured by a composite index), and the household disaggregation in the HIECS sample is based on the distribution of household income per capita.

[a] The 2003 DHS is an interim DHS and contains 3,850 observations. It excludes the Frontier Governorates and oversampled Menia Governorate (located in Upper Egypt) and the slum areas of Greater Cairo (belonging to the Metropolitan area). The 2008 DHS data yield implausible subnational prevalence estimates.

[b] The 2008 DHS data yield implausible subnational prevalence rates.

[c] Estimates for Frontier Governorates are not reported because of insufficient observations.

TABLE A.8 Prevalence of stunted and overweight children and annual average change in Egypt

	2000 (%)	2003[a] (%)	2005 (%)	2008[b] (%)	2011 (%)	2000–2011 (percentage points)	2005–2011 (percentage points)
Total	8.8	5.0	7.6	13.7	14.0	0.5	1.1
By region and residential area[c]							
Metropolitan	2.4	7.5	7.5	12.0	15.6	1.2	1.4
Lower Egypt	9.2	3.9	6.1	20.2	12.7	0.3	1.1
Urban	9.3	3.8	5.3	23.5	11.9	0.2	1.1
Rural	9.1	3.9	6.4	19.3	12.9	0.3	1.1
Upper Egypt	11.2	5.2	9.0	7.1	14.3	0.3	0.9
Urban	8.8	4.9	7.4	6.5	16.2	0.7	1.5
Rural	12.2	5.3	9.6	7.4	13.7	0.1	0.7
By wealth/income quintile and residential area							
Quintile 1 (poorest)	12.0	4.9	11.6	8.1	14.6	0.2	0.5
Quintile 2	10.5	3.9	7.9	12.9	15.0	0.4	1.2
Quintile 3	8.5	5.4	7.5	14.6	11.9	0.3	0.7
Quintile 4	8.5	4.5	6.2	15.9	12.5	0.4	1.0
Quintile 5 (richest)	4.6	6.0	5.8	15.9	15.9	1.0	1.7
Urban	6.3	5.6	6.9	13.7	15.1	0.8	1.4
Quintile 1 (poorest)	8.4	5.2	8.4	10.4	13.2	0.4	0.8
Quintile 2	8.1	3.9	6.8	13.2	16.6	0.8	1.6
Quintile 3	6.5	5.5	5.9	14.6	16.3	0.9	1.7
Quintile 4	4.5	5.6	6.5	14.2	14.1	0.9	1.3
Quintile 5 (richest)	4.1	7.5	6.9	15.2	15.4	1.0	1.4

	2000 (%)	2003[a] (%)	2005 (%)	2008[b] (%)	2011 (%)	2000–2011 (percentage points)	2005–2011 (percentage points)
Rural	10.6	4.6	8.0	13.7	13.4	0.3	0.9
Quintile 1 (poorest)	12.2	4.3	12.1	7.8	13.9	0.2	0.3
Quintile 2	10.6	5.0	8.7	10.8	14.5	0.4	1.0
Quintile 3	11.8	3.7	8.3	13.7	12.1	0.0	0.6
Quintile 4	9.4	5.5	7.6	16.1	11.7	0.2	0.7
Quintile 5 (richest)	9.2	4.4	5.1	18.9	14.7	0.5	1.6

Source: Authors' estimation based on DHS data (2000–2008) (MOH, El-Zanaty and Associates, and Macro International 2008; MOHP, NPC, and ORC Macro 2000; MOHP et al. 2003; MOHP et al. 2005) and data from CAPMAS and WFP (2011).

Note: The samples include children ages 6–59 months with biologically plausible height-for-age z-scores (HAZs) ($-6 \leq$ HAZ ≤ 6) and biologically plausible body-mass-index-for-age z-scores (BMIZs) ($-5 \leq$ BMIZ ≤ 5). The prevalence rate of stunted and overweight children is defined as the proportion of children with HAZs below −2 and BMIZs equal to 2 or above.

The Demographic and Health Surveys (DHSs) from 2000, 2005, and 2008 (MOH, El-Zanaty and Associates, and Macro International 2008; MOHP, NPC, and ORC Macro 2000; MOHP et al. 2003; MOHP et al. 2005) are standard DHSs, and the respective samples contain 8,255, 10,612, and 8,263 observations from all governorates in Egypt. The 2011 Household Income, Expenditure, and Consumption Survey (HIECS) sample (CAPMAS and WFP 2011) contains 3,577 observations from all governorates. The household disaggregation by wealth/income quintile in the DHS samples is based on the distribution of asset wealth (measured by a composite index), and the household disaggregation in the HIECS sample is based on the distribution of household income per capita.

[a] The 2003 DHS is an interim DHS and contains 5,148 observations. It excludes the Frontier Governorates and oversampled Menia Governorate (located in Upper Egypt) and the slum areas of Greater Cairo (belonging to the Metropolitan area).

[b] The 2008 DHS data yield implausible subnational prevalence rates.

[c] Estimates for Frontier Governorates are not reported because of insufficient observations.

TABLE A.9 Subsidized commodities, unit quantities, and unit prices under the ration-card program, as of January 2015

Commodity	Packaging unit (kg)	Amount deductible from ration card (EGP)	Beneficiary copayment (EGP)
Cooking oil			
Sunflower	0.92	9.75	0.25
Vegetable	0.92	8.45	0.25
Shortening			
Al-Mothida, Arma, Safola, Al-Diyar	0.8	7.00	0.25
Rotana, Al-Haloub	0.7	30.00	1.50
Al-Mothida, Arma, Safola	0.45	4.00	0.25
Sugar	1	4.50	0.25
Rice			
12% broken	1	2.25	0.15
5% broken	1	3.75	0.25
Wheat flour	1	3.60	0.15
Pasta			
Large	0.8	2.90	0.10
Small	0.35	1.32	0.03
Black tea			
Brook Bond, Al-Aroosa	0.04	1.30	0.05
Al-Safwa, Captain Tea	0.04	1.20	0.05
Lipton	0.02	0.73	0.03
Lentils (cracked)	0.5	3.35	0.15
Fava beans	1	4.60	0.40
Tomato paste (Al-Rashidi, Royal, Heinz, Edfina, Kaha)			
Large	0.32	2.80	0.20
Small	0.05	0.72	0.02
Fish			
Catfish, Shabar (frozen)	1	6.75	0.25
Tuna (canned)	0.14	5.85	0.15
Meat (frozen)	1	29.00	1.00

Commodity	Packaging unit (kg)	Amount deductible from ration card (EGP)	Beneficiary copayment (EGP)
Chicken (frozen)			
Whole	1	14.25	0.75
Breast (local)	1	17.50	0.50
White cheese			
Domti in plastic tub (various types)	1	14.75	0.25
Domti in Tetrapak (various types)			
Large	1	11.60	0.40
Medium	0.5	6.22	0.20
Small	0.25	3.23	0.15
Obour Land in Tetrapak (various types)			
Medium	0.5	6.80	0.20
Small	0.25	3.50	0.15
Milk (Al–Marae)	1	7.45	0.25
Milk powder	0.063	3.85	0.15
Ready meal			
Regular (canned)	0.8	11.50	0.25
Spicy (canned)	0.8	11.50	0.25
Nescafe (3 in 1)	0.019	0.56	0.04
Chicken bouillon (1 pack)	—	6.00	0.15
Hand soap	0.125	1.60	0.15
Washing machine detergent (Rabso, Savo, Cecil, Zal)			
Automatic	1	6.90	0.35
Standard	1	5.15	0.27
Bleach (Clorox)	1	2.00	0.10

Source: Authors' representation, based on MSIT (2015).

Note: — = data not available; EGP = Egyptian pounds; kg = kilograms.

TABLE A.10 Prevalence of anemia among nonpregnant women and children and average annual change in Egypt

	Children			Women		
	2000 (%)	2005 (%)	Change (percentage points)	2000 (%)	2005 (%)	Change (percentage points)
Total	**30.3**	**48.6**	**3.7**	**27.6**	**39.6**	**2.4**
By region and residential area[a]						
Metropolitan	17.5	42.4	5.0	29.1	40.7	2.3
Lower Egypt	29.3	43.1	2.8	26.6	36.1	1.9
Urban	25.2	38.4	2.6	25.2	36.4	2.2
Rural	30.6	44.6	2.8	27.1	36.0	1.8
Upper Egypt	36.1	55.3	3.8	27.9	42.8	3.0
Urban	32.8	49.3	3.3	23.5	43.4	4.0
Rural	37.4	57.6	4.0	30.1	42.4	2.5
By wealth/income quintile and residential area						
Quintile 1 (poorest)	36.3	55.3	3.8	30.3	41.6	2.3
Quintile 2	33.8	56.9	4.6	28.7	40.3	2.3
Quintile 3	34.8	49.0	2.8	29.5	37.0	1.5
Quintile 4	27.7	44.8	3.4	27.4	41.0	2.7
Quintile 5 (richest)	18.6	39.5	4.2	22.0	38.4	3.3
Urban	24.4	43.6	3.9	26.7	40.5	2.8
Quintile 1 (poorest)	31.0	47.1	3.2	30.4	42.6	2.5
Quintile 2	27.7	51.3	4.7	30.2	41.2	2.2
Quintile 3	25.7	44.7	3.8	29.2	43.4	2.8
Quintile 4	20.7	37.5	3.4	23.0	37.7	2.9
Quintile 5 (richest)	17.8	38.5	4.1	20.7	37.8	3.4

	Children			Women		
	2000 (%)	2005 (%)	Change (percentage points)	2000 (%)	2005 (%)	Change (percentage points)
Rural	34.0	51.4	3.5	28.4	38.9	2.1
Quintile 1 (poorest)	36.8	58.2	4.3	32.7	41.7	1.8
Quintile 2	37.5	56.9	3.9	26.8	38.3	2.3
Quintile 3	31.8	56.7	5.0	27.2	40.9	2.7
Quintile 4	36.2	48.9	2.5	29.9	37.7	1.6
Quintile 5 (richest)	28.3	41.1	2.6	25.8	36.9	2.2

Source: Authors' estimation based on 2000 and 2005 DHS data (MOH, El-Zanaty and Associates, and Macro International 2008; MOHP, NPC, and ORC Macro 2000; MOHP et al. 2003; MOHP et al. 2005).

Note: The samples include children ages 6–59 months and nonpregnant women 20–49 years of age (MOH, El-Zanaty and Associates, and Macro International 2008; MOHP, NPC, and ORC Macro 2000; MOHP et al. 2003; MOHP et al. 2005). The prevalence rate of anemia is defined as the proportion of children and women with hemoglobin concentration in the blood below 110 grams per liter (g/l) and 120 g/l, respectively.

The 2000 Demographic and Health Survey (DHS) sample contains observations from 4,809 children and 6,715 nonpregnant women. The 2005 DHS sample contains observations from 3,915 children and 5,505 nonpregnant women.

The household disaggregation by wealth/income quintile in the DHS samples is based on the distribution of asset wealth (measured by a composite index), and the household disaggregation in the Household Income, Expenditure, and Consumption Survey (HIECS) sample (CAPMAS and WFP 2011) is based on the distribution of household income per capita.

[a] Estimates for Frontier Governorates are not reported because of insufficient observations.

TABLE A.11 Descriptive statistics of estimation variables

	Urban		Rural	
	Mean	Std. dev.	Mean	Std. dev.
Nutrition and dietary quality outcomes				
Child nutrition				
Height-for-age z-score (HAZ)	–0.920	1.973	–0.930	1.926
Stunting (yes = 1, no = 0)	0.279	0.449	0.272	0.445
Body-mass-index-for-age z-score (BMIZ)	1.023	1.768	1.040	1.714
Overweight (yes = 1, no = 0)	0.282	0.450	0.293	0.455
Stunting & overweight (yes = 1, no = 0)	0.145	0.352	0.133	0.339
Maternal nutrition				
Body mass index (BMI) (kg/m^2)	29.09	5.25	28.25	5.18
Overweight (yes = 1, no = 0)	0.783	0.412	0.703	0.457
Double burden of malnutrition				
Child stunting & maternal overweight (yes = 1, no = 0)	0.230	0.421	0.189	0.391
Child overweight & maternal overweight (yes = 1, no = 0)	0.241	0.428	0.215	0.411
Household diet quality at the family level				
Household Dietary Diversity Score (HDDS) (max = 12)	10.67	1.13	10.43	1.17
Consumption frequency (days)				
Vegetables	3.254	2.046	3.559	2.106
Legumes	4.337	2.423	4.293	2.341
Meat & fish	2.995	1.728	2.605	1.481
Milk & dairy products	4.941	2.272	4.452	2.366
Treatment				
Ration card program				
Ration card (yes = 1, no = 0)	0.399	0.490	0.611	0.488
Per capita calorie consumption from oil, sugar, rice (kcal/d)	534.5	237.6	516.8	194.4
Baladi bread & flour program				
Per capita calorie consumption from Baladi bread & flour (kcal/d)	800.4	509.6	802.5	532.0
Independent variables: Household characteristics				
Per capita household income (EGP/d)	14.72	8.17	11.20	4.31
Household size (persons)	4.847	1.555	5.316	2.219
Single-mother household (yes = 1, no = 0)	0.047	0.212	0.050	0.218
Age of household head (years)	38.92	10.58	38.89	12.05

	Urban		Rural	
	Mean	Std. dev.	Mean	Std. dev.
Education of household head (attained level)				
None	0.271	0.445	0.397	0.489
Primary	0.162	0.369	0.100	0.299
Secondary	0.400	0.490	0.381	0.486
Higher	0.167	0.373	0.122	0.328
Pension or social benefits (yes = 1, no = 0)	0.172	0.447	0.212	0.492
Public-sector employment (yes = 1, no = 0)	0.243	0.498	0.244	0.506
Farm household (yes = 1, no = 0)			0.803	1.109
Governorate (aggregate) (yes = 1, no = 0)				
01	0.241	0.428	0.118	0.323
02	0.154	0.361	0.125	0.331
03	0.063	0.244	0.058	0.234
04	0.061	0.239	0.043	0.202
05	0.061	0.239	0.072	0.258
06	0.050	0.218	0.059	0.236
07	0.052	0.223	0.078	0.269
08	0.048	0.214	0.068	0.251
09	0.123	0.329	0.096	0.295
10	0.057	0.233	0.095	0.293
11	0.041	0.197	0.059	0.236
12	0.050	0.218	0.056	0.229
13			0.073	0.261

Source: Authors' calculation based on data from CAPMAS and WFP (2011).

Note: EGP/d = Egyptian pounds per day; kcal/d = kilocalories per day; kg/m^2 = kilograms per square meter.

The descriptive statistics for the independent variables are reported for the household datasets, of which the child and mother samples are subsamples.

TABLE A.12 Logistic regression results of the binary propensity score estimations for child nutrition indicators

	Urban				Rural			
	Coef.	Std. err.	z	P > |z|	Coef.	Std. err.	z	P > |z|
Per capita household income								
Quintile 2	−0.017	0.236	−0.07	0.941	0.135	0.202	0.67	0.502
Quintile 3	−0.358	0.249	−1.44	0.151	0.111	0.208	0.53	0.593
Quintile 4	−0.144	0.253	−0.57	0.570	0.001	0.219	0.01	0.996
Quintile 5 (richest)	−0.704	0.287	−2.45	0.014	−0.293	0.234	−1.25	0.211
Household size								
4	0.474	0.273	1.74	0.082	0.652	0.180	3.62	0.000
5	1.037	0.280	3.70	0.000	1.322	0.196	6.74	0.000
6	1.665	0.314	5.30	0.000	1.674	0.243	6.90	0.000
≥ 7	1.421	0.347	4.09	0.000	2.104	0.255	8.25	0.000
Single-mother household	1.201	0.529	2.27	0.023	0.988	0.528	1.87	0.061
Age of household head								
39–48	0.301	0.184	1.64	0.102	0.548	0.164	3.35	0.001
49–58	1.234	0.318	3.88	0.000	1.271	0.326	3.90	0.000
≥ 59	1.602	0.409	3.92	0.000	1.610	0.343	4.69	0.000
Education of household head								
Primary	−0.002	0.245	−0.01	0.993	−0.267	0.207	−1.29	0.199
Secondary	−0.072	0.201	−0.36	0.721	0.104	0.150	0.69	0.489
Higher	−0.453	0.289	−1.57	0.117	0.192	0.225	0.85	0.393
Pension or social benefits	0.951	0.241	3.94	0.000	1.318	0.223	5.91	0.000
Public-sector employment	0.390	0.201	1.94	0.052	0.632	0.166	3.81	0.000
Farm household					0.428	0.131	3.26	0.001

	Urban				Rural			
	Coef.	Std. err.	z	P > |z|	Coef.	Std. err.	z	P > |z|
Governorate (aggregate)								
02	−1.079	0.270	−4.00	0.000	−0.255	0.228	−1.12	0.265
03	0.302	0.344	0.88	0.379	−0.748	0.305	−2.45	0.014
04	0.197	0.339	0.58	0.561	0.244	0.345	0.71	0.480
05	0.028	0.356	0.08	0.938	0.562	0.280	2.01	0.045
06	−0.066	0.378	−0.18	0.860	−0.091	0.302	−0.30	0.762
07	0.484	0.342	1.41	0.157	0.853	0.269	3.16	0.002
08	0.491	0.355	1.38	0.166	−0.143	0.277	−0.52	0.606
09	−0.525	0.281	−1.87	0.061	−0.134	0.265	−0.51	0.613
10	0.055	0.354	0.16	0.877	−0.307	0.268	−1.15	0.252
11	−0.385	0.414	−0.93	0.353	−0.755	0.309	−2.44	0.015
12	0.932	0.385	2.42	0.016	−1.305	0.313	−4.16	0.000
13					0.155	0.276	0.56	0.575
Constant	−1.473	0.364	−4.04	0.000	−1.318	0.310	−4.26	0.000
Observations		1,006				1,765		
LR chi-sq.		297.4				588.3		
Prob. > chi-sq.		0.000				0.000		
Pseudo R-sq.		0.221				0.250		

Source: Authors' estimation based on data from CAPMAS and WFP (2011).

TABLE A.13 Logistic regression results of the binary propensity score estimations for maternal nutrition indicators

	Urban				Rural			
	Coef.	Std. err.	z	P > |z|	Coef.	Std. err.	z	P > |z|
Per capita household income								
Quintile 2	−0.143	0.222	−0.65	0.519	0.198	0.197	1.00	0.316
Quintile 3	−0.587	0.232	−2.53	0.011	0.158	0.203	0.78	0.435
Quintile 4	−0.359	0.239	−1.50	0.134	0.127	0.213	0.60	0.550
Quintile 5 (richest)	−0.931	0.272	−3.42	0.001	−0.274	0.228	−1.20	0.229
Household size								
4	0.331	0.249	1.33	0.184	0.619	0.180	3.43	0.001
5	0.816	0.257	3.17	0.002	1.403	0.195	7.18	0.000
6	1.509	0.287	5.27	0.000	1.680	0.237	7.09	0.000
≥ 7	1.093	0.319	3.43	0.001	2.078	0.251	8.28	0.000
Single-mother household	0.997	0.491	2.03	0.042	1.240	0.578	2.14	0.032
Age of household head								
39–48	0.243	0.175	1.39	0.165	0.490	0.157	3.12	0.002
49–58	1.155	0.290	3.98	0.000	1.199	0.315	3.81	0.000
≥ 59	1.502	0.376	3.99	0.000	1.883	0.376	5.01	0.000
Education of household head								
Primary	−0.075	0.231	−0.32	0.746	−0.210	0.204	−1.03	0.304
Secondary	−0.130	0.192	−0.68	0.499	0.071	0.148	0.48	0.629
Higher	−0.606	0.271	−2.24	0.025	−0.005	0.218	−0.02	0.983
Pension or social benefits	1.075	0.231	4.65	0.000	1.169	0.214	5.46	0.000
Public-sector employment	0.356	0.188	1.89	0.059	0.689	0.164	4.19	0.000
Farm household					0.417	0.129	3.25	0.001

	Urban				Rural			
	Coef.	Std. err.	z	P > |z|	Coef.	Std. err.	z	P > |z|
Governorate (aggregate)								
02	−0.997	0.251	−3.97	0.000	−0.533	0.225	−2.37	0.018
03	0.433	0.317	1.37	0.172	−0.777	0.297	−2.61	0.009
04	0.472	0.319	1.48	0.139	0.306	0.349	0.88	0.381
05	−0.152	0.333	−0.45	0.649	0.489	0.282	1.74	0.083
06	0.129	0.355	0.36	0.717	−0.299	0.294	−1.02	0.308
07	0.530	0.334	1.59	0.113	0.559	0.260	2.15	0.031
08	0.508	0.342	1.48	0.138	−0.265	0.268	−0.99	0.324
09	−0.541	0.259	−2.09	0.037	−0.121	0.264	−0.46	0.647
10	0.123	0.341	0.36	0.718	−0.454	0.264	−1.72	0.085
11	−0.125	0.378	−0.33	0.740	−0.922	0.303	−3.05	0.002
12	0.987	0.356	2.77	0.006	−1.229	0.304	−4.04	0.000
13					−0.031	0.274	−0.11	0.909
Constant	−1.109	0.336	−3.30	0.001	−1.209	0.304	−3.98	0.000
Observations	1,140				1,823			
LR chi-sq.	341.8				590.7			
Prob. > chi-sq.	0.000				0.000			
Pseudo R-sq.	0.224				0.244			

Source: Authors' estimation based on data from CAPMAS and WFP (2011).

TABLE A.14 Logistic regression results of the binary propensity score estimations for indicators of the double burden of malnutrition at the family level and coexisting child and maternal overweight

	Urban				Rural			
	Coef.	Std. err.	z	P > |z|	Coef.	Std. err.	z	P > |z|
Per capita household income								
Quintile 2	−0.007	0.242	−0.03	0.976	0.138	0.208	0.66	0.507
Quintile 3	−0.420	0.256	−1.64	0.101	0.144	0.216	0.67	0.506
Quintile 4	−0.224	0.261	−0.86	0.392	0.047	0.228	0.21	0.837
Quintile 5 (richest)	−0.675	0.298	−2.27	0.024	−0.263	0.243	−1.08	0.279
Household size								
4	0.408	0.281	1.45	0.146	0.632	0.191	3.31	0.001
5	0.932	0.290	3.21	0.001	1.328	0.206	6.43	0.000
6	1.657	0.321	5.16	0.000	1.666	0.253	6.59	0.000
≥ 7	1.440	0.354	4.06	0.000	2.120	0.266	7.96	0.000
Single-mother household	1.182	0.534	2.21	0.027	1.169	0.582	2.01	0.045
Age of household head								
39–48	0.297	0.188	1.58	0.114	0.580	0.168	3.45	0.001
49–58	1.155	0.325	3.55	0.000	1.178	0.336	3.50	0.000
≥ 59	1.475	0.415	3.55	0.000	1.786	0.382	4.67	0.000
Education of household head								
Primary	−0.035	0.251	−0.14	0.888	−0.246	0.214	−1.15	0.250
Secondary	−0.076	0.209	−0.36	0.717	0.067	0.156	0.43	0.665
Higher	−0.443	0.300	−1.48	0.140	0.137	0.233	0.59	0.557
Pension or social benefits	0.993	0.251	3.96	0.000	1.287	0.229	5.61	0.000
Public-sector employment	0.328	0.207	1.59	0.112	0.674	0.175	3.86	0.000
Farm household					0.471	0.136	3.45	0.001

	Urban				Rural			
	Coef.	Std. err.	z	P > |z|	Coef.	Std. err.	z	P > |z|
Governorate (aggregate)								
02	−1.016	0.278	−3.65	0.000	−0.366	0.238	−1.54	0.124
03	0.345	0.350	0.99	0.324	−0.838	0.315	−2.66	0.008
04	0.342	0.351	0.97	0.330	0.267	0.360	0.74	0.458
05	0.029	0.369	0.08	0.938	0.570	0.293	1.95	0.052
06	0.132	0.388	0.34	0.734	−0.211	0.317	−0.67	0.505
07	0.621	0.355	1.75	0.081	0.739	0.276	2.67	0.007
08	0.570	0.362	1.58	0.115	−0.172	0.290	−0.59	0.552
09	−0.420	0.285	−1.47	0.141	−0.043	0.279	−0.15	0.877
10	0.147	0.371	0.39	0.693	−0.494	0.282	−1.75	0.080
11	−0.282	0.419	−0.67	0.501	−0.773	0.320	−2.42	0.016
12	1.086	0.397	2.73	0.006	−1.288	0.323	−3.99	0.000
13					0.067	0.287	0.23	0.814
Constant	−1.477	0.380	−3.88	0.000	−1.286	0.324	−3.97	0.000
Observations	961				1,659			
LR chi-sq.	284.7				556.7			
Prob. > chi-sq.	0.000				0.000			
Pseudo R-sq.	0.223				0.253			

Source: Authors' estimation based on data from CAPMAS and WFP (2011).

TABLE A.15 Logistic regression results of the binary propensity score estimations for household diet quality indicators

	Urban				Rural			
	Coef.	Std. err.	z	P > lzl	Coef.	Std. err.	z	P > lzl
Per capita household income								
Quintile 2	−0.143	0.222	−0.64	0.519	0.228	0.193	1.18	0.238
Quintile 3	−0.422	0.232	−1.82	0.069	0.108	0.198	0.55	0.584
Quintile 4	−0.200	0.237	−0.84	0.399	0.152	0.209	0.73	0.467
Quintile 5 (richest)	−0.747	0.268	−2.78	0.005	−0.226	0.223	−1.01	0.311
Household size								
4	0.524	0.253	2.07	0.039	0.656	0.172	3.80	0.000
5	0.985	0.261	3.78	0.000	1.459	0.188	7.74	0.000
6	1.655	0.293	5.65	0.000	1.741	0.230	7.56	0.000
≥ 7	1.287	0.325	3.96	0.000	2.146	0.245	8.75	0.000
Single-mother household	1.160	0.509	2.28	0.023	0.835	0.492	1.70	0.090
Age of household head								
39–48	0.286	0.174	1.64	0.101	0.439	0.155	2.83	0.005
49–58	1.076	0.292	3.69	0.000	1.292	0.313	4.13	0.000
≥ 59	1.603	0.383	4.19	0.000	1.551	0.324	4.79	0.000
Education of household head								
Primary	−0.040	0.230	−0.17	0.863	−0.271	0.201	−1.35	0.178
Secondary	−0.138	0.189	−0.73	0.464	0.069	0.144	0.48	0.631
Higher	−0.668	0.274	−2.44	0.015	0.031	0.213	0.15	0.883
Pension or social benefits	1.002	0.227	4.41	0.000	1.249	0.212	5.90	0.000
Public-sector employment	0.429	0.187	2.29	0.022	0.637	0.158	4.03	0.000
Farm household					0.405	0.125	3.23	0.001

	Urban				Rural			
	Coef.	Std. err.	z	P > |z|	Coef.	Std. err.	z	P > |z|
Governorate (aggregate)								
02	−1.007	0.248	−4.06	0.000	−0.374	0.219	−1.71	0.088
03	0.259	0.321	0.81	0.420	−0.652	0.290	−2.25	0.024
04	0.401	0.316	1.27	0.205	0.275	0.338	0.81	0.416
05	−0.226	0.338	−0.67	0.504	0.553	0.273	2.03	0.043
06	0.024	0.353	0.07	0.947	−0.103	0.286	−0.36	0.718
07	0.444	0.328	1.35	0.176	0.706	0.255	2.77	0.006
08	0.552	0.345	1.60	0.110	−0.186	0.260	−0.71	0.475
09	−0.483	0.262	−1.84	0.066	−0.158	0.253	−0.63	0.531
10	0.064	0.337	0.19	0.850	−0.262	0.254	−1.03	0.301
11	−0.058	0.372	−0.16	0.876	−0.907	0.296	−3.06	0.002
12	0.781	0.354	2.21	0.027	−1.276	0.300	−4.25	0.000
13					0.101	0.266	0.38	0.705
Constant	−1.307	0.337	−3.88	0.000	−1.324	0.296	−4.48	0.000
Observations	1,130				1,911			
LR chi-sq.	336.2				620.7			
Prob. > chi-sq.	0.000				0.000			
Pseudo R-sq.	0.221				0.243			

Source: Authors' estimation based on data from CAPMAS and WFP (2011).

TABLE A.16 Balancing property test statistics of the binary propensity score estimations for child nutrition indicators

	Urban					Rural				
	Mean			t-test		Mean			t-test	
	Treated	Control	%-bias	t	P > |t|	Treated	Control	%-bias	t	P > |t|
Per capita household income										
Quintile 1 (poorest)	0.254	0.281	−6.8	−0.81	0.419	0.224	0.248	−5.9	−1.22	0.221
Quintile 2	0.230	0.221	2.3	0.29	0.773	0.221	0.195	6.7	1.44	0.149
Quintile 3	0.180	0.156	6.1	0.84	0.400	0.202	0.194	2.0	0.45	0.653
Quintile 4	0.198	0.196	0.4	0.05	0.959	0.183	0.200	−4.2	−0.94	0.347
Quintile 5 (richest)	0.139	0.146	−2.0	−0.28	0.779	0.170	0.164	1.4	0.34	0.737
Household size										
≤ 3	0.086	0.078	2.2	0.37	0.713	0.096	0.097	−0.2	−0.06	0.952
4	0.209	0.217	−1.6	−0.23	0.819	0.196	0.194	0.5	0.11	0.914
5	0.304	0.339	−8.0	−0.99	0.324	0.249	0.243	1.4	0.30	0.762
6	0.233	0.217	4.5	0.50	0.614	0.179	0.181	−0.6	−0.11	0.910
≥ 7	0.168	0.149	5.7	0.66	0.507	0.280	0.286	−1.3	−0.25	0.804
Single-mother household	0.027	0.027	−0.4	−0.07	0.945	0.036	0.037	−0.7	−0.18	0.861
Age of household head										
≤ 38	0.460	0.463	−0.7	−0.08	0.933	0.523	0.533	−2.2	−0.43	0.666
39–48	0.339	0.326	2.9	0.36	0.720	0.280	0.261	5.0	0.97	0.332
49–58	0.124	0.139	−5.2	−0.57	0.571	0.103	0.115	−4.6	−0.83	0.409
≥ 59	0.077	0.072	1.8	0.25	0.806	0.093	0.091	0.7	0.14	0.885
Education of household head										
None	0.307	0.303	0.8	0.10	0.918	0.416	0.369	9.6	2.09	0.036
Primary	0.168	0.170	−0.6	−0.07	0.942	0.089	0.096	−2.2	−0.53	0.598
Secondary	0.413	0.410	0.6	0.08	0.939	0.367	0.418	−10.3	−2.28	0.023
Higher	0.112	0.117	−1.3	−0.18	0.856	0.128	0.117	3.4	0.74	0.459
Pension or social benefits	0.195	0.177	4.8	0.58	0.559	0.203	0.210	−2.2	−0.42	0.673
Public-sector employment	0.227	0.214	3.3	0.42	0.672	0.237	0.209	7.2	1.51	0.132
Farm household						0.526	0.492	7.0	1.51	0.130

	Urban					Rural				
	Mean			t-test		Mean			t-test	
	Treated	Control	%-bias	t	P > |t|	Treated	Control	%-bias	t	P > |t|
Governorate (aggregate)										
01	0.245	0.262	−4.2	−0.53	0.598	0.105	0.106	−0.3	−0.07	0.941
02	0.103	0.094	2.7	0.42	0.676	0.118	0.099	5.6	1.33	0.184
03	0.065	0.070	−2.0	−0.26	0.797	0.050	0.051	−0.5	−0.13	0.898
04	0.065	0.065	0.1	0.01	0.989	0.053	0.039	7.0	1.50	0.134
05	0.056	0.050	2.5	0.34	0.732	0.084	0.090	−2.2	−0.45	0.650
06	0.050	0.046	2.1	0.28	0.780	0.051	0.041	4.3	1.04	0.300
07	0.077	0.079	−1.1	−0.13	0.896	0.092	0.090	0.6	0.13	0.896
08	0.074	0.072	0.8	0.09	0.928	0.061	0.068	−2.7	−0.60	0.547
09	0.097	0.104	−2.1	−0.29	0.768	0.106	0.116	−3.5	−0.70	0.482
10	0.059	0.054	2.0	0.26	0.796	0.093	0.109	−5.4	−1.15	0.251
11	0.041	0.035	3.3	0.45	0.654	0.054	0.060	−2.5	−0.58	0.564
12	0.068	0.069	−0.6	−0.06	0.949	0.045	0.039	2.7	0.72	0.473
13						0.086	0.090	−1.7	−0.35	0.728
Pseudo R-sq.	0.005					0.010				
LR chi-sq.	4.67					28.23				
Prob. > chi-sq.	1.000					0.558				
Mean bias	2.6					3.4				
Median bias	2.1					2.5				
Rubin's B	16.6					24.1				
Rubin's R	0.97					1.11				

Source: Authors' estimation based on data from CAPMAS and WFP (2011).

TABLE A.17 Balancing property test statistics of the binary propensity score estimations for maternal nutrition indicators

	Urban					Rural				
	Mean			t-test		Mean			t-test	
	Treated	Control	%-bias	t	P > |t|	Treated	Control	%-bias	t	P > |t|
Per capita household income										
Quintile 1 (poorest)	0.264	0.263	0.1	0.02	0.986	0.223	0.246	−5.6	−1.18	0.239
Quintile 2	0.231	0.219	3.1	0.42	0.677	0.219	0.213	1.5	0.32	0.752
Quintile 3	0.188	0.179	2.3	0.33	0.744	0.205	0.199	1.7	0.37	0.714
Quintile 4	0.188	0.186	0.3	0.05	0.962	0.186	0.181	1.3	0.30	0.763
Quintile 5 (richest)	0.129	0.153	−6.1	−0.94	0.348	0.166	0.162	1.2	0.28	0.778
Household size										
≤ 3	0.094	0.090	1.0	0.18	0.858	0.090	0.098	−2.1	−0.62	0.537
4	0.208	0.216	−1.7	−0.26	0.794	0.196	0.182	3.4	0.82	0.410
5	0.277	0.299	−5.1	−0.69	0.489	0.259	0.251	1.9	0.41	0.679
6	0.249	0.229	5.3	0.65	0.519	0.186	0.186	−0.1	−0.01	0.989
≥ 7	0.173	0.166	2.0	0.25	0.805	0.268	0.282	−3.7	−0.71	0.478
Single-mother household	0.036	0.043	−3.5	−0.57	0.570	0.028	0.035	−3.6	−0.89	0.372
Age of household head										
≤ 38	0.452	0.450	0.4	0.05	0.958	0.537	0.539	−0.6	−0.11	0.910
39–48	0.325	0.311	3.1	0.41	0.679	0.289	0.272	4.2	0.84	0.402
49–58	0.142	0.150	−2.6	−0.31	0.759	0.100	0.113	−5.0	−0.91	0.361
≥ 59	0.081	0.089	−3.0	−0.40	0.692	0.074	0.076	−0.7	−0.15	0.883
Education of household head										
None	0.322	0.303	4.3	0.58	0.562	0.408	0.368	8.4	1.84	0.066
Primary	0.157	0.165	−1.9	−0.27	0.785	0.089	0.091	−0.6	−0.13	0.893
Secondary	0.406	0.400	1.3	0.18	0.860	0.369	0.417	−9.8	−2.19	0.029
Higher	0.114	0.132	−5.0	−0.78	0.438	0.133	0.124	2.8	0.63	0.528
Pension or social benefits	0.201	0.192	2.3	0.30	0.768	0.191	0.190	0.3	0.06	0.953
Public-sector employment	0.234	0.212	5.1	0.71	0.478	0.238	0.217	5.4	1.13	0.257
Farm household						0.525	0.502	4.6	1.02	0.310

	Urban					Rural				
	Mean			t-test		Mean			t-test	
	Treated	Control	%-bias	t	P > |t|	Treated	Control	%-bias	t	P > |t|
Governorate (aggregate)										
01	0.239	0.247	−2.0	−0.28	0.776	0.110	0.111	−0.2	−0.03	0.972
02	0.104	0.094	2.9	0.47	0.637	0.113	0.105	2.5	0.60	0.551
03	0.074	0.093	−7.8	−0.99	0.322	0.051	0.066	−6.2	−1.42	0.154
04	0.066	0.065	0.5	0.07	0.942	0.051	0.036	7.6	1.63	0.104
05	0.053	0.050	1.2	0.18	0.855	0.081	0.085	−1.6	−0.33	0.739
06	0.051	0.044	2.9	0.42	0.677	0.051	0.040	4.5	1.13	0.259
07	0.069	0.069	−0.1	−0.01	0.992	0.095	0.092	1.2	0.26	0.797
08	0.063	0.069	−2.6	−0.33	0.742	0.066	0.073	−2.7	−0.61	0.544
09	0.099	0.109	−3.0	−0.44	0.657	0.104	0.098	2.2	0.47	0.636
10	0.058	0.042	7.4	1.08	0.281	0.094	0.110	−5.5	−1.17	0.241
11	0.048	0.041	3.8	0.52	0.605	0.054	0.063	−3.9	−0.89	0.373
12	0.076	0.077	−0.4	−0.05	0.957	0.047	0.045	0.8	0.21	0.838
13						0.082	0.076	2.4	0.52	0.601
Pseudo R-sq.	0.007					0.009				
LR chi-sq.	7.23					25.65				
Prob. > chi-sq.	1.000					0.693				
Mean bias	2.9					3.1				
Median bias	2.6					2.5				
Rubin's B	19.2					22.7				
Rubin's R	1.10					1.25				

Source: Authors' estimation based on data from CAPMAS and WFP (2011).

TABLE A.18 Balancing property test statistics of the binary propensity score estimations for indicators of the double burden of malnutrition at the family level and coexisting child and maternal overweight

	Urban					Rural				
	Mean			t-test		Mean			t-test	
	Treated	Control	%-bias	t	P > |t|	Treated	Control	%-bias	t	P > |t|
Per capita household income										
Quintile 1 (poorest)	0.252	0.277	−6.1	−0.71	0.478	0.224	0.251	−6.8	−1.35	0.176
Quintile 2	0.240	0.232	1.9	0.23	0.821	0.218	0.205	3.3	0.69	0.493
Quintile 3	0.180	0.159	5.3	0.70	0.483	0.204	0.189	3.6	0.78	0.435
Quintile 4	0.189	0.184	1.4	0.18	0.859	0.184	0.187	−0.8	−0.19	0.852
Quintile 5 (richest)	0.139	0.148	−2.4	−0.33	0.741	0.171	0.168	0.7	0.16	0.876
Household size										
≤ 3	0.085	0.080	1.4	0.22	0.826	0.092	0.098	−1.7	−0.48	0.633
4	0.208	0.214	−1.3	−0.18	0.858	0.195	0.187	1.9	0.45	0.655
5	0.290	0.321	−6.9	−0.84	0.402	0.256	0.246	2.5	0.51	0.610
6	0.243	0.233	2.7	0.29	0.770	0.184	0.185	−0.4	−0.08	0.938
≥ 7	0.174	0.152	6.6	0.74	0.458	0.274	0.284	−2.8	−0.50	0.614
Single-mother household	0.022	0.030	−3.5	−0.61	0.539	0.033	0.037	−2.1	−0.48	0.628
Age of household head										
≤ 38	0.461	0.460	0.0	0.00	0.998	0.534	0.546	−2.7	−0.51	0.611
39–48	0.347	0.333	3.1	0.37	0.709	0.286	0.251	8.6	1.65	0.100
49–58	0.120	0.134	−5.1	−0.55	0.585	0.102	0.121	−7.6	−1.30	0.193
≥ 59	0.073	0.072	0.1	0.01	0.989	0.079	0.082	−1.2	−0.24	0.807
Education of household head										
None	0.300	0.299	0.2	0.03	0.976	0.414	0.375	8.1	1.70	0.090
Primary	0.170	0.171	−0.1	−0.02	0.988	0.091	0.096	−1.8	−0.40	0.687
Secondary	0.416	0.416	0.0	0.00	0.999	0.363	0.409	−9.5	−2.02	0.043
Higher	0.114	0.114	−0.2	−0.02	0.983	0.132	0.120	3.9	0.82	0.413
Pension or social benefits	0.189	0.167	6.1	0.72	0.471	0.189	0.203	−4.0	−0.74	0.457
Public-sector employment	0.224	0.208	4.0	0.50	0.620	0.237	0.207	7.8	1.58	0.114
Farm household						0.527	0.497	6.1	1.28	0.200

	Urban					Rural				
	Mean			t-test		Mean			t-test	
	Treated	Control	%-bias	t	P > |t|	Treated	Control	%-bias	t	P > |t|
Governorate (aggregate)										
01	0.237	0.251	−3.4	−0.41	0.679	0.105	0.112	−2.3	−0.51	0.609
02	0.101	0.097	1.0	0.15	0.885	0.115	0.097	5.3	1.24	0.216
03	0.066	0.074	−3.3	−0.40	0.692	0.049	0.055	−2.3	−0.53	0.599
04	0.066	0.064	1.0	0.13	0.899	0.054	0.039	7.4	1.53	0.126
05	0.054	0.049	2.0	0.26	0.794	0.086	0.094	−2.8	−0.54	0.586
06	0.050	0.045	2.3	0.29	0.770	0.050	0.040	4.7	1.11	0.266
07	0.079	0.081	−1.1	−0.12	0.908	0.096	0.091	2.0	0.40	0.690
08	0.076	0.075	0.3	0.03	0.977	0.063	0.075	−4.8	−1.00	0.318
09	0.104	0.108	−1.2	−0.16	0.871	0.106	0.104	0.9	0.17	0.862
10	0.057	0.046	4.9	0.64	0.525	0.090	0.104	−5.0	−1.03	0.304
11	0.041	0.037	1.9	0.25	0.801	0.051	0.066	−6.1	−1.35	0.176
12	0.069	0.072	−1.1	−0.12	0.904	0.047	0.040	3.0	0.76	0.445
13						0.086	0.084	0.9	0.18	0.857
Pseudo R-sq.			0.005					0.011		
LR chi-sq.			4.54					28.38		
Prob. > chi-sq.			1.000					0.550		
Mean bias			2.5					3.9		
Median bias			1.9					3.0		
Rubin's B			16.9					25.0		
Rubin's R			1.06					1.12		

Source: Authors' estimation based on data from CAPMAS and WFP (2011).

TABLE A.19 Balancing property test statistics of the binary propensity score estimations for household diet quality indicators

	Urban					Rural				
	Mean			t-test		Mean			t-test	
	Treated	Control	%-bias	t	P > |t|	Treated	Control	%-bias	t	P > |t|
Per capita household income										
Quintile 1 (poorest)	0.259	0.268	−2.2	−0.29	0.772	0.222	0.253	−7.8	−1.67	0.094
Quintile 2	0.221	0.214	1.7	0.23	0.815	0.221	0.200	5.4	1.20	0.230
Quintile 3	0.186	0.173	3.3	0.49	0.626	0.202	0.196	1.6	0.38	0.706
Quintile 4	0.198	0.194	1.0	0.15	0.884	0.190	0.193	−0.7	−0.16	0.875
Quintile 5 (richest)	0.136	0.151	−3.9	−0.61	0.541	0.165	0.159	1.4	0.36	0.717
Household size										
≤ 3	0.085	0.078	2.0	0.37	0.712	0.092	0.091	0.3	0.10	0.922
4	0.211	0.218	−1.6	−0.24	0.813	0.195	0.194	0.3	0.07	0.946
5	0.284	0.317	−7.4	−1.01	0.315	0.255	0.250	1.3	0.29	0.775
6	0.246	0.217	8.0	0.98	0.326	0.184	0.179	1.7	0.34	0.735
≥ 7	0.173	0.170	0.9	0.11	0.911	0.274	0.287	−3.6	−0.69	0.490
Single-mother household	0.033	0.042	−4.2	−0.72	0.472	0.036	0.039	−1.8	−0.44	0.661
Age of household head										
≤ 38	0.452	0.459	−1.4	−0.19	0.846	0.525	0.523	0.5	0.11	0.914
39–48	0.329	0.316	2.9	0.39	0.696	0.280	0.274	1.5	0.30	0.763
49–58	0.138	0.140	−0.8	−0.09	0.927	0.102	0.113	−4.5	−0.85	0.395
≥ 59	0.080	0.084	−1.4	−0.20	0.844	0.093	0.090	1.2	0.26	0.795
Education of household head										
None	0.322	0.310	2.7	0.37	0.714	0.417	0.370	9.8	2.22	0.027
Primary	0.156	0.162	−1.8	−0.26	0.797	0.086	0.090	−1.5	−0.38	0.707
Secondary	0.415	0.404	2.2	0.31	0.759	0.372	0.419	−9.9	−2.26	0.024
Higher	0.108	0.124	−4.5	−0.71	0.478	0.126	0.121	1.7	0.39	0.699
Pension or social benefits	0.209	0.201	2.1	0.27	0.784	0.207	0.208	−0.4	−0.08	0.933
Public-sector employment	0.239	0.219	4.7	0.66	0.512	0.239	0.217	5.5	1.19	0.232
Farm household						0.529	0.495	6.9	1.56	0.120

	Urban					Rural				
	Mean			t-test		Mean			t-test	
	Treated	Control	%-bias	t	P > |t|	Treated	Control	%-bias	t	P > |t|
Governorate (aggregate)										
01	0.236	0.248	−2.8	−0.40	0.691	0.108	0.100	2.5	0.62	0.533
02	0.111	0.097	3.7	0.61	0.541	0.114	0.102	3.6	0.89	0.376
03	0.068	0.087	−7.7	−1.00	0.320	0.054	0.062	−3.3	−0.79	0.431
04	0.068	0.066	0.7	0.09	0.927	0.050	0.037	6.6	1.46	0.143
05	0.053	0.048	1.8	0.28	0.783	0.079	0.083	−1.7	−0.36	0.717
06	0.055	0.049	2.7	0.37	0.709	0.053	0.043	4.2	1.08	0.282
07	0.068	0.069	−0.4	−0.05	0.959	0.093	0.089	1.6	0.33	0.739
08	0.065	0.070	−2.3	−0.29	0.773	0.064	0.067	−1.0	−0.24	0.814
09	0.095	0.101	−1.6	−0.25	0.803	0.107	0.115	−2.6	−0.56	0.576
10	0.060	0.051	3.9	0.56	0.573	0.098	0.117	−6.5	−1.42	0.155
11	0.050	0.045	2.6	0.36	0.722	0.054	0.065	−4.7	−1.11	0.268
12	0.070	0.068	1.2	0.15	0.883	0.045	0.041	1.7	0.46	0.646
13						0.082	0.080	0.6	0.13	0.896
Pseudo R-sq.			0.006					0.010		
LR chi-sq.			6.55					30.13		
Prob. > chi-sq.			1.000					0.459		
Mean bias			2.8					3.1		
Median bias			2.2					1.7		
Rubin's B			18.2					23.9		
Rubin's R			0.98					1.20		

Source: Authors' estimation based on data from CAPMAS and WFP (2011).

TABLE A.20 GLM results of the generalized propensity score estimations for child nutrition indicators and ration-card-program subsidies

	Urban				Rural			
	Coef.	Robust std. err.	z	P > |z|	Coef.	Robust std. err.	z	P > |z|
Per capita household income								
Quintile 2	0.034	0.107	0.31	0.754	0.036	0.065	0.55	0.584
Quintile 3	0.187	0.111	1.69	0.092	0.160	0.069	2.32	0.020
Quintile 4	0.180	0.141	1.28	0.202	0.215	0.072	3.00	0.003
Quintile 5 (richest)	0.325	0.145	2.24	0.025	0.283	0.080	3.53	0.000
Household size								
4	−0.289	0.209	−1.39	0.166	−0.168	0.109	−1.54	0.123
5	−0.226	0.200	−1.13	0.258	−0.293	0.104	−2.82	0.005
6	−0.473	0.201	−2.35	0.019	−0.353	0.109	−3.23	0.001
≥ 7	−0.479	0.211	−2.27	0.023	−0.675	0.111	−6.09	0.000
Single-mother household	−0.079	0.152	−0.52	0.604	−0.038	0.086	−0.44	0.657
Age of household head								
39–48	0.124	0.106	1.17	0.241	0.225	0.054	4.19	0.000
49–58	0.288	0.138	2.08	0.037	0.105	0.078	1.35	0.177
≥ 59	0.404	0.162	2.49	0.013	0.126	0.074	1.70	0.089
Education of household head								
Primary	−0.229	0.143	−1.60	0.110	−0.095	0.080	−1.19	0.236
Secondary	0.079	0.094	0.84	0.400	−0.119	0.058	−2.05	0.040
Higher	0.032	0.182	0.18	0.860	−0.085	0.079	−1.07	0.282
Pension or social benefits	0.073	0.109	0.67	0.504	0.093	0.051	1.82	0.069
Public-sector employment	−0.099	0.101	−0.99	0.324	−0.017	0.054	−0.31	0.755
Farm household					0.056	0.048	1.16	0.244

	Urban				Rural			
	Coef.	Robust std. err.	z	P > |z|	Coef.	Robust std. err.	z	P > |z|
Governorate (aggregate)								
02	−0.200	0.190	−1.05	0.293	0.353	0.094	3.74	0.000
03	0.038	0.172	0.22	0.827	0.652	0.126	5.17	0.000
04	−0.211	0.169	−1.25	0.212	−0.570	0.097	−5.85	0.000
05	0.001	0.187	0.01	0.994	0.104	0.096	1.09	0.275
06	0.230	0.155	1.49	0.137	0.165	0.114	1.44	0.148
07	−0.291	0.169	−1.71	0.086	−0.010	0.109	−0.09	0.930
08	−0.126	0.150	−0.84	0.403	−0.432	0.112	−3.85	0.000
09	−0.262	0.156	−1.68	0.093	−0.151	0.099	−1.52	0.128
10	−0.398	0.161	−2.48	0.013	−0.193	0.093	−2.08	0.038
11	−0.507	0.171	−2.96	0.003	−0.074	0.117	−0.63	0.530
12	−0.281	0.154	−1.82	0.068	−0.044	0.116	−0.38	0.703
13					−0.109	0.105	−1.04	0.299
Constant	−0.090	0.254	−0.35	0.724	0.137	0.132	1.04	0.300
Observations	390				1,082			
Deviance	0.168				0.134			
Pearson	0.145				0.117			

Source: Authors' estimation based on data from CAPMAS and WFP (2011).

Note: GLM = generalized linear model.

TABLE A.21 GLM results of the generalized propensity score estimations for maternal nutrition indicators and ration-card-program subsidies

	Urban				Rural			
	Coef.	Robust std. err.	z	P > |z|	Coef.	Robust std. err.	z	P > |z|
Per capita household income								
Quintile 2	0.084	0.100	0.84	0.399	0.059	0.061	0.97	0.333
Quintile 3	0.311	0.106	2.93	0.003	0.154	0.067	2.28	0.023
Quintile 4	0.264	0.129	2.06	0.040	0.213	0.071	2.99	0.003
Quintile 5 (richest)	0.313	0.133	2.36	0.018	0.303	0.079	3.81	0.000
Household size								
4	−0.382	0.179	−2.13	0.033	−0.189	0.113	−1.68	0.094
5	−0.222	0.174	−1.28	0.201	−0.269	0.108	−2.50	0.012
6	−0.503	0.177	−2.84	0.004	−0.284	0.114	−2.50	0.012
≥ 7	−0.532	0.190	−2.80	0.005	−0.640	0.114	−5.63	0.000
Single-mother household	−0.083	0.143	−0.58	0.562	−0.017	0.087	−0.20	0.841
Age of household head								
39–48	0.150	0.098	1.53	0.126	0.222	0.052	4.31	0.000
49–58	0.335	0.132	2.54	0.011	0.135	0.076	1.78	0.075
≥ 59	0.516	0.153	3.36	0.001	0.103	0.074	1.40	0.163
Education of household head								
Primary	−0.336	0.132	−2.55	0.011	−0.095	0.077	−1.22	0.221
Secondary	0.044	0.090	0.49	0.626	−0.132	0.056	−2.34	0.019
Higher	0.113	0.164	0.69	0.493	−0.050	0.080	−0.63	0.528
Pension or social benefits	0.022	0.100	0.22	0.825	0.068	0.050	1.36	0.174
Public-sector employment	−0.084	0.089	−0.93	0.350	−0.047	0.052	−0.90	0.367
Farm household					0.057	0.047	1.22	0.221

	Urban				Rural			
	Coef.	Robust std. err.	z	P > |z|	Coef.	Robust std. err.	z	P > |z|
Governorate (aggregate)								
02	−0.117	0.174	−0.67	0.503	0.324	0.092	3.51	0.000
03	0.100	0.139	0.72	0.470	0.598	0.115	5.22	0.000
04	−0.235	0.150	−1.56	0.119	−0.574	0.095	−6.02	0.000
05	−0.025	0.181	−0.14	0.892	0.096	0.092	1.04	0.299
06	0.174	0.149	1.17	0.241	0.107	0.110	0.97	0.331
07	−0.349	0.169	−2.06	0.040	0.037	0.104	0.36	0.718
08	−0.062	0.139	−0.45	0.654	−0.401	0.106	−3.77	0.000
09	−0.219	0.138	−1.59	0.111	−0.098	0.097	−1.01	0.312
10	−0.329	0.153	−2.16	0.031	−0.195	0.093	−2.10	0.035
11	−0.483	0.176	−2.75	0.006	−0.052	0.111	−0.47	0.640
12	−0.235	0.149	−1.58	0.113	−0.028	0.120	−0.23	0.816
13					−0.088	0.104	−0.85	0.398
Constant	−0.128	0.222	−0.58	0.563	0.108	0.132	0.81	0.415
Observations	445				1,127			
Deviance	0.163				0.134			
Pearson	0.140				0.117			

Source: Authors' estimation based on data from CAPMAS and WFP (2011).

Note: GLM = generalized linear model.

TABLE A.22 GLM results of the generalized propensity score estimations for indicators of the double burden of malnutrition at the family level and coexisting child and maternal overweight and ration-card-program subsidies

	Urban				Rural			
	Coef.	Robust std. err.	z	P > |z|	Coef.	Robust std. err.	z	P > |z|
Per capita household income								
Quintile 2	−0.011	0.112	−0.10	0.924	0.044	0.065	0.67	0.502
Quintile 3	0.205	0.114	1.80	0.072	0.155	0.070	2.23	0.026
Quintile 4	0.175	0.148	1.18	0.237	0.210	0.073	2.88	0.004
Quintile 5 (richest)	0.267	0.151	1.77	0.077	0.304	0.082	3.69	0.000
Household size								
4	−0.243	0.215	−1.13	0.258	−0.195	0.118	−1.65	0.099
5	−0.166	0.208	−0.80	0.424	−0.280	0.113	−2.47	0.014
6	−0.433	0.207	−2.10	0.036	−0.322	0.119	−2.71	0.007
≥ 7	−0.418	0.218	−1.92	0.055	−0.647	0.120	−5.41	0.000
Single-mother household	−0.079	0.158	−0.50	0.615	−0.023	0.092	−0.25	0.802
Age of household head								
39–48	0.171	0.107	1.59	0.111	0.235	0.054	4.35	0.000
49–58	0.339	0.147	2.31	0.021	0.136	0.080	1.70	0.089
≥ 59	0.431	0.167	2.58	0.010	0.134	0.077	1.73	0.083
Education of household head								
Primary	−0.272	0.150	−1.82	0.069	−0.068	0.082	−0.84	0.401
Secondary	0.091	0.099	0.93	0.354	−0.109	0.058	−1.86	0.063
Higher	0.134	0.188	0.71	0.476	−0.055	0.080	−0.69	0.491
Pension or social benefits	0.096	0.113	0.85	0.396	0.076	0.053	1.43	0.153
Public-sector employment	−0.100	0.104	−0.97	0.334	−0.051	0.056	−0.92	0.356
Farm household					0.052	0.049	1.05	0.292

	Urban				Rural			
	Coef.	Robust std. err.	z	P > |z|	Coef.	Robust std. err.	z	P > |z|
Governorate (aggregate)								
02	−0.068	0.204	−0.33	0.738	0.328	0.099	3.30	0.001
03	0.118	0.177	0.67	0.506	0.599	0.127	4.71	0.000
04	−0.203	0.181	−1.12	0.261	−0.568	0.102	−5.56	0.000
05	0.043	0.201	0.22	0.829	0.093	0.098	0.95	0.343
06	0.226	0.159	1.42	0.155	0.135	0.119	1.13	0.258
07	−0.272	0.175	−1.56	0.120	0.002	0.113	0.02	0.987
08	−0.068	0.154	−0.44	0.660	−0.394	0.114	−3.46	0.001
09	−0.188	0.158	−1.19	0.235	−0.138	0.103	−1.34	0.180
10	−0.349	0.168	−2.08	0.038	−0.187	0.100	−1.86	0.062
11	−0.442	0.174	−2.54	0.011	−0.080	0.120	−0.67	0.503
12	−0.246	0.157	−1.57	0.117	−0.049	0.119	−0.41	0.684
13					−0.132	0.107	−1.23	0.220
Constant	−0.191	0.267	−0.72	0.474	0.120	0.142	0.85	0.397
Observations	367				1,028			
Deviance	0.170				0.135			
Pearson	0.145				0.118			

Source: Authors' estimation based on data from CAPMAS and WFP (2011).

Note: GLM = generalized linear model.

TABLE A.23 GLM results of the generalized propensity score estimations for household diet quality indicators and ration-card-program subsidies

	Urban				Rural			
	Coef.	Robust std. err.	z	P > lzl	Coef.	Robust std. err.	z	P > lzl
Per capita household income								
Quintile 2	0.097	0.099	0.98	0.329	0.034	0.061	0.56	0.577
Quintile 3	0.275	0.105	2.61	0.009	0.153	0.066	2.31	0.021
Quintile 4	0.270	0.125	2.15	0.031	0.213	0.071	3.02	0.003
Quintile 5 (richest)	0.396	0.133	2.97	0.003	0.284	0.078	3.64	0.000
Household size								
4	−0.271	0.184	−1.47	0.140	−0.134	0.106	−1.27	0.203
5	−0.127	0.178	−0.71	0.477	−0.256	0.100	−2.56	0.011
6	−0.434	0.182	−2.38	0.017	−0.287	0.106	−2.71	0.007
≥ 7	−0.466	0.193	−2.41	0.016	−0.640	0.106	−6.03	0.000
Single-mother household	−0.060	0.141	−0.42	0.671	−0.031	0.085	−0.37	0.713
Age of household head								
39–48	0.114	0.098	1.16	0.247	0.204	0.051	3.99	0.000
49–58	0.279	0.126	2.22	0.027	0.107	0.074	1.44	0.149
≥ 59	0.516	0.148	3.48	0.000	0.095	0.071	1.35	0.178
Education of household head								
Primary	−0.272	0.128	−2.13	0.033	−0.133	0.077	−1.72	0.086
Secondary	0.013	0.089	0.15	0.882	−0.137	0.056	−2.46	0.014
Higher	0.005	0.169	0.03	0.977	−0.073	0.079	−0.92	0.359
Pension or social benefits	−0.027	0.098	−0.28	0.781	0.082	0.049	1.67	0.095
Public-sector employment	−0.038	0.088	−0.43	0.667	−0.014	0.051	−0.27	0.784
Farm household					0.053	0.046	1.15	0.248

	Urban				Rural			
	Coef.	Robust std. err.	z	P > lzl	Coef.	Robust std. err.	z	P > lzl
Governorate (aggregate)								
02	−0.178	0.167	−1.07	0.286	0.348	0.089	3.90	0.000
03	0.073	0.146	0.50	0.615	0.653	0.114	5.70	0.000
04	−0.167	0.145	−1.15	0.250	−0.571	0.093	−6.17	0.000
05	0.037	0.179	0.20	0.838	0.120	0.092	1.31	0.191
06	0.243	0.147	1.65	0.098	0.146	0.107	1.37	0.172
07	−0.232	0.156	−1.49	0.136	0.042	0.101	0.41	0.681
08	−0.056	0.141	−0.40	0.692	−0.428	0.106	−4.03	0.000
09	−0.231	0.140	−1.65	0.099	−0.109	0.094	−1.15	0.250
10	−0.351	0.152	−2.31	0.021	−0.186	0.087	−2.12	0.034
11	−0.465	0.173	−2.69	0.007	−0.031	0.111	−0.28	0.782
12	−0.212	0.149	−1.42	0.155	0.033	0.113	0.29	0.769
13					−0.063	0.103	−0.61	0.544
Constant	−0.209	0.227	−0.92	0.358	0.105	0.126	0.83	0.406
Observations	453				1,171			
Deviance	0.161				0.133			
Pearson	0.138				0.116			

Source: Authors' estimation based on data from CAPMAS and WFP (2011).

Note: GLM = generalized linear model.

TABLE A.24 Dose-response function estimates for the effect of ration-card-program subsidies on child HAZ

	Urban				Rural			
	Coef.	Std. err.	t	P > |t|	Coef.	Std. err.	t	P > |t|
Fraction	−0.490	3.226	−0.15	0.879	−3.895	2.302	−1.69	0.091
Fraction sq.	−2.558	2.023	−1.26	0.207	1.365	1.278	1.07	0.286
GPS	−0.912	12.697	−0.07	0.943	22.713	6.226	3.65	0.000
GPS sq.	1.549	16.528	0.09	0.925	−23.869	7.632	−3.13	0.002
Fraction x GPS	4.021	8.579	0.47	0.640	4.969	5.155	0.96	0.335
Constant	−0.726	2.537	−0.29	0.775	−5.873	1.392	−4.22	0.000
Observations	390				1,082			
F	1.10				4.20			
Prob. > F	0.359				0.001			
R-sq.	0.014				0.019			
Adj. R-sq.	0.001				0.015			

Source: Authors' estimation based on data from CAPMAS and WFP (2011).

Note: GPS = generalized propensity score; HAZ = height-for-age z-score.

TABLE A.25 Dose-response function estimates for the effect of ration-card-program subsidies on child stunting

	Urban				Rural			
	Coef.	Std. err.	z	P > |z|	Coef.	Std. err.	z	P > |z|
Fraction	0.470	4.200	0.11	0.911	5.244	2.793	1.88	0.060
Fraction sq.	−1.189	2.638	−0.45	0.652	−3.437	1.785	−1.93	0.054
GPS	6.548	16.358	0.40	0.689	−23.246	7.055	−3.30	0.001
GPS sq.	−14.113	22.063	−0.64	0.522	22.800	8.832	2.58	0.010
Fraction x GPS	5.544	11.397	0.49	0.627	−3.505	6.362	−0.55	0.582
Constant	−2.263	3.159	−0.72	0.474	3.963	1.568	2.53	0.012
Observations	390				1,082			
LR chi-sq.	8.28				28.70			
Prob. > chi-sq.	0.141				0.000			
Pseudo R-sq.	0.019				0.023			

Source: Authors' estimation based on data from CAPMAS and WFP (2011).

Note: GPS = generalized propensity score.

TABLE A.26 Dose-response function estimates for the effect of ration-card-program subsidies on child BMIZ

	Urban				Rural			
	Coef.	Std. err.	t	P > |t|	Coef.	Std. err.	t	P > |t|
Fraction	5.516	3.017	1.83	0.068	−1.661	2.061	−0.81	0.420
Fraction sq.	4.055	1.892	2.14	0.033	−1.406	1.144	−1.23	0.219
GPS	−29.263	11.873	−2.46	0.014	−8.477	5.574	−1.52	0.129
GPS sq.	38.663	15.455	2.50	0.013	6.236	6.834	0.91	0.362
Fraction x GPS	−17.881	8.022	−2.23	0.026	5.579	4.616	1.21	0.227
Constant	6.250	2.373	2.63	0.009	3.441	1.246	2.76	0.006
Observations	390				1,082			
F	3.30				1.32			
Prob. > F	0.006				0.253			
R-sq.	0.041				0.006			
Adj. R-sq.	0.029				0.002			

Source: Authors' estimation based on data CAPMAS and WFP (2011).

Note: BMIZ = body-mass-index-for-age z-score; GPS = generalized propensity score.

TABLE A.27 Dose-response function estimates for the effect of ration-card-program subsidies on child overweight

	Urban				Rural			
	Coef.	Std. err.	z	P > |z|	Coef.	Std. err.	z	P > |z|
Fraction	6.989	3.815	1.83	0.067	−2.666	2.776	−0.96	0.337
Fraction sq.	3.007	2.457	1.22	0.221	−3.800	1.692	−2.25	0.025
GPS	−19.764	14.751	−1.34	0.180	−2.647	7.159	−0.37	0.712
GPS sq.	28.495	19.178	1.49	0.137	−2.200	9.059	−0.24	0.808
Fraction x GPS	−18.002	10.015	−1.80	0.072	12.301	6.584	1.87	0.062
Constant	1.715	2.956	0.58	0.562	0.234	1.571	0.15	0.881
Observations	390				1,082			
LR chi-sq.	11.13				8.54			
Prob. > chi-sq.	0.049				0.129			
Pseudo R-sq.	0.025				0.007			

Source: Authors' estimation based on data from CAPMAS and WFP (2011).

Note: GPS = generalized propensity score.

TABLE A.28 Dose-response function estimates for the effect of ration-card-program subsidies on mother's BMI

	Urban				Rural			
	Coef.	Std. err.	t	P > |t|	Coef.	Std. err.	t	P > |t|
Fraction	26.614	7.838	3.40	0.001	5.464	6.328	0.86	0.388
Fraction sq.	5.359	4.525	1.18	0.237	−0.418	3.455	−0.12	0.904
GPS	−25.695	28.145	−0.91	0.362	10.218	18.217	0.56	0.575
GPS sq.	79.795	35.681	2.24	0.026	−1.507	22.388	−0.07	0.946
Fraction x GPS	−74.116	19.941	−3.72	0.000	−11.594	14.541	−0.80	0.425
Constant	26.946	5.764	4.67	0.000	23.924	4.031	5.94	0.000
Observations	445				1,127			
F	6.42				0.87			
Prob. > F	0.000				0.503			
R-sq.	0.068				0.004			
Adj. R-sq.	0.058				−0.001			

Source: Authors' estimation based on data from CAPMAS and WFP (2011).

Note: BMI = body mass index; GPS = generalized propensity score.

TABLE A.29 Dose-response function estimates for the effect of ration-card-program subsidies on maternal overweight

	Urban				Rural			
	Coef.	Std. err.	z	P > |z|	Coef.	Std. err.	z	P > |z|
Fraction	26.044	5.886	4.42	0.000	0.582	2.667	0.22	0.827
Fraction sq.	1.359	2.794	0.49	0.627	1.506	1.577	0.96	0.340
GPS	−68.751	22.316	−3.08	0.002	17.928	7.481	2.40	0.017
GPS sq.	110.787	32.298	3.43	0.001	−14.632	9.371	−1.56	0.118
Fraction x GPS	−60.201	16.817	−3.58	0.000	−4.577	6.373	−0.72	0.473
Constant	10.100	3.911	2.58	0.010	−3.902	1.638	−2.38	0.017
Observations	445				1,127			
LR chi-sq.	37.82				11.19			
Prob. > chi-sq.	0.000				0.048			
Pseudo R-sq.	0.088				0.008			

Source: Authors' estimation based on data from CAPMAS and WFP (2011).

Note: GPS = generalized propensity score.

TABLE A.30 Dose-response function estimates for the effect of ration-card-program subsidies on child stunting and overweight

	Urban				Rural			
	Coef.	Std. err.	z	P > |z|	Coef.	Std. err.	z	P > |z|
Fraction	8.799	4.876	1.80	0.071	-4.013	4.006	–1.00	0.316
Fraction sq.	0.836	3.230	0.26	0.796	–8.435	3.138	–2.69	0.007
GPS	–18.363	18.270	–1.01	0.315	–7.747	9.315	–0.83	0.406
GPS sq.	25.531	23.702	1.08	0.281	–3.712	12.631	–0.29	0.769
Fraction x GPS	–15.307	12.281	–1.25	0.213	22.084	10.539	2.10	0.036
Constant	0.050	3.675	0.01	0.989	1.524	1.958	0.78	0.436
Observations	390				1,082			
LR chi-sq.	12.91				20.38			
Prob. > chi-sq.	0.024				0.001			
Pseudo R-sq.	0.042				0.025			

Source: Authors' estimation based on data from CAPMAS and WFP (2011).

Note: GPS = generalized propensity score.

TABLE A.31 Dose-response function estimates for the effect of ration-card-program subsidies on child stunting and maternal overweight

	Urban				Rural			
	Coef.	Std. err.	z	P > |z|	Coef.	Std. err.	z	P > |z|
Fraction	–1.167	4.756	–0.25	0.806	–2.952	3.044	–0.97	0.332
Fraction sq.	–6.922	4.029	–1.72	0.086	3.582	1.430	2.50	0.012
GPS	–7.875	16.383	–0.48	0.631	9.754	9.339	1.04	0.296
GPS sq.	–1.024	21.679	–0.05	0.962	–6.798	11.093	–0.61	0.540
Fraction x GPS	17.836	14.155	1.26	0.208	–2.185	6.847	–0.32	0.750
Constant	0.895	3.280	0.27	0.785	–3.518	2.128	–1.65	0.098
Observations	367				1,028			
LR chi-sq.	4.35				13.79			
Prob. > chi-sq.	0.500				0.017			
Pseudo R-sq.	0.011				0.014			

Source: Authors' estimation based on data from CAPMAS and WFP (2011).

Note: GPS = generalized propensity score.

TABLE A.32 Dose-response function estimates for the effect of ration-card-program subsidies on child overweight and maternal overweight

	Urban				Rural			
	Coef.	Std. err.	z	P > |z|	Coef.	Std. err.	z	P > |z|
Fraction	−1.361	4.956	−0.27	0.784	−5.133	3.164	−1.62	0.105
Fraction sq.	−2.544	3.259	−0.78	0.435	1.276	1.536	0.83	0.406
GPS	27.515	17.852	1.54	0.123	14.579	9.652	1.51	0.131
GPS sq.	−34.339	23.231	−1.48	0.139	−16.933	11.628	−1.46	0.145
Fraction x GPS	8.764	13.907	0.63	0.529	6.842	7.277	0.94	0.347
Constant	−6.971	3.648	−1.91	0.056	−3.927	2.166	−1.81	0.070
Observations	367				1,028			
LR chi-sq.	3.66				6.54			
Prob. > chi-sq.	0.600				0.257			
Pseudo R-sq.	0.009				0.007			

Source: Authors' estimation based on data from CAPMAS and WFP (2011).

Note: GPS = generalized propensity score.

TABLE A.33 Dose-response function estimates for the effect of ration-card-program subsidies on household dietary diversity

	Urban				Rural			
	Coef.	Std. err.	t	P > |t|	Coef.	Std. err.	t	P > |t|
Fraction	−2.419	1.476	−1.64	0.102	0.929	1.461	0.64	0.525
Fraction sq.	2.146	0.978	2.19	0.029	1.688	0.852	1.98	0.048
GPS	−1.492	5.684	−0.26	0.793	−5.314	3.799	−1.40	0.162
GPS sq.	1.330	7.403	0.18	0.857	8.767	4.714	1.86	0.063
Fraction x GPS	1.233	3.852	0.32	0.749	−5.808	3.286	−1.77	0.077
Constant	11.156	1.113	10.02	0.000	11.317	0.853	13.26	0.000
Observations	453				1,171			
F	2.14				1.51			
Prob. > F	0.060				0.183			
R-sq.	0.023				0.007			
Adj. R-sq.	0.013				0.002			

Source: Authors' estimation based on data from CAPMAS and WFP (2011).

Note: GPS = generalized propensity score.

TABLE A.34 Dose-response function estimates for the effect of ration-card-program subsidies on frequency of household vegetable consumption

	Urban				Rural			
	Coef.	Std. err.	t	P > |t|	Coef.	Std. err.	t	P > |t|
Fraction	5.864	2.687	2.18	0.030	1.459	2.450	0.60	0.552
Fraction sq.	2.752	1.781	1.55	0.123	5.123	1.428	3.59	0.000
GPS	7.757	10.349	0.75	0.454	−15.322	6.370	−2.41	0.016
GPS sq.	2.835	13.478	0.21	0.834	26.058	7.905	3.30	0.001
Fraction x GPS	−18.381	7.014	−2.62	0.009	−14.248	5.510	−2.59	0.010
Constant	−0.256	2.027	−0.13	0.899	6.012	1.431	4.20	0.000
Observations	453				1,171			
F	3.12				8.15			
Prob. > F	0.009				0.000			
R-sq.	0.034				0.034			
Adj. R-sq.	0.023				0.030			

Source: Authors' estimation based on data from CAPMAS and WFP (2011).

Note: GPS = generalized propensity score.

TABLE A.35 Dose-response function estimates for the effect of ration-card-program subsidies on frequency of household legume consumption

	Urban				Rural			
	Coef.	Std. err.	t	P > |t|	Coef.	Std. err.	t	P > |t|
Fraction	−9.651	3.184	−3.03	0.003	−2.633	2.803	−0.94	0.348
Fraction sq.	4.684	2.110	2.22	0.027	0.226	1.635	0.14	0.890
GPS	9.023	12.264	0.74	0.462	9.858	7.289	1.35	0.177
GPS sq.	−22.821	15.972	−1.43	0.154	−11.931	9.045	−1.32	0.187
Fraction x GPS	11.548	8.311	1.39	0.165	4.396	6.305	0.70	0.486
Constant	5.751	2.402	2.39	0.017	2.561	1.637	1.56	0.118
Observations	453				1,171			
F	6.71				0.45			
Prob. > F	0.000				0.816			
R-sq.	0.070				0.002			
Adj. R-sq.	0.059				−0.002			

Source: Authors' estimation based on data from CAPMAS and WFP (2011).

Note: GPS = generalized propensity score.

TABLE A.36 Dose-response function estimates for the effect of ration-card-program subsidies on frequency of household meat and fish consumption

	Urban				Rural			
	Coef.	Std. err.	t	P > |t|	Coef.	Std. err.	t	P > |t|
Fraction	−3.354	2.223	−1.51	0.132	2.333	1.653	1.41	0.158
Fraction sq.	1.042	1.474	0.71	0.480	2.692	0.964	2.79	0.005
GPS	25.707	8.565	3.00	0.003	−13.380	4.297	−3.11	0.002
GPS sq.	−25.744	11.154	−2.31	0.021	18.939	5.332	3.55	0.000
Fraction x GPS	3.215	5.804	0.55	0.580	−9.684	3.717	−2.61	0.009
Constant	−2.721	1.677	−1.62	0.106	4.954	0.965	5.13	0.000
Observations	453				1,171			
F	5.48				4.04			
Prob. > F	0.000				0.001			
R-sq.	0.058				0.017			
Adj. R-sq.	0.047				0.013			

Source: Authors' estimation based on data from CAPMAS and WFP (2011).

Note: GPS = generalized propensity score.

TABLE A.37 Dose-response function estimates for the effect of ration-card-program subsidies on frequency of household milk and dairy product consumption

	Urban				Rural			
	Coef.	Std. err.	t	P > |t|	Coef.	Std. err.	t	P > |t|
Fraction	–8.795	3.031	–2.90	0.004	6.132	2.880	2.13	0.033
Fraction sq.	–1.614	2.009	–0.80	0.422	2.329	1.679	1.39	0.166
GPS	1.189	11.674	0.10	0.919	2.943	7.488	0.39	0.694
GPS sq.	–7.135	15.203	–0.47	0.639	5.207	9.292	0.56	0.575
Fraction x GPS	19.794	7.911	2.50	0.013	–17.263	6.476	–2.67	0.008
Constant	5.998	2.286	2.62	0.009	2.347	1.682	1.40	0.163
Observations	453				1,171			
F	3.51				2.05			
Prob. > F	0.004				0.069			
R-sq.	0.038				0.009			
Adj. R-sq.	0.027				0.005			

Source: Authors' estimation based on data from CAPMAS and WFP (2011).

Note: GPS = generalized propensity score.

TABLE A.38 GLM results of the generalized propensity score estimations for child nutrition indicators and Baladi bread and flour subsidies

	Urban				Rural			
	Coef.	Robust std. err.	z	P > |z|	Coef.	Robust std. err.	z	P > |z|
Per capita household income								
Quintile 2	−0.071	0.085	−0.83	0.405	0.063	0.074	0.85	0.393
Quintile 3	−0.071	0.089	−0.80	0.426	0.122	0.076	1.60	0.109
Quintile 4	−0.234	0.089	−2.63	0.009	−0.164	0.083	−1.96	0.050
Quintile 5 (richest)	−0.353	0.118	−3.00	0.003	−0.084	0.094	−0.89	0.372
Household size								
4	−0.146	0.105	−1.40	0.162	−0.195	0.084	−2.31	0.021
5	−0.094	0.109	−0.86	0.391	−0.150	0.085	−1.77	0.077
6	0.005	0.126	0.04	0.966	−0.191	0.098	−1.94	0.052
≥ 7	−0.147	0.144	−1.02	0.308	−0.336	0.098	−3.41	0.001
Single-mother household	−0.042	0.166	−0.25	0.802	0.005	0.125	0.04	0.970
Age of household head								
39–48	0.123	0.074	1.65	0.098	0.077	0.064	1.20	0.231
49–58	0.009	0.116	0.08	0.940	0.274	0.100	2.74	0.006
≥ 59	0.040	0.153	0.26	0.793	0.181	0.098	1.85	0.064
Education of household head								
Primary	0.105	0.097	1.08	0.282	−0.157	0.088	−1.79	0.073
Secondary	−0.092	0.077	−1.19	0.236	−0.048	0.062	−0.78	0.437
Higher	−0.204	0.118	−1.74	0.082	−0.141	0.090	−1.57	0.117
Pension or social benefits	0.271	0.096	2.82	0.005	0.079	0.066	1.20	0.230
Public-sector employment	0.043	0.078	0.54	0.586	0.130	0.058	2.26	0.024
Farm household					−0.078	0.053	−1.48	0.138

	Urban				Rural			
	Coef.	Robust std. err.	z	P > |z|	Coef.	Robust std. err.	z	P > |z|
Governorate (aggregate)								
02	−0.149	0.099	−1.51	0.132	0.220	0.092	2.38	0.017
03	−0.150	0.125	−1.20	0.231	0.751	0.117	6.40	0.000
04	0.043	0.128	0.33	0.739	−0.575	0.124	−4.63	0.000
05	−0.182	0.118	−1.53	0.125	0.166	0.106	1.57	0.118
06	−0.246	0.164	−1.50	0.135	0.395	0.103	3.83	0.000
07	−0.206	0.135	−1.52	0.127	−0.176	0.126	−1.40	0.161
08	−0.541	0.137	−3.94	0.000	0.906	0.119	7.64	0.000
09	−0.107	0.125	−0.86	0.392	1.092	0.105	10.36	0.000
10	0.859	0.148	5.79	0.000	0.771	0.103	7.49	0.000
11	0.553	0.149	3.71	0.000	0.674	0.141	4.77	0.000
12	0.281	0.137	2.05	0.041	0.481	0.139	3.46	0.001
13					0.755	0.125	6.03	0.000
Constant	−0.468	0.135	−3.46	0.001	−0.904	0.132	−6.87	0.000
Observations	1,006				1,765			
Deviance	0.241				0.246			
Pearson	0.199				0.204			

Source: Authors' estimation based on data from CAPMAS and WFP (2011).

Note: GLM = generalized linear model.

TABLE A.39 GLM results of the generalized propensity score estimations for maternal nutrition indicators and Baladi bread and flour subsidies

	Urban				Rural			
	Coef.	Robust std. err.	z	P > |z|	Coef.	Robust std. err.	z	P > |z|
Per capita household income								
Quintile 2	−0.008	0.081	−0.10	0.919	0.046	0.074	0.62	0.534
Quintile 3	−0.036	0.083	−0.43	0.664	0.130	0.077	1.69	0.091
Quintile 4	−0.208	0.085	−2.45	0.014	−0.146	0.085	−1.72	0.086
Quintile 5 (richest)	−0.262	0.109	−2.41	0.016	−0.109	0.094	−1.15	0.249
Household size								
4	−0.137	0.097	−1.41	0.158	−0.172	0.087	−1.97	0.048
5	−0.141	0.102	−1.38	0.168	−0.132	0.087	−1.51	0.132
6	0.024	0.117	0.21	0.837	−0.226	0.101	−2.23	0.026
≥ 7	−0.182	0.135	−1.35	0.176	−0.328	0.101	−3.23	0.001
Single-mother household	−0.090	0.155	−0.58	0.561	0.011	0.127	0.08	0.933
Age of household head								
39–48	0.150	0.070	2.13	0.033	0.089	0.064	1.39	0.165
49–58	0.052	0.116	0.45	0.655	0.286	0.102	2.81	0.005
≥ 59	0.082	0.141	0.58	0.562	0.205	0.098	2.09	0.036
Education of household head								
Primary	0.074	0.093	0.79	0.429	−0.133	0.088	−1.51	0.131
Secondary	−0.065	0.075	−0.87	0.387	−0.054	0.063	−0.87	0.387
Higher	−0.292	0.110	−2.65	0.008	−0.143	0.089	−1.61	0.107
Pension or social benefits	0.272	0.092	2.95	0.003	0.089	0.066	1.35	0.178
Public-sector employment	0.036	0.073	0.49	0.623	0.116	0.058	1.98	0.048
Farm household					−0.105	0.053	−1.96	0.050

	Urban				Rural			
	Coef.	Robust std. err.	z	P > |z|	Coef.	Robust std. err.	z	P > |z|
Governorate (aggregate)								
02	−0.150	0.093	−1.61	0.107	0.186	0.094	1.99	0.047
03	−0.110	0.117	−0.94	0.345	0.715	0.116	6.19	0.000
04	0.137	0.125	1.10	0.272	−0.541	0.126	−4.30	0.000
05	−0.157	0.105	−1.50	0.133	0.174	0.107	1.63	0.103
06	−0.216	0.160	−1.35	0.178	0.326	0.102	3.18	0.001
07	−0.147	0.130	−1.13	0.258	−0.182	0.125	−1.46	0.145
08	−0.408	0.136	−2.99	0.003	0.888	0.119	7.47	0.000
09	−0.098	0.111	−0.88	0.377	1.097	0.109	10.04	0.000
10	0.886	0.137	6.47	0.000	0.776	0.105	7.39	0.000
11	0.551	0.145	3.81	0.000	0.711	0.142	5.02	0.000
12	0.440	0.141	3.13	0.002	0.430	0.139	3.09	0.002
13					0.692	0.129	5.37	0.000
Constant	−0.543	0.128	−4.25	0.000	−0.863	0.135	−6.41	0.000
Observations	1,140				1,823			
Deviance	0.243				0.258			
Pearson	0.201				0.213			

Source: Authors' estimation based on data from CAPMAS and WFP (2011).

Note: GLM = generalized linear model.

TABLE A.40 GLM results of the generalized propensity score estimations for indicators of the double burden of malnutrition at the family level and coexisting child and maternal overweight and Baladi bread and flour subsidies

	Urban				Rural			
	Coef.	Robust std. err.	z	P > |z|	Coef.	Robust std. err.	z	P > |z|
Per capita household income								
Quintile 2	−0.071	0.087	−0.82	0.415	0.068	0.076	0.89	0.372
Quintile 3	−0.044	0.091	−0.48	0.631	0.162	0.079	2.06	0.039
Quintile 4	−0.251	0.090	−2.78	0.006	−0.156	0.088	−1.77	0.077
Quintile 5 (richest)	−0.283	0.120	−2.35	0.019	−0.084	0.098	−0.85	0.393
Household size								
4	−0.164	0.107	−1.53	0.126	−0.196	0.091	−2.16	0.031
5	−0.119	0.113	−1.06	0.290	−0.147	0.091	−1.62	0.105
6	−0.013	0.129	−0.10	0.922	−0.188	0.105	−1.79	0.073
≥ 7	−0.172	0.146	−1.18	0.240	−0.318	0.105	−3.05	0.002
Single-mother household	−0.054	0.167	−0.32	0.747	0.020	0.130	0.15	0.880
Age of household head								
39–48	0.113	0.075	1.50	0.132	0.085	0.066	1.29	0.197
49–58	−0.009	0.119	−0.08	0.938	0.263	0.106	2.48	0.013
≥ 59	0.003	0.158	0.02	0.986	0.145	0.102	1.42	0.155
Education of household head								
Primary	0.088	0.100	0.89	0.375	−0.150	0.090	−1.68	0.093
Secondary	−0.090	0.080	−1.13	0.260	−0.069	0.064	−1.07	0.283
Higher	−0.258	0.122	−2.12	0.034	−0.139	0.093	−1.50	0.133
Pension or social benefits	0.266	0.100	2.65	0.008	0.088	0.068	1.30	0.194
Public-sector employment	0.061	0.080	0.76	0.448	0.110	0.060	1.83	0.067
Farm household					−0.111	0.055	−2.01	0.044

	Urban				Rural			
	Coef.	Robust std. err.	z	P > |z|	Coef.	Robust std. err.	z	P > |z|
Governorate (aggregate)								
02	−0.169	0.102	−1.66	0.097	0.216	0.098	2.19	0.028
03	−0.160	0.127	−1.26	0.207	0.705	0.122	5.81	0.000
04	0.091	0.130	0.70	0.485	−0.543	0.129	−4.22	0.000
05	−0.212	0.122	−1.73	0.083	0.173	0.111	1.56	0.120
06	−0.273	0.174	−1.57	0.116	0.355	0.107	3.32	0.001
07	−0.175	0.138	−1.27	0.205	−0.149	0.130	−1.15	0.251
08	−0.533	0.141	−3.79	0.000	0.885	0.126	7.04	0.000
09	−0.114	0.129	−0.89	0.374	1.092	0.113	9.70	0.000
10	0.843	0.154	5.47	0.000	0.762	0.111	6.89	0.000
11	0.558	0.152	3.68	0.000	0.692	0.146	4.76	0.000
12	0.310	0.138	2.24	0.025	0.442	0.146	3.03	0.002
13					0.711	0.132	5.38	0.000
Constant	−0.449	0.142	−3.16	0.002	−0.893	0.141	−6.32	0.000
Observations		961				1,659		
Deviance			0.241				0.247	
Pearson			0.198				0.205	

Source: Authors' estimation based on data from CAPMAS and WFP (2011).

Note: GLM = generalized linear model.

TABLE A.41 GLM results of the generalized propensity score estimations for household diet quality indicators and Baladi bread and flour subsidies

	Urban				Rural			
	Coef.	Robust std. err.	z	P > |z|	Coef.	Robust std. err.	z	P > |z|
Per capita household income								
Quintile 2	−0.053	0.082	−0.65	0.518	0.029	0.072	0.41	0.684
Quintile 3	−0.034	0.082	−0.41	0.682	0.085	0.075	1.14	0.253
Quintile 4	−0.236	0.085	−2.77	0.006	−0.160	0.082	−1.95	0.051
Quintile 5 (richest)	−0.333	0.109	−3.05	0.002	−0.106	0.091	−1.16	0.247
Household size								
4	−0.128	0.099	−1.30	0.193	−0.171	0.082	−2.08	0.037
5	−0.129	0.102	−1.26	0.208	−0.146	0.083	−1.76	0.079
6	−0.005	0.114	−0.05	0.963	−0.232	0.096	−2.41	0.016
≥ 7	−0.188	0.136	−1.38	0.168	−0.359	0.097	−3.71	0.000
Single-mother household	−0.079	0.158	−0.50	0.618	0.010	0.122	0.08	0.934
Age of household head								
39–48	0.144	0.070	2.06	0.039	0.089	0.063	1.41	0.159
49–58	0.070	0.118	0.60	0.550	0.316	0.098	3.23	0.001
≥ 59	0.098	0.140	0.70	0.482	0.256	0.094	2.73	0.006
Education of household head								
Primary	0.090	0.093	0.97	0.331	−0.135	0.087	−1.56	0.119
Secondary	−0.076	0.073	−1.04	0.298	−0.030	0.061	−0.49	0.624
Higher	−0.257	0.110	−2.34	0.019	−0.120	0.087	−1.37	0.170
Pension or social benefits	0.261	0.091	2.88	0.004	0.075	0.064	1.16	0.244
Public-sector employment	0.036	0.072	0.51	0.613	0.130	0.056	2.31	0.021
Farm household					−0.078	0.052	−1.50	0.133

	Urban				Rural			
	Coef.	Robust std. err.	z	P > |z|	Coef.	Robust std. err.	z	P > |z|
Governorate (aggregate)								
02	−0.126	0.093	−1.35	0.176	0.174	0.089	1.95	0.051
03	−0.084	0.118	−0.71	0.479	0.735	0.112	6.57	0.000
04	0.107	0.124	0.86	0.389	−0.591	0.122	−4.83	0.000
05	−0.113	0.104	−1.09	0.278	0.123	0.102	1.20	0.230
06	−0.133	0.153	−0.87	0.385	0.345	0.099	3.50	0.000
07	−0.163	0.129	−1.26	0.206	−0.221	0.121	−1.82	0.068
08	−0.408	0.134	−3.04	0.002	0.910	0.113	8.07	0.000
09	−0.068	0.114	−0.60	0.551	1.082	0.103	10.51	0.000
10	0.920	0.139	6.60	0.000	0.768	0.098	7.83	0.000
11	0.543	0.142	3.83	0.000	0.696	0.137	5.06	0.000
12	0.417	0.139	3.00	0.003	0.468	0.133	3.52	0.000
13					0.715	0.122	5.84	0.000
Constant	−0.515	0.126	−4.10	0.000	−0.851	0.127	−6.71	0.000
Observations	1,130				1,911			
Deviance	0.242				0.256			
Pearson	0.200				0.211			

Source: Authors' estimation based on data from CAPMAS and WFP (2011).

Note: GLM = generalized linear model.

TABLE A.42 Dose-response function estimates for the effect of Baladi bread and flour subsidies on child HAZ

	Urban				Rural			
	Coef.	Std. err.	t	P > |t|	Coef.	Std. err.	t	P > |t|
Fraction	−0.081	1.365	−0.06	0.953	−0.197	0.917	−0.22	0.830
Fraction sq.	0.459	0.997	0.46	0.645	1.194	0.721	1.66	0.098
GPS	6.153	4.980	1.24	0.217	−4.117	3.166	−1.30	0.194
GPS sq.	−8.862	7.070	−1.25	0.210	7.561	4.915	1.54	0.124
Fraction x GPS	−0.401	3.856	−0.10	0.917	−2.223	2.506	−0.89	0.375
Constant	−1.868	0.902	−2.07	0.039	−0.310	0.513	−0.60	0.545
Observations	1,006				1,765			
F	0.68				1.06			
Prob. > F	0.641				0.381			
R-sq.	0.003				0.003			
Adj. R-sq.	−0.002				0.000			

Source: Authors' estimation based on data from CAPMAS and WFP (2011).

Note: GPS = generalized propensity score; HAZ = height-for-age z-score.

TABLE A.43 Dose-response function estimates for the effect of Baladi bread and flour subsidies on child stunting

	Urban				Rural			
	Coef.	Std. err.	z	P > |z|	Coef.	Std. err.	z	P > |z|
Fraction	0.917	1.514	0.61	0.545	−2.579	1.108	−2.33	0.020
Fraction sq.	−0.457	1.123	−0.41	0.684	−1.263	0.891	−1.42	0.156
GPS	−3.016	5.460	−0.55	0.581	10.472	3.884	2.70	0.007
GPS sq.	6.490	7.657	0.85	0.397	−18.006	6.171	−2.92	0.004
Fraction x GPS	−1.124	4.194	−0.27	0.789	8.950	3.270	2.74	0.006
Constant	−0.853	1.000	−0.85	0.394	−2.302	0.618	−3.73	0.000
Observations	1,006				1,765			
LR chi-sq.	5.42				14.56			
Prob. > chi-sq.	0.366				0.012			
Pseudo R-sq.	0.005				0.007			

Source: Authors' estimation based on data from CAPMAS and WFP (2011).

Note: GPS = generalized propensity score.

TABLE A.44 Dose-response function estimates for the effect of Baladi bread and flour subsidies on child BMIZ

	Urban				Rural			
	Coef.	Std. err.	t	P > |t|	Coef.	Std. err.	t	P > |t|
Fraction	−1.531	1.208	−1.27	0.205	0.595	0.817	0.73	0.467
Fraction sq.	0.403	0.883	0.46	0.648	−1.002	0.643	−1.56	0.119
GPS	2.935	4.407	0.67	0.505	6.605	2.821	2.34	0.019
GPS sq.	−3.515	6.256	−0.56	0.574	−10.870	4.379	−2.48	0.013
Fraction x GPS	2.770	3.413	0.81	0.417	0.865	2.233	0.39	0.698
Constant	0.513	0.798	0.64	0.521	0.040	0.457	0.09	0.930
Observations	1,006				1,765			
F	1.00				2.33			
Prob. > F	0.417				0.041			
R-sq.	0.005				0.007			
Adj. R-sq.	0.000				0.004			

Source: Authors' estimation based on data from CAPMAS and WFP (2011).

Note: BMIZ = body mass index-for-age z-score; GPS = generalized propensity score.

TABLE A.45 Dose-response function estimates for the effect of Baladi bread and flour subsidies on child overweight

	Urban				Rural			
	Coef.	Std. err.	z	P > |z|	Coef.	Std. err.	z	P > |z|
Fraction	−0.273	1.476	−0.18	0.853	−0.052	1.042	−0.05	0.960
Fraction sq.	1.371	1.061	1.29	0.196	−0.386	0.811	−0.48	0.635
GPS	−1.446	5.483	−0.26	0.792	8.226	3.694	2.23	0.026
GPS sq.	3.275	7.716	0.42	0.671	−12.616	5.768	−2.19	0.029
Fraction x GPS	−1.704	4.097	−0.42	0.678	0.843	2.895	0.29	0.771
Constant	−0.795	0.997	−0.80	0.426	−2.100	0.596	−3.52	0.000
Observations	1,006				1,765			
LR chi-sq.	2.58				6.23			
Prob. > chi-sq.	0.764				0.284			
Pseudo R-sq.	0.002				0.003			

Source: Authors' estimation based on data from CAPMAS and WFP (2011).

Note: GPS = generalized propensity score.

TABLE A.46 Dose-response function estimates for the effect of Baladi bread and flour subsidies on mother's BMI

	Urban				Rural			
	Coef.	Std. err.	t	P > |t|	Coef.	Std. err.	t	P > |t|
Fraction	−0.931	2.903	−0.32	0.748	1.026	2.252	0.46	0.649
Fraction sq.	−3.059	2.214	−1.38	0.167	0.212	2.004	0.11	0.916
GPS	9.114	12.020	0.76	0.448	9.510	8.112	1.17	0.241
GPS sq.	−22.548	17.213	−1.31	0.190	−21.641	12.389	−1.75	0.081
Fraction x GPS	14.554	8.225	1.77	0.077	0.659	6.590	0.10	0.920
Constant	27.875	2.116	13.18	0.000	27.243	1.336	20.39	0.000
Observations	1,140				1,823			
F	1.80				4.53			
Prob. > F	0.110				0.000			
R-sq.	0.008				0.012			
Adj. R-sq.	0.004				0.010			

Source: Authors' estimation based on data from CAPMAS and WFP (2011).

Note: BMI = body mass index; GPS = generalized propensity score.

TABLE A.47 Dose-response function estimates for the effect of Baladi bread and flour subsidies on maternal overweight

	Urban				Rural			
	Coef.	Std. err.	z	P > |z|	Coef.	Std. err.	z	P > |z|
Fraction	1.062	1.429	0.74	0.458	−0.471	0.971	−0.49	0.627
Fraction sq.	−1.576	1.128	−1.40	0.162	0.054	0.855	0.06	0.949
GPS	2.249	5.898	0.38	0.703	4.184	3.439	1.22	0.224
GPS sq.	−7.419	8.328	−0.89	0.373	−9.210	5.192	−1.77	0.076
Fraction x GPS	4.305	3.950	1.09	0.276	1.405	2.784	0.50	0.614
Constant	0.959	1.040	0.92	0.357	0.615	0.573	1.07	0.283
Observations	1,140				1,823			
LR chi-sq.	16.62				17.14			
Prob. > chi-sq.	0.005				0.004			
Pseudo R-sq.	0.015				0.008			

Source: Authors' estimation based on data from CAPMAS and WFP (2011).

Note: GPS = generalized propensity score.

TABLE A.48 Dose-response function estimates for the effect of Baladi bread and flour subsidies on child stunting and overweight

	Urban				Rural			
	Coef.	Std. err.	z	P > |z|	Coef.	Std. err.	z	P > |z|
Fraction	−1.423	1.831	−0.78	0.437	−2.326	1.528	−1.52	0.128
Fraction sq.	1.719	1.304	1.32	0.187	−1.469	1.214	−1.21	0.226
GPS	4.188	7.080	0.59	0.554	15.893	5.526	2.88	0.004
GPS sq.	−3.224	9.818	−0.33	0.743	−25.682	8.796	−2.92	0.004
Fraction x GPS	0.444	4.994	0.09	0.929	8.410	4.587	1.83	0.067
Constant	−2.691	1.299	−2.07	0.038	−4.073	0.879	−4.63	0.000
Observations	1,006				1,765			
LR chi-sq.	5.31				12.08			
Prob. > chi-sq.	0.379				0.034			
Pseudo R-sq.	0.007				0.009			

Source: Authors' estimation based on data from CAPMAS and WFP (2011).

Note: GPS = generalized propensity score.

TABLE A.49 Dose-response function estimates for the effect of Baladi bread and flour subsidies on child stunting and maternal overweight

	Urban				Rural			
	Coef.	Std. err.	z	P > |z|	Coef.	Std. err.	z	P > |z|
Fraction	−0.703	1.652	−0.43	0.670	3.236	1.256	2.58	0.010
Fraction sq.	0.583	1.227	0.48	0.635	−1.885	1.069	−1.76	0.078
GPS	3.822	6.097	0.63	0.531	3.173	4.057	0.78	0.434
GPS sq.	−5.909	8.993	−0.66	0.511	−6.430	6.423	−1.00	0.317
Fraction x GPS	0.989	5.024	0.20	0.844	−3.806	3.565	−1.07	0.286
Constant	−1.826	1.081	−1.69	0.091	−2.004	0.651	−3.08	0.002
Observations	961				1,659			
LR chi-sq.	0.81				25.47			
Prob. > chi-sq.	0.976				0.000			
Pseudo R-sq.	0.001				0.016			

Source: Authors' estimation based on data from CAPMAS and WFP (2011).

Note: GPS = generalized propensity score.

TABLE A.50 Dose-response function estimates for the effect of Baladi bread and flour subsidies on child overweight and maternal overweight

	Urban				Rural			
	Coef.	Std. err.	z	P > |z|	Coef.	Std. err.	z	P > |z|
Fraction	−3.871	1.686	−2.30	0.022	1.631	1.170	1.39	0.163
Fraction sq.	1.712	1.186	1.44	0.149	−1.082	0.992	−1.09	0.275
GPS	4.497	6.486	0.69	0.488	5.397	3.937	1.37	0.170
GPS sq.	−13.404	10.270	−1.31	0.192	−11.525	6.327	−1.82	0.069
Fraction x GPS	7.082	5.437	1.30	0.193	−1.192	3.423	−0.35	0.728
Constant	−0.878	1.080	−0.81	0.416	−1.858	0.620	−3.00	0.003
Observations	961				1,659			
LR chi-sq.	15.45				28.69			
Prob. > chi-sq.	0.009				0.000			
Pseudo R-sq.	0.014				0.016			

Source: Authors' estimation based on data from CAPMAS and WFP (2011).

Note: GPS = generalized propensity score.

TABLE A.51 Dose-response function estimates for the effect of Baladi bread and flour subsidies on household dietary diversity

	Urban				Rural			
	Coef.	Std. err.	t	P > |t|	Coef.	Std. err.	t	P > |t|
Fraction	0.336	0.644	0.52	0.602	−0.003	0.502	−0.01	0.995
Fraction sq.	0.371	0.507	0.73	0.464	−1.158	0.419	−2.77	0.006
GPS	1.771	2.501	0.71	0.479	2.923	1.775	1.65	0.100
GPS sq.	−2.679	3.574	−0.75	0.454	−6.693	2.606	−2.57	0.010
Fraction x GPS	−0.467	1.823	−0.26	0.798	3.178	1.375	2.31	0.021
Constant	10.311	0.447	23.06	0.000	10.049	0.299	33.58	0.000
Observations	1,130				1,911			
F	1.83				5.03			
Prob. > F	0.105				0.000			
R-sq.	0.008				0.013			
Adj. R-sq.	0.004				0.010			

Source: Authors' estimation based on data from CAPMAS and WFP (2011).

Note: GPS = generalized propensity score.

TABLE A.52 Dose-response function estimates for the effect of Baladi bread and flour subsidies on frequency of household vegetable consumption

	Urban				Rural			
	Coef.	Std. err.	t	P > |t|	Coef.	Std. err.	t	P > |t|
Fraction	1.507	1.240	1.21	0.225	−2.248	0.861	−2.61	0.009
Fraction sq.	0.158	0.977	0.16	0.872	0.003	0.718	0.00	0.996
GPS	−21.716	4.818	−4.51	0.000	−9.976	3.042	−3.28	0.001
GPS sq.	24.340	6.885	3.54	0.000	1.181	4.466	0.26	0.791
Fraction x GPS	−2.128	3.512	−0.61	0.545	6.914	2.356	2.93	0.003
Constant	7.481	0.861	8.69	0.000	6.847	0.513	13.35	0.000
Observations	1,130				1,911			
F	7.93				46.76			
Prob. > F	0.000				0.000			
R-sq.	0.034				0.109			
Adj. R-sq.	0.030				0.107			

Source: Authors' estimation based on data from CAPMAS and WFP (2011).

Note: GPS = generalized propensity score.

TABLE A.53 Dose-response function estimates for the effect of Baladi bread and flour subsidies on frequency of household legume consumption

	Urban				Rural			
	Coef.	Std. err.	t	P > |t|	Coef.	Std. err.	t	P > |t|
Fraction	4.230	1.437	2.94	0.003	−0.349	0.986	−0.35	0.723
Fraction sq.	−3.066	1.132	−2.71	0.007	−0.859	0.822	−1.05	0.296
GPS	−8.736	5.581	−1.57	0.118	16.157	3.484	4.64	0.000
GPS sq.	16.885	7.974	2.12	0.034	−18.499	5.115	−3.62	0.000
Fraction x GPS	−1.754	4.067	−0.43	0.666	4.038	2.699	1.50	0.135
Constant	4.536	0.997	4.55	0.000	0.773	0.587	1.32	0.188
Observations	1,130				1,911			
F	11.30				21.20			
Prob. > F	0.000				0.000			
R-sq.	0.048				0.053			
Adj. R-sq.	0.044				0.050			

Source: Authors' estimation based on data from CAPMAS and WFP (2011).

Note: GPS = generalized propensity score.

TABLE A.54 Dose-response function estimates for the effect of Baladi bread and flour subsidies on frequency of household meat and fish consumption

	Urban				Rural			
	Coef.	Std. err.	t	P > |t|	Coef.	Std. err.	t	P > |t|
Fraction	−0.002	1.047	0.00	0.999	0.309	0.611	0.51	0.613
Fraction sq.	0.851	0.825	1.03	0.303	−1.422	0.510	−2.79	0.005
GPS	−21.063	4.066	−5.18	0.000	−13.800	2.160	−6.39	0.000
GPS sq.	20.852	5.809	3.59	0.000	11.843	3.172	3.73	0.000
Fraction x GPS	−0.764	2.963	−0.26	0.797	1.832	1.673	1.09	0.274
Constant	7.613	0.727	10.48	0.000	5.791	0.364	15.90	0.000
Observations	1,130				1,911			
F	16.88				54.04			
Prob. > F	0.000				0.000			
R-sq.	0.070				0.124			
Adj. R-sq.	0.066				0.122			

Source: Authors' estimation based on data from CAPMAS and WFP (2011).

Note: GPS = generalized propensity score.

TABLE A.55 Dose-response function estimates for the effect of Baladi bread and flour subsidies on frequency of household milk and dairy product consumption

	Urban				Rural			
	Coef.	Std. err.	t	P > |t|	Coef.	Std. err.	t	P > |t|
Fraction	−2.636	1.339	−1.97	0.049	1.175	1.002	1.17	0.241
Fraction sq.	3.187	1.055	3.02	0.003	1.320	0.836	1.58	0.114
GPS	−14.817	5.202	−2.85	0.004	−18.362	3.542	−5.18	0.000
GPS sq.	15.029	7.432	2.02	0.043	24.230	5.200	4.66	0.000
Fraction x GPS	1.243	3.791	0.33	0.743	−6.395	2.744	−2.33	0.020
Constant	8.528	0.930	9.17	0.000	7.836	0.597	13.12	0.000
Observations	1,130				1,911			
F	6.08				12.89			
Prob. > F	0.000				0.000			
R-sq.	0.026				0.033			
Adj. R-sq.	0.022				0.030			

Source: Authors' estimation based on data from CAPMAS and WFP (2011).

Note: GPS = generalized propensity score.

Authors

Olivier Ecker (o.ecker@cgiar.org) is a research fellow in the Development Strategy and Governance Division of the International Food Policy Research Institute (IFPRI), Washington, DC.

Perrihan Al-Riffai (p.al-riffai@cgiar.org) is a senior research analyst in the Development Strategy and Governance Division of IFPRI, Washington, DC.

Clemens Breisinger (c.breisinger@cgiar.org) is a senior research fellow in the Development Strategy and Governance Division of IFPRI and the leader of IFPRI's Egypt Country Program based in Cairo.

Rawia El-Batrawy (rawia_batrawy@yahoo.com) is the former head of the Demographic and Census Sector and the Social Demographic Research and Studies Center of the Egypt Central Agency for Public Mobilization and Statistics (CAPMAS), Cairo.

Olivier Ecker, Perrihan Al-Riffai, and Clemens Breisinger also coauthored two IFPRI Food Policy Reports, *Beyond the Arab Awakening: Policies and Investments for Poverty Reduction and Food Security* (Breisinger et al. 2012) and *How to Build Resilience to Conflict: The Role of Food Security* (Breisinger et al. 2014).

Index

Page numbers for entries occurring in boxes are followed by a *b*; those for entries in figures, by an *f*; those for entries in notes, by an *n*; and those for entries in tables, by a *t*.

Made in the USA
Las Vegas, NV
04 November 2026

57431639R00169